Edwards and the Edwardseans

"Sometimes, if they're lucky—or blessed—a historian can look back over the course of their life and realize that their work has coherence, meaning, and brings continual discovery. Happily, David Kling shares his instructive and ever-deepening odyssey into the world of Jonathan Edwards and generations of his followers in this volume. In these pages, Kling emerges as an insightful guide to the profound importance of Edwards and the Edwardseans not only in American but in global religious history."

—Kenneth P. Minkema, executive editor,
Jonathan Edwards Center, Yale University

"In this collection of previously published works by this respected historian, Kling traces the impact of Jonathan Edwards on and through the New Divinity thinkers that followed. From early chapters that demonstrate the significance of conversion and missions in Edwards's thought through several case studies of his influence on the next generation of Christian leaders, this work summarizes not only the impact of Edwards on his successors but the influence of Kling's historiography on students of Edwards."

—Glenn R. Kreider, professor of theological studies,
Dallas Theological Seminary

"David Kling's book wonderfully brings together features not normally found in one volume: theological wisdom combined with outstanding historical research, a reading of Edwards that does not pit him against the Edwardseans, and astute scholarly reflection coupled with a robust concern for Christian spirituality and mission. A masterful set of essays that illuminates the global reach of Edwards's ministry. I will be consulting it for years to come."

—Robert W. Caldwell III, professor of church history,
Southwestern Baptist Theological Seminary

"As Jonathan Edwards was fond to say, 'By their fruits ye shall know them.' The rich fruit gathered in this volume confirms David Kling's place as a groundbreaking scholar of the Edwardsean tradition. Each essay is superb, and collected together, they form a new narrative that significantly enlarges our understanding of Edwards and his legacy."

—Ava Chamberlain, professor emerita of religion,
Wright State University

"A rich harvest of the fruits of many years of scholarship by a leading authority in the field, this volume greatly adds to our understanding of Jonathan Edwards and especially the history and significance of the Edwardsean tradition. David Kling sheds much new light on the formidable influence of Edwards's heirs on so many facets of American religion and culture in the nineteenth century and beyond."

— JAN STIEVERMANN, professor of the history of Christianity in the US, Heidelberg University

Edwards and the Edwardseans

Jonathan Edwards, the New Divinity,
and the Making of a Theological Culture

DAVID W. KLING

Foreword by DOUGLAS A. SWEENEY

◆PICKWICK Publications · Eugene, Oregon

EDWARDS AND THE EDWARDSEANS
Jonathan Edwards, the New Divinity, and the Making of a Theological Culture

Copyright © 2024 David W. Kling. All rights reserved. Except for brief quotations in critical publications or reviews, no part of this book may be reproduced in any manner without prior written permission from the publisher. Write: Permissions, Wipf and Stock Publishers, 199 W. 8th Ave., Suite 3, Eugene, OR 97401.

Pickwick Publications
An Imprint of Wipf and Stock Publishers
199 W. 8th Ave., Suite 3
Eugene, OR 97401

www.wipfandstock.com

PAPERBACK ISBN: 979-8-3852-0374-1
HARDCOVER ISBN: 979-8-3852-0375-8
EBOOK ISBN: 979-8-3852-0376-5

Cataloguing-in-Publication data:

Names: Kling, David W., 1950– [author] | Sweeney, Douglas A. [foreword writer].

Title: Edwards and the Edwardseans : Jonathan Edwards, the new divinity, and the making of a theological culture / David W. Kling.

Description: Eugene, OR: Pickwick Publications, 2024 | Includes bibliographical references and index.

Identifiers: ISBN 979-8-3852-0374-1 (paperback) | ISBN 979-8-3852-0375-8 (hardcover) | ISBN 979-8-3852-0376-5 (ebook)

Subjects: LCSH: Edwards, Jonathan, 1703–1758. | Edwards, Jonathan, 1703–1758—Influence. | New England theology—History. | Calvinism. | Theology—United States—History.

Classification: BX7260.E3 K55 2024 (print) | BX7260.E3 (ebook)

The chapters in this volume were originally published in slightly different form in the following journals and books:

Chapter 1: Kling, David W. "Puritans and the Great Awakening in America (1630–1790)." In David W. Kling, *A History of Christian Conversion*, 356–77. New York: Oxford University Press, 2020. Reproduced by permission of Oxford University Press. https://global.oup.com/academic/search?q=Kling%2C+David+W.&cc=us&lang=en.

Chapter 2: Kling, David W. "Jonathan Edwards, the Bible, and Conversion." In *Jonathan Edwards and Scripture: Biblical Exegesis in British North America*, edited by David P. Barshinger and Douglas A. Sweeney, 212–32. New York: Oxford University Press, 2018. Reproduced by permission of Oxford University Press. https://global.oup.com/academic/search?q=Kling%2C+David+W.&cc=us&lang=en.

Chapter 3: Kling, David W. "Jonathan Edwards, Petitionary Prayer, and the Cognitive Science of Religion," *Theology and Science* 17 (2019) 1–24. © Center for Theology and the Natural Sciences. Reprinted by permission of Taylor & Francis Ltd, http://www.tandfonline.com, on behalf of the Center for Theology and the Natural Sciences. This chapter is adapted from an address by the author delivered at the Carl F. H. Henry Center for Theological Understanding, Trinity Evangelical Divinity School, Deerfield, IL, Oct. 18, 2018.

Chapter 4: Kling, David W. "Edwards in the Context of International Revivals and Missions." In *The Oxford Handbook of Jonathan Edwards*, edited by Jan Stievermann and Douglas A. Sweeney, 51–68. New York: Oxford University Press, 2021. Reproduced by permission of Oxford University Press. https://global.oup.com/academic/search?q=Kling%2C+David+W.&cc=us&lang=en.

Chapter 5: Kling, David W. "Edwards in the Second Great Awakening: The New Divinity Contributions of Edward Dorr Griffin and Asahel Nettleton." In *After Edwards: The Courses of the New England Theology*, edited by Oliver D. Crisp and Douglas A. Sweeney, 130–41. New York: Oxford University Press, 2012. Reproduced by permission of Oxford University Press. https://global.oup.com/academic/search?q=Kling%2C+David+W.&cc=us&lang=en.

Chapter 6: Kling, David W. "The New Divinity and the Origins of the American Board of Commissioners for Foreign Missions." *Church History* 72 (2003) 791–819. © Cambridge University Press, reproduced with permission.

Chapter 7: Kling, David W. "New Divinity Schools of the Prophets, 1750–1825: A Case Study in Ministerial Education." *History of Education Quarterly* 37 (1997) 185–206. © History of Education Society 2019. Reprinted by permission.

Chapter 8: Kling, David W. "The New Divinity and Williams College, 1793–1836." *Religion and American Culture: A Journal of Interpretation* 6 (1996) 195–223. Reprinted by permission.

Unless otherwise noted or within a quoted source, all Scripture quotations contained herein are from the Authorized (King James) Version. Rights in the Authorized Version in the United Kingdom are vested in the Crown. Reproduced by permission of the Crown's patentee, Cambridge University Press.

To Daniel L. Pals and Douglas A. Sweeney

Contents

List of Figures | xi
Foreword by Douglas A. Sweeney | xiii
Preface | xvii
Acknowledgments | xx
Abbreviations | xxi
Introduction | xxiii

PART ONE: *Jonathan Edwards*

Chapter 1   The Puritans, Jonathan Edwards, and the Great Awakening in America, 1630–1790 | 3

Chapter 2   Edwards, the Bible, and Conversion | 38

Chapter 3   Edwards, Petitionary Prayer, and the Cognitive Science of Religion | 58

Chapter 4   Edwards in the Context of International Revivals and Missions | 88

PART TWO: *The Edwardseans*

Chapter 5   Edwards in the Second Great Awakening: The New Divinity Contributions of Edward Dorr Griffin and Asahel Nettleton | 111

Chapter 6   The New Divinity and the Origins of the American Board of Commissioners for Foreign Missions | 128

Chapter 7 New Divinity Schools of the Prophets, 1750–1825:
            A Case Study in Ministerial Education | 157

Chapter 8 The New Divinity and Williams College, 1793–1836 | 181

Bibliography | 207
Index | 229

List of Figures

Figure 1. Jonathan Edwards's sermons and his usage of the term "conversion." | 49

Figure 2. New Divinity schools of the prophets, 1750–1825. | 167

Foreword

FIFTY YEARS AGO, WHEN David Kling enrolled in graduate school, scholarship on Jonathan Edwards and his "New Divinity" heirs[1] was enthralled by the work of a recently deceased Presbyterian theologian, Joseph Haroutunian (1904–68), who had spent his final years at the University of Chicago. A devotee of "neo-orthodox" cultural criticism, Haroutunian had published, while still in his twenties, a benchmark essay on the legacy of Edwards, *Piety versus Moralism: The Passing of the New England Theology* (1932), which, forty years later, still dominated the field. Dissatisfied with much of modern Western theology, impatient with the vagaries of history on the ground, Haroutunian took a macro-level view of social history, interpreting its modern American ecclesiastical subjects in light of his ideology. His profound respect for Edwards and valiant quest to battle against the forces of Enlightenment gave rise to a withering critique of Edwards's heirs. Those who fitted Edwards's theocentric vision to the lives of more humanistic, independent, early national Americans—framing it in relation to republican concerns for civil liberty, virtue, and noncoercive moral government—were treated with suspicion and portrayed as accomplices in the steady degradation of Western culture.[2]

It should go without saying that this cavalier take on Edwards's ministerial legacy militated against careful, sympathetic study of its everyday proponents. Those convinced in advance of historical declension rarely pay due attention to the figures they blame. Fortunately,

---

1. Edwards's pastoral ministry, his network of colleagues, and his theological writings gave birth to the first indigenous school of Christian thought in colonial American history. This school and its leaders went by several different names, especially as they grew and spread across the new nation: the New Divinity movement, Consistent Calvinists, New England Theologians, and, most broadly, Edwardseans. They played a major role in the spread of North American evangelicalism. By the nineteenth century, the school had grown quite large and internally diverse.

2. Haroutunian, *Piety versus Moralism*.

however, Haroutunian was eclipsed during the late twentieth century—in no small part by another Presbyterian at the University of Chicago, the author of the essays you are holding in your hands. Beginning with his doctoral dissertation at Chicago, and continuing with a long series of ground-breaking articles on Edwards and his legacies, David Kling has demonstrated crucial continuities between Edwards himself and his New Divinity heirs—continuities that energized revivals, missions, undergraduate education, the rise of modern seminaries, and serious theology in the new United States, not to mention pastoral ministry all over the Western world. I encountered Kling's work as a graduate student at Vanderbilt and became one of many younger colleagues for whom Kling's scholarship was formative.[3]

Permit me a page or two to put Kling's work in historical perspective. In 1965, in a little-known essay by historian Richard Birdsall, the seeds of revisionary interpretation of Edwards and his followers were sown.[4] A handful of scholars soon paid close attention to at least the best-known of the New Divinity preachers. But not until the publication of Joseph Conforti's *Samuel Hopkins and the New Divinity Movement* (1981) did scholars circumvent the force of Haroutunian's paradigm. Like Birdsall, Conforti called for better social history of the New Divinity movement. By ignoring its social context and focusing instead on its "intellectual rigor and commitment to consistency," Conforti contended, many falsely assumed that the New Divinity clergy "became divorced from social reality and the dynamic piety of the [Great] Awakening." Conforti admitted that the New Divinity "radically extended and modified" Edwards's theological program. But he argued that it "stopped far short of transforming Calvinist piety into Christian moralism." He went on in later studies to discuss other Edwardseans, highlighting their "cultural revival" in the first half of the nineteenth century. Impelled by the revivals of the Second Great Awakening, their movement grew "in size and influence to a position of dominance within New England Congregationalism." It even played a major part in nineteenth-century history south and west of New England. So much for the "passing" of the Edwardsean tradition.[5]

---

3. The most important of the articles are published in this volume. The dissertation was published as Kling, *Field of Divine Wonders*.

4. Birdsall, "Ezra Stiles," 248–58. Cf. Birdsall, "Second Great Awakening," where he argues in similar fashion for the historical (and moral) significance of Edwardsean revivalism.

5. Conforti, *Samuel Hopkins*, 4–6, 192, 48; Conforti, "Invention of the Great

Several scholars followed Conforti's lead in taking the Edwardseans themselves more seriously as actors on the ground with their own religious concerns. And a few, most importantly the author of these essays, answered his call for more and better social history of the New Divinity movement. Looking closely at the third generation of its clergy in northwestern Connecticut, Kling discovered that his subjects were engaging small-town pastors and successful revivalists. Their achievements in the practice of parish ministry, in fact, suggested to Kling that the "piety of . . . Edwards did not give way to the [allegedly] bland moralism" of his followers. The New Divinity clergy stayed true to the promotion of heartfelt Edwardsean piety and, in doing so, they "dominated theological discourse in New England."[6]

Others joined Birdsall, Conforti, and Kling in paying heed to the New Divinity clergy, slowly reassembling the puzzle of Edwards's theological legacy. William Breitenbach investigated the New Divinity notion of human moral accountability, affirming that "Hopkinsian theology lay squarely within the New England Calvinist tradition." Many "obstinately continue to impose the piety-versus-moralism paradigm on . . . New England religious history," Breitenbach observed, but the "dominant New England theological tradition, the clerical orthodoxy, was one of piety and moralism." Each of the "so-called peculiarities and innovations of the New Divinity," moreover, were continuations of "Edwards' most creative and important contributions to New England theology." Mark Noll and Bruce Kuklick remained somewhat beholden to Haroutunian's perspective. But they, too, studied New England with sensitivity to Edwardsean priorities. Noll insisted that while Edwards had no true "successors," he enjoyed faithful "guardians" in nineteenth-century New England. And while Kuklick depicted Haroutunian's paradigm as "at least formally accurate," he portrayed the New England Theology as a legitimate extension of the thought of its progenitor, "the most sustained, systematic, and creative intellectual tradition" the nation had ever produced.[7]

Awakening," 108, 101. Conforti's many other publications on New Divinity history culminated in Conforti, *Jonathan Edwards*.

6. Kling, *Field of Divine Wonders*, 88, 25.

7. Breitenbach, "Piety and Moralism," 178–79, 190–91; Breitenbach, "New Divinity Theology," 102–11; Breitenbach, "Consistent Calvinism," 243–64; Breitenbach, "Unregenerate Doings"; Noll, "Jonathan Edwards"; Noll, "Contested Legacy"; Noll, "Moses Mather"; Noll, *America's God*; Kuklick, "Jonathan Edwards," 257; Kuklick, *Churchmen and Philosophers*, 63–64.

Allen Guelzo treated New Divinity thought most fully. In his highly acclaimed book entitled *Edwards on the Will: A Century of American Theological Debate* (1989), he maintained that Edwardsean theology derived "almost entirely from the ... agendas of [Edwards's] *Freedom of the Will*" (1754). For Guelzo, as for others who would follow in his steps, if the Edwardseans were "moral rigorists, it was because Edwards gave them a mandate for rigorism which they took with uncompromising seriousness." New Divinity doctrine was not an innovative departure from the work of its progenitor. It "was hardly more than a set of variations on certain Edwardsean themes."[8]

I, too, on my own and in combined work with others, have followed Kling and company, revisiting the history of the New Divinity movement. Kling's bright scholarly light has illuminated the field in which many have now labored. It is an honor to pay him tribute in this foreword.[9]

David Kling has been a field-changing scholar. And the chapters in this volume will introduce readers to horizons of New England and American social history he has opened for many. He would be the first to say that much work remains to be done on the Edwardsean tradition. The next generation of those who work on Edwards's legacies will no doubt contribute far more detailed, colorful, and clear-eyed portrayals of the New Divinity movement. They will do so, however, because they stand on the shoulders of David Kling.

Douglas A. Sweeney
Beeson Divinity School
Samford University

---

8. Guelzo, *Edwards on the Will*, 87–93, 135–36; Guelzo, "Oberlin Perfectionism."

9. Sweeney, *Nathaniel Taylor*; Kling and Sweeney, *Jonathan Edwards at Home and Abroad*; Sweeney and Guelzo, *New England Theology*; Crisp and Sweeney, *After Jonathan Edwards*.

Preface

THE LAST HALF-CENTURY HAS witnessed an unprecedented outpouring of scholarship on Jonathan Edwards and the Edwardseans (also known as the New Divinity).[1] Unquestionably, the Jonathan Edwards Center[2] at Yale University has been the engine driving this scholarship. The Yale letterpress edition of Edwards's works reached its completion at twenty-six volumes in 2008, and the seventy-three-volume online version contains the entire corpus of Edwards's works, including unpublished computerized manuscripts. In addition, eleven global centers promote research on Edwards; published works about Edwards number in the thousands, and although those about the New Divinity are considerably fewer, they are nonetheless substantial. An online journal is devoted to Edwards studies, Edwards conferences continue to attract scholars from around the world, and thorough assessments of Edwards and his influence have appeared in the past two decades (see the introduction). My contribution to this thriving cottage industry is at best modest, but I hope that it will serve as an introduction to theological matters that meant the most to Edwards and his disciples: spiritual revival, conversion, the Bible, prayer, and extending the kingdom of God.

The chapters in this book appeared in previously published books and journals over the course of nearly thirty years. In this day of the proliferation of easily accessed online publications, the reader may rightly question why I have chosen to gather these writings into a single volume. My answer is fourfold. First, approachability of the subject. Taken together, these chapters serve as an introduction to the central spiritual and theological interests of Edwards and to the long shadow these interests

---

1. For a succinct summary of the New Divinity movement—its theology, social bonds, and institutional presence—see Sweeney, "New Divinity," 400–404.
2. http://edwards.yale.edu.

cast on his eponymous followers. This book is meant to be suitable as either a basic or supplementary text for interested lay people and graduate students, and especially for use in seminaries where Edwards and the Edwardseans are a focus of interest.

Second, coherence of the chapters. The whole (the book) is greater than the sum of its parts (the chapters) insofar as the pages of this book trace a well-defined theological movement from Edwards to his second- and especially third-generation followers. The impact of this movement resulted in the creation of a distinct theological culture that, over two generations, was institutionalized in informal seminaries or "schools of the prophets," in colleges attended by New Divinity students and staffed by New Divinity presidents, and in missionary outreach both at home and abroad.

Third, symmetry to the chapters. When I initially considered gathering the various chapters and articles into a single volume, I realized that there was a natural symmetry to the eight chapters that comprise this book. The first four (Part One) focus on Jonathan Edwards—his formative role in the Great Awakening, his biblical understanding of conversion, his perspective on petitionary prayer, and his influence on missionary endeavors. The next four chapters (Part Two) focus on the appropriation of Edwards by his disciples in the Second Great Awakening and their creation of both informal and formal institutions that bore the Edwardsean imprint into the 1840s.

Fourth, affordability of the book. Not all college, university, or seminary libraries have the financial resources to purchase either online subscriptions or hard copies of the journals and books in which the chapters in this book first appeared. Thanks to Wipf and Stock's pricing policy, this book makes these collected articles and chapters available at reasonable cost.

On a personal note, I came to the study of Edwards and the New Divinity through a circuitous route. My own religious background was in the free church, pietistic, Arminian tradition, far removed from the Reformed or Calvinist orbit. The trajectory of my interest in Edwards and the New Divinity was launched initially in my graduate studies at the University of Chicago. Although I had no clear research agenda or dissertation topic at the ready when I matriculated, coursework and conversations with Martin Marty and Jerald Brauer piqued my interest in America's revivalist tradition. During my years at Chicago, to my later regret, I never took a course from or had a conversation with the great Edwards scholar Thomas Schaefer, who was teaching at McCormick Theological Seminary, just across the street from the University's Divinity School. In any event, I completed a dissertation on the Second Great Awakening in Connecticut that was published in revised form in 1993.[3] Subsequent journal publications grew out of themes and subjects discussed in the monograph (chapters 6, 7, and 8 in this volume) that had not been fully fleshed out in my book.

To grasp the theological significance of the Awakening, I had to work back chronologically to understand the influence of Edwards's writings on the leaders of the revival. A focused attention on Edwards came later, largely due to collaborations with and invitations from Douglas Sweeney, an Edwards scholar par excellence. Together, we co-edited a volume on Edwards that grew out of a conference that convened in Miami in 2000.[4] Subsequent invitations from Doug to contribute chapters to edited volumes and an invitation to deliver a paper at Trinity Evangelical Divinity School's Henry Center for Theological Understanding in 2018 drove me deeper into the writings of Edwards. Immersing myself more deeply in Edwards's works enabled me to more fully understand the connective links from Edwards to his disciples.

---

3. Kling, *Field of Divine Wonders*.
4. Kling and Sweeney, *Jonathan Edwards at Home and Abroad*.

Acknowledgments

I HAVE BENEFITTED IMMENSELY from those many colleagues who, over the past three decades, responded to my questions, read drafts, shared their work, offered suggestions, corrected errors, critiqued arguments, gave encouragement, and included me in the ever-enlarging circle of Edwards scholars. My thanks and acknowledgements extend to David Barshinger, Ava Chamberlain, Charles Cohen, Joe Conforti, Oliver Crisp, Allen Guelzo, Michael McClymond, Gerald McDermott, Kenneth Minkema, Mark Noll, Lewis Rambo, Jan Stievermann, the late Stephen Stein, and Harry Stout.

I am also indebted to Kathy McKay, copy editor extraordinaire and, serendipitously, a graduate of Williams College (the focus of chapter 8). She transformed the many styles in which the individual chapters in this book first appeared to meet Wipf and Stock's style guidelines. Her keen eye and valuable suggestions improved both the style and content of this book.

Edwards and the Edwardseans is dedicated to two dear friends and colleagues who have had a profound impact on my professional career. During his years as chair of the Department of Religious Studies at the University of Miami, Dan Pals guided me through the tenure process, created an environment for scholarship to flourish, and applied his expert editorial pen (now Track Changes) to nearly all of my scholarly writings. I could not ask for a better departmental colleague. In the last two decades, as I ventured into other book projects, Doug Sweeney kept me firmly planted in the Edwardsean world, inviting me to return to my first scholarly love. Our first encounter at the Annual Meeting of the American Academy of Religion in 1994 led to shared scholarly interests, critiques of each other's works, and, along the way, an enduring friendship. I could not ask for a better collaborative colleague.

Abbreviations

ABCFM	American Board of Commissioners for Foreign Missions
Gratz Collection	Simon Gratz Collection, Historical Society of Pennsylvania, Philadelphia, Pennsylvania
Plumer Papers	William Swan Plumer Papers, Presbyterian Church (USA), Department of History, Montreat, North Carolina
Williamsiana Collection	Williamsiana Collection, Williams College Archives, Williamstown, Massachusetts
WJE	Edwards, Jonathan. *Works of Jonathan Edwards.* 26 vols. New Haven, CT: Yale University Press, 1957–2006.
WJE 1	*Freedom of the Will*
WJE 2	*A Treatise Concerning Religious Affections*
WJE 3	*Original Sin*
WJE 4	*The Great Awakening*
WJE 5	*Apocalyptic Writings*
WJE 6	*Scientific and Philosophical Writings*
WJE 7	*The Life of David Brainerd*
WJE 8	*Ethical Writings*
WJE 9	*A History of the Work of Redemption*
WJE 10	*Sermons and Discourses, 1720–1723*
WJE 11	*Typological Writings*

WJE 12	*Ecclesiastical Writings*
WJE 13	*The "Miscellanies": Nos. a–z, aa–zz, 1–500*
WJE 14	*Sermons and Discourses, 1723–1729*
WJE 15	*Notes on Scripture*
WJE 16	*Letters and Personal Writings*
WJE 17	*Sermons and Discourses 1730–1733*
WJE 18	*The "Miscellanies": Nos. 501–832*
WJE 19	*Sermons and Discourses, 1734–1738*
WJE 20	*The "Miscellanies": Nos. 833–1132*
WJE 21	*Writings on the Trinity, Grace and Faith*
WJE 22	*Sermons and Discourses, 1739–1742*
WJE 23	*The "Miscellanies": Nos. 1153–1360*
WJE 24	*The "Blank Bible"*
WJE 25	*Sermons and Discourses, 1743–1758*
WJEO	Works of Jonathan Edwards Online. Jonathan Edwards Center at Yale University. http://edwards.yale.edu/archive.
WPE	*The Works of President Edwards*. 8 vols. 1817, 2 suppl. vols. 1847. Reprint of all 10 vols. by New York: Burt Franklin, 1968.

Introduction

"Of making many books there is no end" (Eccl 12:12). Certainly, these words of the sage Kohelet are true of the publication history of books and articles about Jonathan Edwards in the last half century. According to the calculations of Kenneth Minkema, the executive editor of Yale's Edwards project, "The number of secondary publications on Edwards fast approaches 4,000, making him one of the most studied figures in Christian thought and *the* most studied American intellectual figure before 1800."[1] And in the years since M. X. Lesser concluded his massive annotated Edwards bibliography in 2005, an estimated 450 publications have appeared.[2] I need not go into the reasons for this explosion (some who refer to it as a renaissance minimize this reality), for these have been sufficiently discussed by others.[3] What I want to emphasize is that in the past two decades, beginning with George Marsden's authoritative biography of Edwards in 2003, scholarship on Edwards and the Edwardseans clearly reached a pinnacle. In addition to Marsden's award-winning book, Gerald McDermott and Michael McClymond offered a magisterial account of Edwards's theology in 2012, and the more recent *Jonathan Edwards Encyclopedia* (2017) and the *Oxford Handbook of Jonathan Edwards* (2021) supplied the most up-to-date critical analyses of Edwards and the Edwardseans.[4] All of which is to say that what is offered in this

---

1. Minkema, "Jonathan Edwards," 678.

2. Lesser, *Reading Jonathan Edwards*. I am adding speculatively to the list of 406 publications compiled by Doug Sweeney for the years from 2005 to 2018. See Sweeney, "Edwards Studies Today," 569–70.

3. For examples, see Minkema, "Jonathan Edwards," 659–87; Marsden, "Old, Rested, and Reformed." On the history of interpretation of Edwards, see Sweeney, "Edwards and His Mantle."

4. Marsden, *Jonathan Edwards* (see also his *Short Life of Jonathan Edwards*); McClymond and McDermott, *Theology of Jonathan Edwards*; Stout et al., *Jonathan Edwards Encyclopedia*; Sweeney and Stievermann, *Oxford Handbook of Jonathan Edwards*. For

book will find amplification, clarification, and perhaps revision in these more recent works. And of course, since scholarship is always in the process of discovering new sources, proposing new directions, and challenging interpretations, of the making many books and articles on Jonathan Edwards and the Edwardseans there will be no end—to the point where, as the sage continues, "much study is a weariness of the flesh." And so, I offer a beginning, an entrée into the spiritual and theological world of Edwards and his followers.

Part One takes up issues dear to Edwards: conversion, prayer, and missions. Chapter 1 serves as an introduction to Edwards, narrating the larger context of his views of conversion, beginning with the necessity and nature of conversion from the earliest New England Puritan communities in the seventeenth century to the mid-eighteenth-century colonies-wide Great Awakening. Following an examination of the conversionary views of Thomas Shepard and briefly exploring the phenomenon of the Great Awakening, I turn to an extended discussion of the centrality of conversion in the life and writings of Edwards, with particular attention to his *Personal Narrative* and *Religious Affections*. Despite the Awakening's many variations, the unifying theme that transcended denominational boundaries was its focus on a "heart-centered," conversion-oriented religion. Indeed, thanks in large part to Edwards, the legacy of the Awakening—what made it truly "great"—was the formation of an American evangelical culture whose touchstone was the conversion experience and whose influence has stretched into our own time and expanded around the world.

Chapter 2 narrows the scope of chapter 1 to examine the exegetical foundations of Edwards's understanding of conversion. I probe this topic by, first, treating the role of the Bible in Edwards's own conversion, distinct as it was from the reigning model in the Puritan tradition; second, considering the place of conversion in Edwards's discussion of revivals; and third, examining the intersection of Scripture and conversion in three representative awakening sermons. In Edwards's view, the Bible taught that conversion is real, that it transforms not only the soul but also the body, and that it involves both a "first conversion" and an ongoing process.

Chapter 3 takes the reader beyond traditional historical analysis to extend the findings of cognitive science to an examination of petitionary

---

accessible works on Edwards's ministry and theology, see Sweeney, *Jonathan Edwards*; Lucas, *God's Grand Design*.

prayer in the sermons and writings of Edwards. The contemporary field of cognitive science proposes (among other things) that religion involves a two-step model of reasoning that moves from basic beliefs in God ("natural religion") to a more particularized theological elaboration of those beliefs. The transition from natural religion to theology can lead to a tension, if not a contradiction, in thinking. An analysis of Edwards's writings on petitionary prayer uncovers this difficulty, both among his Northampton parishioners in their "prayer bids" and in Edwards himself in his pleas for petitionary prayer that God grant the British victory over the French at Cape Breton.

Chapter 4 moves from Edwards "at home" to his influence abroad in the context of international revivals and missions—an influence that is entirely dependent on the reception of his writings. In the context of the early stages of a transatlantic evangelical awakening, Edwards's efforts to advance the gospel were both immediate and delayed—immediate insofar as his writings, particularly the *Faithful Narrative*, inspired Scottish Presbyterian and German and Dutch Pietist evangelical contemporaries to promote revival and delayed insofar as his impact on foreign missions was not felt until the end of the eighteenth and well into the nineteenth century. Edwards's most important contributions to international missions are derived from his conception of cosmic redemption (*Humble Attempt, History of the Work of Redemption*), his distinction between moral and natural ability (*Freedom of the Will*), and his presentation of an archetypical missionary model (*Life of David Brainerd*).

Part Two presents four cases studies demonstrating Edwards's enduring impact. Continuing Edwards's preoccupation with revival, chapter 5 argues that his followers were not only thinkers but doers and not only speculative theologians (for which they earned the label New Divinity) but engaged revivalists. Their concern with spiritual awakening was particularly evident among the third generation of Edwardseans, a postrevolutionary cohort whose ministry extended from the 1790s to the 1820s. Among the revivalists of the Second Great Awakening in New England, Edward Dorr Griffin and Asahel Nettleton excelled at the craft. Griffin, the "prince of preachers," who held several pastorates and then presided over Williams College (the subject of chapter 8), wielded the sermonic conventions of his day with "tenderness and tears" to lead sinners to Christ. As an itinerant evangelist who specialized in personal group "conference meetings," Nettleton far exceeded Griffin's success. In the words of Francis Wayland, "I suppose no minister of his time was the means of so many conversions."

Chapter 6 moves from the individual efforts of Griffin and Nettleton to the collective influence of the New Divinity in the formation and character of the American Board of Commissioners for Foreign Missions (ABCFM), the first foreign missionary organization in the United States. The New Divinity's foray into missions abroad may be seen as a continuation and extension of local revivals and frontier missions. Though devoid of explicit doctrinal standards, the ABCFM "was a New Divinity creation, rooted in New Divinity theology, inspired by New Divinity revivals, and staffed by a well-established New Divinity social and institutional network." By 1850, the ABCFM had become the first (created in 1810) and the largest (sponsoring 40 percent of all missionary personnel in the United States) missionary organization in the United States.

Chapter 7 turns to ministerial education and the commanding presence of New Divinity theological instructors from 1750 to 1825. Before the creation of theological seminaries (Andover Theological Seminary was the first, organized in 1808), post-baccalaureate theological education was conducted primarily in informal academies known as "schools of the prophets." Despite monopolizing theological training for well over half a century, the New Divinity schools of the prophets have either been overlooked or, more often, underappreciated. From 1750 to 1825, over five hundred clerical aspirants studied in these Edwardsean home schools—indeed, many of the students lived with their theological instructor. Largely due to the impact of these schools, the New Divinity attained cultural, theological, and missiological preeminence throughout New England and abroad.

Chapter 8 rounds out the book by examining a third instance of New Divinity institutionalization—collegiate education, in particular at Williams College. Although Williams became known as the celebrated site of the Haystack Prayer Meeting where in 1806 Samuel J. Mills Jr. and four other students consecrated their lives to overseas missions, the college was never, in a legal or formal sense, a religious institution. Moreover, the college's founder, Ephraim Williams, was a Calvinist, but an Edwardsean he was not. And yet the history of Williams College, from the college's beginnings in 1793 to 1836 (encompassing the presidencies of three New Divinity men), exemplified the cultural revival of Jonathan Edwards. The formation of Williams coincided with the maturation of the New Divinity movement to create an institution with a distinct Edwardsean ethos.

Alert readers will detect that in several chapters I reiterate theological themes crucial to the New Divinity's appropriation of Edwards. Because these essays were originally written as standalone pieces whose themes often intersected, I frequently drew from the content in previous essays in discussing major theological convictions linking Edwards to his followers. Although I have revised my discussion of these themes in some of the chapters as they originally appeared so as not to "self-plagiarize," overlap in content and to some extent verbiage could not always be avoided. Three recurring themes stand out. Two define the New Divinity movement's theological agenda: the appropriation of Edwards's view of the will and his emphasis on the necessity of immediate repentance. The third is the modification of Edwards's "disinterested benevolence" by Samuel Hopkins and the consequent implications this "improvement" (as Hopkins called it) had for missionary and social activism.

PART ONE

Jonathan Edwards

1

The Puritans, Jonathan Edwards, and the Great Awakening in America, 1630–1790

SHORTLY AFTER ARRIVING AT the Massachusetts Bay Colony in the 1630s, Puritan ministers instituted an unprecedented requirement for prospective members of the church. To the standard admission requirement of affirming Reformed doctrine and giving evidence of an upright life, they now insisted that those seeking admittance must give a credible public testimony of the genuineness and reality of divine grace in their lives. Although English Puritans placed conversion at the center of religious experience, they rarely made it a litmus test for church membership. All Puritans, whether in England, in exile on the Continent, or in America, began with the premise that the church should consist of the faithful—those who had voluntarily entered into a covenant—and yet no uniform criteria were applied in determining who were the faithful.

By 1600, a few Puritan independent churches in England required candidates for full membership to give their verbal assent to the doctrinal standards of the church. Radical separatists, particularly those living in exile on the Continent, went a step further. They expected their members to submit to the church and live an upright life and then added the crucial requirement of making a profession of faith that was not merely a pro forma assent but one that evidenced understanding and belief. Still, although they "considered saving faith necessary for entrance into the invisible church they did not attempt to discern it in those admitted to the visible church," for "saving faith lay in the heart, where only God could see it."[1] But New England Puritans decided to "play God" by coming as close as humanly possible to ensuring that "visible saints" (members of the church by virtue of their giving convincing proof that they were among the elect) were among the "invisible saints" (the elect known only to God). By taking upon themselves this awesome task, they envisioned becoming a true gathered community modeled on the New Testament church. Why a conversion narrative became a requirement for church admission has never been answered satisfactorily—Puritan divines gave no explicit reasons—but historians speculate that an effort to maintain doctrinal orthodoxy by scrutinizing the nature of the candidates' conversion is a plausible reason.[2] For several generations, the insistence on a church of visible saints remained a distinguishing mark of New England Puritan churches. Although the concept fell into disrepute in some churches, its most basic feature—the necessity of a conversion experience—came to define an emerging evangelical movement in the 1730s and 1740s. To this day, it has endured as a centerpiece of evangelicalism in America and around the world.

Puritanism, of course, cannot take sole credit for the rise of evangelicalism. The early evangelical movement included the contributions of Continental Pietism and English Methodism, but American Puritanism's uniquely profound and lasting contribution merits our attention in this chapter. Here, we examine Puritan views of conversion in the colonial period by focusing on the Great Awakening and, in particular, on the life and writings of Jonathan Edwards (1703–58), considered "the most influential thinker in all of evangelical history."[3]

BACK TO THE FUTURE: VISIBLE SAINTHOOD

One of the earliest American Puritan examples of the requirement of giving testimony to God's work of grace is found in the "Relations" or "Confessions," transcriptions of the oral testimonies of aspiring communicants recorded by Thomas Shepard (1605–49), pastor of First Church in Cambridge, Massachusetts. Prospective church members who had recently arrived as refugees from England presented themselves for examination, privately before the minister and publicly before the congregation. They

---

1. Morgan, *Visible Saints*, 47.
2. Winship, *Making Heretics*, 80.
3. Sweeney, *Jonathan Edwards*, 17.

were charged, noted Shepard, to "make known to the congregation the work of grace upon [their] souls."[4] Their accounts, "practiced at home, coached by the minister, and vetted by senior saints," reflected the unique circumstances of the individual, and yet they generally followed the well-established model of conversion devised by English Puritans. That model, however, as Patricia Caldwell observes, "emerges from an angle of vision and not from an arrangement of steps. It is a literary morphology, a total way of perceiving and talking about experiences rather than a particular predetermined mold."[5]

Indeed, while the Puritan William Perkins (1558–1602), the leading English systematic theologian in his day, formulated a ten-step process, Shepard noted only four, and, as we will see, Jonathan Edwards, like the English Nonconformist Richard Baxter (1615–91), questioned a strict morphology of conversion, mainly because his own conversion did not conform to such. At the end of his *Parable of the Ten Virgins* sermon series, Shepard gave his Cambridge congregation a simple formula for proper confession: "Thus was I humbled, then thus was I called, then thus have I walked, though with many weaknesses since; and such special providences of God have I seen, temptations gone through; and thus the Lord hath delivered me."[6] The brief conversion narrative of Edward Hall conforms to this blueprint. Hall testified that after he heard Shepard preach from John 3 concerning the new birth, he saw more of his miserable, sinful, "Christless" condition. The Lord humbled him and he realized that without Christ he would perish. Shepard "opened" John 5:40 (the words of Jesus: "And ye will not come to me, that ye might have life"). Hall realized that Christ was freely offered, and he was stirred to seek Christ. He embraced the promise that the son of man came to seek that which was lost (Luke 19:10). The Lord made him "loath" himself and he felt "enmity" against the Lord, but as he came to acknowledge the Lord's grace and mercy, the enmity dissipated.[7]

Confessions such as Hall's marked the beginning, not the end, of the Christian's pilgrimage. Shepard's record of his own spiritual experiences and sermons reinforced this view. In his autobiography, Shepard observes that renewed conversions followed his long and stressful first

---

4. McGiffert, *God's Plot*, 137.
5. Caldwell, *Puritan Conversion Narrative*, 178.
6. Shepard, *Parable of the Ten Virgins*, 631.
7. McGiffert, *God's Plot*, 149–50.

conversion as a student at Cambridge.[8] In his lengthy series of sermons entitled *Parable of the Ten Virgins*, he speaks of the first experience of conversion as deceptive: "Many that have had mighty strong affections at first conversion afterward become dry, and wither, and consume, and pine, and die away, and now their hypocrisy is manifest." He concluded his sermon series by echoing the Reformation catchphrase with an added Puritan twist: "Be always converting, and be always converted; turn us again, O Lord. When a man thinks, I was humbled and comforted, I will not lay all by, and so live on old scraps, O, beware of that frame; not that a Christian should be always pulling up the foundations, and ever doubting; but to make sure, be always converting, more humble, more sensible of sin, more near to Christ Jesus."[9] *To make sure.* Shepard's sustained and fervent insistence "on the renewability of conversion," writes Michael McGiffert, "tended to slight the evidential significance of the original experience."[10] His preoccupation with assurance and signs of that assurance had the potential to lead his parishioners to doubt their election and suffer from perpetual spiritual angst. Apparently, the odds were against them. Shepard calculated that for every one of the elect, one thousand were damned![11] He continually reminded his church attenders that no one could know for sure whether God had chosen them. The blessing of assurance—so confidently expressed by the "disorderly" Anne Hutchinson and other American Puritan "antinomians" who appealed to the direct revelation of the Spirit and threatened the stability of the infant colony—belonged to no one.[12] The surest sign of assurance included a sound faith, earnest efforts to be loving and faithful, a desire for heaven, a grateful response to the good news of the gospel—and continued doubts about one's assurance.[13] The most a Christian could hope for was conditional assurance. A state of continual struggle characterized the authentically godly. Despite putting his parishioners on "a seesaw of hope and despair," Shepard lightened the psychological burden by appealing more

---

8. Pettit, *Heart Prepared*, 106–7.
9. Shepard, *Parable of the Ten Virgins*, 233, 632.
10. McGiffert, *God's Plot*, 26.
11. Shepard, *Sincere Convert*, 62.
12. The literature on Anne Hutchinson and the "Antinomian Controversy" (more appropriately called the "free grace controversy") is extensive, but see Winship, *Making Heretics*; Winship, *Times and Trials of Anne Hutchinson*.
13. McGiffert, *God's Plot*, 15, 21, 24.

often to God's mercy than to God's wrath.[14] Although a controversial hunter of heresy, his contemporaries recognized him as an exemplary pastor and preacher.

Proof that the number of elect was indeed small became obvious to Puritan leaders when an increasing number of second-generation Puritans were unable to testify to the work of grace in their lives. This falloff in conversions presented a particularly acute ecclesiastical problem when the rising generation married and had children. Given their unconverted status, they were disqualified from presenting their infants for baptism—the initial sign of God's covenant. Puritan leaders faced a quandary unanticipated by the first generation of leaders: the continued demand for a church of visible saints could potentially reduce the number of full church members to an insignificant remnant and destroy the Puritan experiment that envisioned the church and the people of the colony coextensive. After much debate, New England divines created the Half-Way Covenant (1662). Under its terms, sincere and upright though unconverted parents who agreed to submit to the "watch and care" of the church could present their children for baptism and thereby "own" the covenant, but they could not vote on church matters or receive the Lord's Supper (and hence were not "full" members). The architects of this plan anticipated that both the unregenerate parents and the children would testify at some point to God's gracious work in their lives. The historian Edmund Morgan maintained, "The halfway covenant was neither a sign of decline in piety nor a betrayal of the standards of the founding fathers, but an honest attempt to rescue the concept of a church of visible saints from the tangle of problems created in time by human reproduction."[15] The congregational form of church government in New England left the implementation of the Half-Way Covenant in the hands of the local church, and by 1700 most churches had adopted it.

Toward the end of the seventeenth century and into the first decades of the eighteenth century, Puritan pastors responded to the spiritual concerns of their parishioners by relaxing requirements for church membership. Some did so because they concluded the bar of conversion had set admission standards out of the reach of their congregants. Increasingly, pastors composed formalized statements that resembled contracts in place of the oral, introspective presentations given by past candidates.

---

14. Caldwell, *Puritan Conversion Narrative*, 121.
15. Morgan, *Visible Saints*, 137.

Church records indicate that admissions were increasingly linked to important life transitions: spouses joined together, followed a month later by the baptism of their children. Ministers also moderated admission standards for evangelistic reasons. Although the ideal of a gathered church of the converted remained, many adopted a more inclusive policy of membership in the hope of reaching nonmembers. "Gradually, and for the most part imperceptibly," observed Morgan, "New England churches made baptism available to all professing Christians of good behavior and to their children."[16]

More controversial were radical changes made in Communion practices. In the late seventeenth century, Solomon Stoddard (1643–1729), the renowned pastor in Northampton, Massachusetts, abandoned the traditional "fencing of the table" and opened participation in the Lord's Supper to professing Christians of moral standing who had conscientiously absented themselves from the sacrament because, in their minds, "they had not a work of Saving conversion." Stoddard was convinced that the sacrament could be used effectively as a "converting ordinance."[17] Accordingly, writes Brooks Holifield, "The Lord's Supper was a mnemonic ceremony that converted men [and women] by teaching them and stirring their emotions, thereby evoking internal assent to doctrines that they had known before only as cold, lifeless propositions."[18] The sacrament not only *strengthened* grace in the soul—the traditional Puritan view—but, in Stoddard's mind, it could also *produce* grace in the soul. Despite accusations of apostasy, Stoddard was no theological liberal. He urged ministers to preach the "Fear of Hell to restrain [people] from Sin," and no one could match him as a revivalist. Under his evangelistic preaching, his congregation experienced five "harvests" of revival from 1679 to 1718, foreshadowing the outpouring of spiritual fervor in the religious awakening led by his grandson and successor in the Northampton pulpit, Jonathan Edwards. Although Edwards inherited his grandfather's passion for revivals, he eventually repudiated Stoddard's admission policies and denounced the Half-Way Covenant. Edwards and his revivalist confrères reasserted the earlier insistence on a church of visible saints, demanding of communicants a credible testimony of conversion.

---

16. Winiarski, "Religious Experiences in New England," 219–21; Morgan, *Visible Saints*, 145.

17. Quoted in Holifield, *Covenant Sealed*, 213.

18. Holifield, *Covenant Sealed*, 211.

THE GREAT AWAKENING

Sporadic flares of revival, such as were experienced in Stoddard's church, erupted in the last decades of the seventeenth century, but by the mid-1730s the flames of revival had spread up and down the eastern seaboard and into the hinterlands. Many Puritan ministers who had previously expressed worries about flagging spirituality by preaching "jeremiads" (from the lamentations found in the Old Testament book of Jeremiah) and urging congregational "covenant renewals" (rituals of English Puritan origin stressing corporate commitments to God and the covenant) now expressed joy at the apparent widespread outpouring of God's Spirit. The so-called Great Awakening (a label given to the revival movement a century later), perhaps more appropriately described as America's first evangelical movement, reflected the theological traditions growing out of English Puritanism, Scots-Irish Presbyterianism, Continental Pietism, and, by the end of the eighteenth century, Methodism.

Recent studies of the revivals' scattered geographical distribution, chronological unevenness, and denominational pluralism have brought into question the extent to which these spiritual stirrings can be considered a unified, intercolonial, "great" awakening.[19] Yet, however one defines "great," the Awakening was extraordinary in its nature and scope. American revivalists forged links (primarily through print and correspondence) between local awakenings to create an intercolonial movement, and they made connections with their British counterparts to promote revival on both sides of the Atlantic. Beginning as early as the 1720s, intermittent revivals appeared among Lutherans, Presbyterians, and Calvinists in the Middle Colonies. Major seasons of revival erupted among Congregationalists and Baptists in New England from the 1730s to the 1760s. Anglican, Baptist, and Methodist revivals broke out in the South from the 1750s to the 1770s, and a "New Light Stir" flared up in northern New England and Nova Scotia during the American Revolution (1776–83). Those swept up in the religious enthusiasm included British, Dutch, Scots-Irish, French, and German colonists, African Americans (slaves and free), and Native Americans.[20] Thousands were saved—young and old, rich and poor, male and female.

---

19. On the questionable "greatness" of the Awakening, see Butler, "Enthusiasm Described and Decried," 305–25; Lambert, "First Great Awakening," 650–59; Conforti, *Jonathan Edwards*, 4; and esp. Lambert, *Inventing the "Great Awakening."*

20. Kidd, *Great Awakening*.

The revivals spun off radical sects, female preachers, visionaries, and a dizzying array of "come-outers." In the process, the enthusiasts challenged a hierarchical social order characterized by deference and social rank and sparked a communication revolution. The popular, extemporaneous rhetoric of evangelists "proclaimed the power of the spoken word directly to every individual who would hear, and it confirmed a shift in authority by organizing voluntary prayer meetings and justifying them in the religious vocabulary of the day." Taken together, this upsurge in religious enthusiasm constitutes what Thomas Kidd refers to as "the *long* First Great Awakening," spanning over five decades of the eighteenth century.[21] The push for revival continued into the 1790s with the so-called Second Great Awakening and extended to the Civil War and beyond. Revivalism became a fixture in the American evangelical Protestant landscape.

Despite the Awakening's many variations, the unifying theme that transcended denominational boundaries was its attention to "heart-centered," conversion-oriented religion. The evangelical awakeners, notes Kidd, "successfully convinced thousands of Americans that their conversion by the grace of Christ was the single most important goal of their lives." Indeed, the legacy of the Awakening—what made it truly "great"—was the formation of an American evangelical culture whose touchstone was the conversion experience and whose influence has continued into our own time and expanded around the world.[22]

As the Awakening generated thousands of conversions and bulging church membership rolls, it also sowed the seeds of rancor and division. Congregationalists in New England split between pro-revival New Lights and anti-revival Old Lights, and over one hundred separatist New Light churches were created. Similarly, the Presbyterians in the mid-Atlantic region splintered into New Side and Old Side parties. Moderate evangelicals fell somewhere in between. The conversion experience did not unite colonists; it became the flashpoint of controversy.

To spread their evangelical message, revivalists (both lay and clerical, male and female) itinerated throughout the colonies, occasionally marched unannounced into churches, and even declared that "old" party

---

21. Stout, "Religion," 95; Kidd, *Great Awakening*, xix.

22. Kidd, *Great Awakening*, 323. For examples of the global reach of evangelicalism, see Noll, *New Shape of World Christianity*; Wuthnow, *Boundless Faith*; Stanley, *Global Diffusion of Evangelicalism*.

ministers were unsaved.[23] Gilbert Tennent (1703–64), a Presbyterian minister from Freehold, New Jersey, itinerated in the mid-Atlantic and New England colonies and alienated Old Lights with his sermon *The Danger of an Unconverted Ministry* (1740). Tennent likened the spiritually dead clergy to caterpillars who suck the juices out of living churches and spiritually starve them to death. Like the "old Pharisee-Shepherds," these clergy were "ignorant of the New Birth . . . having no Experience of a special Work of the Holy Ghost, upon their souls."[24]

Not to be outdone, James Davenport (1716–57), another Presbyterian minister who was from Southold, Long Island, abandoned his congregation to become an itinerant minister. He visited various parishes in New York and Connecticut, preached in the fields if denied access to a meetinghouse, denounced local ministers if so led by the Spirit, and occasionally stormed the study of a minister to question him about the state of his soul. After joining a group of Congregational New Light separatists in New London, Connecticut, Davenport called the congregation together and proceeded to harangue them for twenty-four hours straight before collapsing in exhaustion. In a public display reminiscent of Luther's burning of a papal bull, Davenport convinced the parishioners to burn their wigs, jewelry, fine clothes, and the works of suspect writers. Fortunately for the cause of the revival, Davenport's New Light colleagues accurately diagnosed his manic-depressive condition, condemned his actions, and approved his temporary dismissal from the ministry. In 1744, Davenport wrote a "Confession and Retraction" and soon after rejoined the Presbyterian Church.

Less aberrant in his behavior but more sensational in his results was the self-assured English revivalist George Whitefield (1717–70), a former member of John Wesley's Holy Club at Oxford University and the "Grand Itinerant" of America's Awakening. Employing a public relations man and providing extensive newspaper copy of previous successes and future colonial tours, Whitefield honed the marketing tactics of the eighteenth-century Anglo-American commercial world to create a revivalist sensation up and down the Atlantic seaboard. Over the course of thirty years, he made seven preaching tours of the colonies, each lasting about a year and extending from Georgia to Massachusetts. Whitefield elevated the new birth to theological preeminence over against the dead formalism

---

23. On colonial itinerancy, see Hall, *Contested Boundaries*.
24. Tennent, *Danger of an Unconverted Ministry*, 72, 74, 78.

of the churches and the spiritual lassitude of the colonialists. In the process, he truncated the Puritan morphology of conversion as a lifelong pilgrimage into a single transformative event, minimized Reformed theology (e.g., the covenant), and assured his auditors that they could find instant relief from their pangs of guilt and fears of death. Whitefield epitomized the changed religious setting over the course of a century—a change aptly described by Charles Cohen: "Conversion became less the initiation into a group charged with a holy mission than a private act of supreme importance."[25]

More than any other Great Awakener, Whitefield wrought a revolution in religious communication. Not only did he "set up" his audiences with advance publicity, but also his theatrical, extemporaneous, and emotional preaching departed from traditional forms of sermonizing. He attracted thousands to his outdoor preaching spectaculars—the most memorable being a sermon delivered on the Boston Common to twenty thousand people. Under conviction and inspired by the Spirit, his auditors groaned and cried, shouted and danced, and soared into flights of religious ecstasy. Whitefield's histrionics were such that the English actor David Garrick remarked that the revivalist could bring tears to the eyes merely by his pronunciation of the word "Mesopotamia."[26]

What was one to think of the "outcries, faintings, and fits," reports of dreams and visions, and lay exhortations? Critics lambasted the increasing number of individuals, lay and clerical, male and female, who, in the words of William Hart, an anti-revivalist Old Light minister, "will resign themselves up to be led and determ'd in their Sentiments about Religious Matters, by *sudden Impressions & Impulses* upon their minds, by *Imagination, Phantasy, and Conceit,* by *Passion* and *Humour,* and *vitious Pretences.*"[27] Charles Chauncy (1705–87), the respected minister of First Church in Boston and a leading critic of revival, wrote of those caught up in the "religious Phrenzy" that "the extraordinary fervor of their minds" is "accompanied by uncommon bodily motions, and an excessive confidence and assurance."[28] They claim that "God himself speaks inwardly and immediately to their souls." It was all delusion, the result of enthusiasm

---

25. Cohen, *God's Caress*, 274. See also Brauer, "Conversion," 238–43.

26. On Whitefield, see Stout, *Divine Dramatist*; Lambert, *"Pedlar in Divinity"*; Hammond and Jones, *George Whitefield*.

27. Minkema, "Whitefield, Jonathan Edwards, and Revival," 124.

28. Chauncy, "Enthusiasm Described," 234.

getting the best of reason.[29] "The plain Truth is," wrote Chauncy, "*an enlightened Mind*, and not *raised Affections*, ought always to be the Guide of those who called themselves Men; and this in the Affairs of Religion, as well as other Things."[30]

How much credence was one to give to "raised affections" as presumed signs of saving grace? Had personal experience transcended Scripture and reason? Was an "immediate witness of the Spirit" indicative of assurance of salvation? Who could tell? *How* could one tell what was of divine origin or human contrivance? Was the excitement a question of acceptable or unacceptable emotional expression? Was the issue simply one of taste? Was the Great Awakening the work of God, the work of Satan, or a combination?

JONATHAN EDWARDS AND CONVERSION

The events of the revival and the controversies they engendered impelled Jonathan Edwards, a preacher, observer, and promoter of revival in his own Northampton church, to think long and hard about the nature of religious experience, authentic and inauthentic religion, and true and false conversions. For over a decade, beginning with letters describing the revival in his own congregation, then in several sermons, and finally in a book-length treatise, *Religious Affections* (1746), Edwards addressed these issues. To this day, *Religious Affections* is rivaled only by William James's *Varieties of Religious Experience* (1902) for its profound insight into the nature of religious experience. This work, notes Stephen Stein, "represents the quintessential Edwards. The issues he addressed continue to be relevant to a world that is very different from eighteenth-century New England. The challenge of distinguishing authentic from inauthentic religion remains at the heart of the religious enterprise and at the center of the effort by those who stand outside this enterprise as critics."[31] *Religious Affections* represents the culmination of Edwards's maturing thought about religious experience as informed by his own conversion, the conversion of others, and the revivals he promoted and witnessed throughout the Connecticut Valley.

---

29. Chauncy, "Enthusiasm Described," 232.
30. Chauncy, "Seasonable Thoughts," 298.
31. Stein, "Introduction," xvii.

In his time, Edwards was considered a leading theologian; in our own, thanks to a single sermon that appears in nearly every anthology of early American literature, Edwards is known for his "hellfire-and-brimstone" preaching in the sermon *Sinners in the Hands of an Angry God* (1741). Hailed as a prototypical expression of Puritan rhetoric, the sermon describes a wrathful God who suspends sinners over the fiery pit of hell, "much as one holds a spider" dangling from a slender thread, "ready every moment to singe it, and burn it asunder." God "is not only able to cast wicked men into hell, but he can most *easily* do it." In fact, this sermon is less about the horrors of the life to come than about the present condition of those who rarely entertain thoughts of their own mortality. Edwards, like many of his colleagues, preached "the whole counsel of God," that is, both God's judgment ("the wrath of almighty God is now undoubtedly hanging over great part of this congregation") and mercy ("Christ has flung the door of mercy wide open").[32] Yet what he is remembered for by many students is his relentless and shocking (to modern ears) emphasis upon an angry God. Unfortunately, if this one sermon is isolated from his more than 1,200 extant sermons and other works (now twenty-six volumes in the Yale print edition and seventy-three in the online edition), the real brilliance of Edwards's thought is overlooked.[33]

Edwards's wide-ranging intellectual pursuits included philosophy, ethics, psychology, history, theology, and biblical studies. Despite his geographical isolation from centers of intellectual life, Edwards read widely, corresponded with the best minds in Europe, and remained conversant with the latest intellectual trends in science and philosophy. He mentored future ministers who became his devoted followers, biographers, and publishers. By the early nineteenth century, a third generation of "Edwardseans" was exerting a powerful influence throughout New England and carrying salient themes in his theology overseas in missionary endeavors, primarily under the auspices of the American Board of Commissioners for Foreign Missions. Edwards's legacy, transmitted through his writings and witnesses, is international in scope.[34]

Edwards's conversion indelibly shaped his life's work and legacy. Avihu Zakai contends, "Perhaps no event can be compared, in terms of

---

32. Edwards, *Sinners in the Hands of an Angry God*, 57, 58, 50, 65, 63.

33. An illuminating guide to this sermon is Kimnach et al., *Jonathan Edwards's "Sinners in the Hands of an Angry God."*

34. Kling and Sweeney, *Jonathan Edwards at Home and Abroad*; and chap. 6 in this volume.

intensity of religious life and spiritual experience, to his conversion. This moment radically shaped his religious consciousness and determined the growth of his universe of thought; it led him to find his vocation in life, and not least, it provided him with the form and content for his lifelong theological and philosophical undertakings."[35]

EDWARDS'S CONVERSION: "PERSONAL NARRATIVE"

Born in East Windsor, Connecticut, Edwards was the fifth of eleven children raised in a family steeped in the evangelical Puritan tradition. His father, Timothy (1669–1758), was a pastor, and his mother, Esther, was the daughter of Solomon Stoddard.[36] Much was expected of this only son. Tutored by an exacting father and nurtured by a theologically astute mother, Jonathan was singled out as the family heir to respectability and fame. As it turned out, he was up to the challenge. A brilliant, precocious, and ambitious lad, he began learning the ancient languages at age six and by his eleventh birthday began recording observations on the natural world. Ideas came to Edwards fast and furious—so much so that his nineteenth-century interpreters propounded the legend that when riding on horseback he pinned notes to his jacket as reminders of these thoughts (it has since been concluded that loose bits of papers were attached to his sermon notes with straight pins).[37]

With ideas came powerful religious experiences that Edwards later recorded in his "Personal Narrative" (ca. 1740) and that provided a lens through which he interpreted other people's religious experiences. This narrative, a brief account of his spiritual pilgrimage from his childhood to his mid-twenties, is suffused with the vocabulary (the "rhetoric of sensation") and major themes that he took up in his published works on revival. Several initial observations concerning Edwards's spiritual autobiography are in order. First, the "Personal Narrative" is a carefully composed, stylized literary reconstruction of events and thoughts that had occurred nearly twenty years previously. Daniel Shea notes in Edwards's narrative a common feature that is found in other conversion narratives—a time gap between the actual experience of conversion and

35. Zakai, *Jonathan Edwards's Philosophy of History*, 53.

36. Biographies of Edwards include Winslow, *Jonathan Edwards*; Miller, *Jonathan Edwards*; Tracy, *Jonathan Edwards, Pastor*; Murray, *Jonathan Edwards*; Marsden, *Jonathan Edwards*.

37. Kimnach, "General Introduction to the Sermons," 101n5.

the later reflection on that experience. Edwards's "Personal Narrative" "is not identical with his spiritual experience but represents a mature articulation of that experience, its form and language determined in varying degrees by the author's reading of sacred and secular writers, interviews with awakened sinners, and his concerns at the time of composition."[38]

Second, the occasion for the "Personal Narrative" was Edwards's keen interest in the perceived spiritual condition of the self—not only in his own life but also in that of his wife, Sarah Pierpont (1710–58), who served as Edwards's paragon of true piety. Edwards considered their religious experiences paradigmatic of the manner in which God effected change (or regeneration) in the soul of an individual. In his "Personal Narrative" he not only "edited his own experiences to fit his prescription of a model saint" but, in his "On Sarah Pierpont" (ca. 1723)—a brief tribute to Sarah's spiritual qualities—he edited hers as well.[39] In both writings, Edwards underscores the principle that supernatural change does not simply provide new knowledge; it also induces a perceptual change that enthralls the heart and mind, even to the point of spiritual ecstasy. Sarah would later describe her own experience of the divine presence—one that lasted five or six hours—as being "swallowed up with light and love," a time when she was "lost in God."[40] Conversion infuses a new and true spiritual perception of reality. That which is "most real" to the self (and metaphysically as well) is spiritual reality, a reality created and sustained by God (philosophically, Edwards was an immaterialist, believing the material or natural order merely reflected the mind of God).

Third, a comprehensive knowledge of the Bible shaped Edwards's view of reality.[41] He notes in his "Personal Narrative" that he took "the greatest delight in the holy Scriptures, of any book whatsoever." The biblical record was the source for apprehending the beauty (or "excellency") of God and of the new spiritual perception of divine things. As the source of divine communication, Scripture touched the soul. "I seemed often to see so much light, exhibited by every sentence, and such a refreshing ravishing food communicated, that I could not get along in reading." He often lingered "long on one sentence, to see the wonders contained in it;

38. Shea, *Spiritual Autobiography in Early America*, 190.
39. Claghorn, "Introduction," 748, 746.
40. Edwards, *WJE* 4:331.
41. On Edwards's engagement with contemporary critical issues of the Bible, see Brown, *Jonathan Edwards and the Bible*; on Edwards's extensive exegetical efforts, see Sweeney, *Edwards the Exegete*.

and yet almost every sentence seemed to be full of wonders." The Bible informed Edwards's lifelong agenda, what Roland Dellatre refers to as the "relentless pursuit of a better perception and grasp of the real, the actual."[42]

Fourth, in a broad sense, Edwards's account of his conversion conforms to traditional conversion narratives insofar as it discloses the movement from despair and humiliation to exaltation and a state of grace, but in significant ways it departs from the evangelical Puritan narrative. Most noticeable is the absence of the chartable stages in the Puritan morphology. As he made clear in other writings, he rejected the Puritan notion of a predictable pattern or form to conversion. God's sovereign and saving ways could not be so confidently calculated. Edwards "made the nature of the spiritual experience rather than the order the discriminating factor in determining whether or not they were gracious." Other aspects of the traditional Puritan conversion narrative are missing as well. Edwards was neither overwhelmed with conviction of sin—deep penitence for sin came long after his conversion—nor did he dwell for any length of time on the condition of his soul. In addition, the typical Puritan preoccupation with the self is absent. His spirituality, observes Michael McClymond was "more outward- than inward-looking."[43] The persistent spiritual anxiety encouraged by Thomas Shepard is nowhere to be found; Edwards's gaze was Other-directed: "The sweetest joys and delights I have experienced," he wrote, "have not been those that have arisen from a hope of my own good estate; but in the glorious things of the gospel."[44]

Edwards's initial interest in religion occurred in his childhood during a revival in his father's congregation. He was "very much affected for many months," prayed five times daily, engaged in religious conversation with other boys, and with his schoolmates built a "prayer booth" in a swamp—"a very secret and retired place." "My affections," he noted, "seemed to be lively and easily moved, and I seemed to be in my element, when engaged in religious duties." Over time, however, he lost his "affections and delights," quit praying, "and returned like a dog to his vomit, and went on in the ways of sin."[45]

---

42. Edwards, "Personal Narrative," 289; Delattre, "Recent Scholarship on Jonathan Edwards," 370.
43. McClymond, *Encounters with God*, 42, 47.
44. Edwards, "Personal Narrative," 292.
45. Edwards, "Personal Narrative," 281, 282.

Not yet thirteen years old, Edwards entered Yale College, then a small, struggling institution that had been recently founded in 1701. He took his degree in 1720 and remained at the college for an additional two years to pursue theological studies. During his later years there, Edwards contracted pleurisy, a common and sometimes fatal disease during colonial times. By his account, "It pleased God . . . to seize me with pleurisy; in which he brought me nigh to the grave, and shook me over the pit of hell." He recovered only to return to his "old ways of sin." His spiritual struggles continued. He vowed to "seek my salvation," yet not with the delight of old; he erected intellectual barriers to the faith, especially objecting to the doctrines of God's sovereignty and electing decrees, which appeared "like a horrible doctrine to me."[46]

Eventually, Edwards passed from resistance to acquiescence and then to a full delight in the "hard doctrines" of Calvinism. There took place "a wonderful alteration in my mind." He took comfort in God's sovereignty; the doctrine appeared "an exceeding pleasant, bright, and sweet doctrine." This new view came to him after reading 1 Tim 1:17, "Now unto the King eternal, immortal, invisible, the only wise God, be honor and glory forever and ever, Amen." While reading these words, Edwards was overcome with "a sense of the glory of the Divine Being; a new sense, quite different from anything I ever experienced before." The language of ecstasy intruded: "I thought with myself, . . . how happy I should be, if I might enjoy that God, and be wrapped up to God in heaven, and be as it were swallowed up in him." His attention turned to Christ's work of redemption: "I had an inward, sweet sense of things." He envisioned "being alone in the mountains, or some solitary wilderness, far from all mankind, sweetly conversing with Christ, and wrapt and swallowed up in God."[47]

After relating these spiritual experiences to his father, he retreated to "a solitary place" outdoors where he "looked up in the sky and the clouds" and was again transfixed by "a sweet sense of the glorious majesty and grace of God." This sense of God reflected in nature, of images inciting the religious imagination to their spiritual significance, became a constant refrain in Edwards's writings. A fundamental shift in his view of reality took place. Nature did not lead to God; Edwards was not a nature mystic. Rather, a new view of God given by God led to a renewed

---

46. Edwards, "Personal Narrative," 282, 283.
47. Edwards, "Personal Narrative," 283, 284.

understanding of nature; the created order reflected the divine attributes of the Creator. "God's excellency, his wisdom, his purity and love, seemed to appear in everything; in the sun, moon, and stars; in the clouds, and blue sky; in the grass, flowers, trees, in the water, and all nature." Whereas in the past thunder and lightning had terrified him, now these "sweet" displays "rejoiced me." So enraptured was Edwards of this majestic Creator and Redeemer that he often broke out into spontaneous singing or chanting. He concluded that these spiritual excitations were "totally of another kind" from those of his childhood. "Those former delights, never reached the heart; and did not arise from any sight of the divine excellency of the things of God; or any taste of the soul-satisfying, and life-giving good, there is in them."[48]

At this point, the "Personal Narrative" shifts geographically from New Haven to New York City, where Edwards ministered briefly (1722–23) at a small Presbyterian church. It also shifts to a new spiritual emphasis on holiness stimulated by a gradual increase in "divine things." "Pure and humble, holy and heavenly Christianity, appeared exceedingly amiable to me. I felt in me a burning desire to be in everything a complete Christian; and conformed to the blessed image of Christ." Edwards described holiness as "a sweet, pleasant, charming, serene, calm nature," bringing "an inexpressible purity" and "ravishment to the soul." He invoked the world of nature to capture the transformation of the soul of a true Christian: in the garden of God, the little white flower of the soul opens its petals "to receive the pleasant beams of the sun's glory." Still, because these heights of religious ecstasy were tempered by the realization that he came so "late" to religion, he was moved "to weep abundantly . . . for a considerable time."[49]

In the spring of 1723, Edwards returned to Connecticut, completed his master's oration, and delivered it at the Yale commencement in September. From the following fall until September 1726, Edwards served as senior tutor and acting rector at Yale. He relates little of his spiritual condition during this time other than to note that during an illness "God was pleased to visit me again with the sweet influence of his Spirit."[50] In the fall of 1726, he became the associate pastor and heir apparent to his aging grandfather. Following Stoddard's death in 1729, Edwards assumed full ministerial duties and served the Northampton church for the next

---

48. Edwards, "Personal Narrative," 285, 286.
49. Edwards, "Personal Narrative," 286, 287, 288.
50. Edwards, "Personal Narrative," 290.

twenty years, rising between four and five in the morning and spending thirteen hours a day in his study. The life of the mind, consecrated to God's service, would shape and define Edwards's career.

The remainder of the "Personal Narrative" (terminating around 1739) uplifts doctrines and conditions of the soul emphasized earlier. Edwards continues his preoccupation with God's holiness, the "sweet and glorious doctrines" of God's absolute sovereignty and free grace, the "glorious and excellent" way of salvation, and "the advancement of Christ's kingdom." In moments of solitude during his pastorate in Northampton, he weeps aloud as he is transported into a state of religious ecstasy, being "emptied and annihilated," "totally wrapped up in the fullness of Christ." At the same time, he is convicted of his wickedness and sin and longs "for a broken heart" and "to lie infinitely low before God."[51] Sanctification—the process of the Spirit making one holy—was premised upon humiliation—the recognition of one's total unworthiness before God. Between these complementary poles of human sin and corruption at one end and God's sovereignty, beauty, and holiness at the other lay the vast realm of religious experience that Edwards pursued so relentlessly throughout his life.

A man of strict morals, unbending conviction, and forceful logic, Edwards was discharged from his Northampton congregation in 1750 after insisting that the reception of the Lord's Supper be restricted to those who could give credible testimony of the inner work of grace in their lives (he had already taken a stand against the Half-Way Covenant). Convinced that Stoddard had erred and fearing that his parishioners professed Christian faith without truly having it, Edwards "fenced the table" by limiting participation in the sacrament of Communion to those who could give a reliable testimony of their conversion.

Following his dismissal, Edwards settled with his large family (now totaling eleven; two of his children had married) in the western frontier outpost of Stockbridge, Massachusetts, where he served as pastor to a local congregation and missionary to the Mohican and Mohawk Indians. It was not a bucolic life. He faced stiff competition from Moravian missionaries; he became embroiled in controversy over control of the mission school; the encroaching Seven Years' War threatened his safety; and he suffered physical setbacks. Yet he found time to return to major writing projects that had been on hold. He completed four lengthy theological

---

51. Edwards, "Personal Narrative," 291, 292, 293 (see also 296), 295.

treatises in the last five years of his life while closeted quite literally in a seven- by three-and-a-half-foot room. In January 1758, he took up duties as the third president of the College of New Jersey (since renamed Princeton) and successor to his son-in-law, Aaron Burr Sr., but three months later, Edwards was dead, the casualty of a reaction to a smallpox vaccination.

EDWARDS AND THE GREAT AWAKENING

Earlier in Edwards's Northampton pastorate, when relations with his parishioners were amicable, a revival unexpectedly occurred, "affecting all sorts, sober and vicious, high and low, rich and poor, wise and unwise." In 1734–35, three hundred believers were added to the church. According to Edwards, several unusual events heightened interest in religion: the unexpected deaths of a young man and woman in April 1734 ignited spiritual interest among the youth; the death of an elderly person "moved and affected" many; and the conversion of a young woman "who had been one of the greatest company-keepers in the whole town" awakened others.[52] Edwards also took note of the "surprising conversions" that resulted after he preached a series of sermons on justification by faith alone (1734). Reiterating the views of Augustine and the Protestant Reformers, Edwards argued against the self-satisfying notion that in some way salvation depended on human "works"—be they a person's right choices or moral deeds. This false "Arminianism," Edwards noted, placed hope for salvation in the idea that God would respect human contributions. Will not God honor my effort, some asked? No, replied Edwards, you cannot convert yourself. There is no necessary causal relationship between obligatory "preparatory works" (or the "means of grace")—practices such as Bible reading (even relying on Scripture), prayer, family devotions, church attendance—and salvation. God normally grants salvation to those who seek or "get in the way" of grace and rarely grants it to non-seekers, but there are no guarantees. Regeneration is solely God's act. Then what must I do to be saved? Have faith and recognize that faith, too, is a gift of God.

The revival soon spread—by word of mouth, letters, and print—and took on a life of its own. Initially, Edwards had no human explanation for the revival other than to invoke the biblical passage that the "Spirit

52. Edwards, *WJE* 4:157, 147–49.

listeth where it will" (John 3:8). By his reading of it, the Great Awakening disclosed the gift of God's dynamic, present action in the Holy Spirit. It was neither contrived nor anticipated but a miracle from God. Pious Christians had engaged in preparatory work but, ultimately, God alone in God's sovereign pleasure determined the timing of seasons of grace. At the same time, Edwards was convinced that news of conversions begat other conversions: "There is no one thing that I know of," he wrote in his *Faithful Narrative of the Surprising Work of God*, "that God has made such a means of promoting his work amongst us, as the news of others' conversion."[53]

Historians of the Great Awakening offer a variety of conflicting interpretations for the surge of conversions. Some point to factors of "social strain" and the consequent threat to the stability of New England life. In an environment of uncertainty, they argue, colonials looked to divine assistance as a way of resolving both personal and collective anxiety—ergo, the revival. Historians who favor this interpretive model cite the social pressures placed on society by disease (e.g., an outbreak of "throat distemper" or diphtheria in the 1730s) and especially by economic uncertainties brought about by a number of developments: Britain's declaration of war on Spain in 1739; concern over an inadequate supply of currency; a rapid expansion of new settlements and the attendant shift from a rural, agricultural life to an acquisitive, commercial economy; and the scarcity of inherited land and the concomitant decline in economic opportunity for young men living in towns. A sense of God's judgment (evidenced by disease), the lusting after wealth (with its consequent feelings of guilt), and the anxiety of displacement (portending an uncertain future) heightened spiritual concerns and eventuated in mass conversions.

Other historians connect America's Great Awakening to the ripple effects of a larger Anglo-European revival dating to the Pietist movement in late seventeenth-century Germany; England's Methodist movement; and transatlantic connections.[54] More recently, a group of "supply-side" sociologists have viewed the Awakening as a series of successful marketing campaigns by religious entrepreneurs such as Whitefield. In an "unregulated market," they contend, Whitefield experienced initial

---

53. Edwards, *WJE* 4:176. On the centrality of conversion in Edwards's life and ministry, see chap. 2 in this volume.

54. See Westerkamp, *Triumph of the Laity*; Schmidt, *Holy Fairs*; Crawford, *Seasons of Grace*; Ward, *Protestant Evangelical Awakening*; Noll et al., *Evangelicalism*; Lambert, *Inventing the "Great Awakening*," chap. 5.

successes. Once the established ministers realized the threat to their religious monopoly, however, they formed a cartel to defend their interests and adroitly halted the expansion of revival. For example, in 1742, following a recommendation of the General Consocation of ministers, the Connecticut legislature passed an act prohibiting itinerancy without the expressed permission of the minister of the particular parish. With this restrictive act, the Great Awakening in Connecticut came to an abrupt end.[55] To Edwards, all of these explanations—if appealed to as primary explanations—fell short. His Calvinist views of divine sovereignty and initiative in the history of redemption admitted that God worked through social and economic forces, but make no mistake: God was the efficient cause of the revival.

Two short-lived revivals at Northampton (1734–35, 1740–41) provided the laboratory for Edwards's examination of the nature of conversion and the excitements of the Awakening. Three works written during or shortly after these revivals highlight Edwards's skills of observation as a religious psychologist and anticipate themes later expanded on in his *Religious Affections*. In his letter entitled *A Faithful Narrative of the Surprising Work of God* (1735; revised for publication in 1737), Edwards chronicled the events leading up to the revival and then described the external behavioral and internal spiritual changes of the converted. Written shortly after the revival commenced, the narrative reflects the excitement of Edwards as both participant and observer. He described conversion as "a great and glorious work of God's power, at once changing the heart and infusing life into the dead soul."[56] Outwardly, the saved abandoned old vices and contentious ways for the bonds of love. Inwardly, they expressed a new or "lively" sense of the divine presence and a new "disposition" toward religious things.

In *The Distinguishing Marks of a Work of the Spirit of God* (1741), Edwards defended the revival as God's work by demonstrating the authenticity of the conversions. He admitted to irregularities and excesses but suggested heeding the advice of the writer of 1 John to "try the spirits whether they be of God" (4:1). To that end, he proposed "signs" (both positive and negative) by which the work of the Holy Spirit might be judged legitimate. Finally, in *Some Thoughts Concerning the Present Revival of Religion in New England* (1742), Edwards expanded his discussion

---

55. Finke and Iannaccone, "Supply-Side Explanations," 27–39. On itinerancy, see Hall, *Contested Boundaries*.

56. Edwards, *Faithful Narrative*, 177.

of "signs," arguing for the identification of the "fruits of the Spirit" in Gal 5:22–23 (love, joy, peace, a long-suffering nature, gentleness, etc.) with "religious affections." Holiness, Edwards argued, has its seat in the heart or will rather than in the understanding, and holy or religious affections are the substance of genuine religion.[57] A *Treatise Concerning Religious Affections* (1746), published two years after Edwards declared that the revival was over, represented Edwards's definitive treatment of the subject of revival, for here he gave systematic attention to the nature of revival and, more broadly, to the nature of religious experience.

EDWARDS ON CONVERSION: *TREATISE CONCERNING RELIGIOUS AFFECTIONS*

Edwards's *Treatise Concerning Religious Affections* describes the spiritual character of the converted, those who grasp the beauty of God and delight in God and God's world. It is a taxonomy of the soul, classifying the attitudes and actions of the regenerate. On the one hand, it shares the Enlightenment's preoccupation with scientific inquiry and empirical proof; on the other, it denies its presupposition of human autonomy and self-confidence. It is at once modern in its methods and traditional in its message. It is polemical in intent, on the one hand defending "true religion" against cold, lifeless, "liberal" religion and on the other attacking enthusiastic, delusional, allegedly evangelical religion that indiscriminately embraced the revival. *Religious Affections* engages a problem that had persisted since the Protestant Reformation, that of external and internal authority, the tension between the objective criterion of the Word of God and the subjective criterion of the testimony of the Spirit.

Briefly stated, *Religious Affections* considers a basic problem, centers upon a key text, and argues a provocative thesis. The central problem is posed as a question: "What are the distinguishing qualifications of those that are in favor with God, and entitled to his eternal rewards?"[58] What are the characteristics of true Christian converts? Expressed abstractly, "What is the nature of true religion?" Edwards raises a basic epistemological question that had preoccupied his Puritan predecessors: How can one know true piety from counterfeit piety? Unlike his earlier revival accounts that described and quantified the Great Awakening as a social

---

57. These three works by Edwards are found in *WJE* 4.
58. Edwards, *WJE* 2:84.

event, *Religious Affections* is almost exclusively concerned with the individual dimension of religious experience. The Awakening as an event provides the canvas for a detailed portrait of the awakening of the individual soul. As Ava Chamberlain has pointed out, the salient issue is that of assurance: How can I know genuine religion in myself, and how can I know it in others? What troubled Edwards was the revival's admixture of good and evil, of fluff and substance, for in this condition "the devil has had his greatest advantage against the cause and kingdom of Christ." Satan's counterfeit spirituality compromised the outpourings of the Spirit of God in the apostolic church, the Reformation, early New England, and now the recent revival. What should one think of excessive emotional outbursts? What about the censoriousness of preachers and parishioners who turned against their pastor? By what criteria, Edwards asked, can we discern the work of the Holy Spirit in ourselves and in others?[59]

To answer these questions, Edwards examined the biblical record and concluded that those who experienced genuine conversions persevered during times of trial and persecution. For his "sermon text," Edwards selected 1 Pet 1:8, wherein the author addresses his fellow Christians regarding Christ: "Whom having not seen, ye love: in whom, though now ye see him not, yet believing, ye rejoice with joy unspeakable and full of glory." "True religion never appears so lovely," Edwards wrote,

> as when it is most oppressed: and the divine excellency of real Christianity, is never exhibited with such advantage, as when under the greatest trials: then it is that true faith appears much more precious than gold . . . that is tried in the fire, is purged from its alloy and all remainders of dross, and comes forth more solid and beautiful . . . and thus also is found unto praise, and honor, and glory.[60]

Trials of faith, which every Christian faces, test the believer's integrity. The solid foundation of a true conversion is built on persevering in Christ-like word, thought, and deed to the glory of God.

In the next several pages, Edwards comments on the believer's love of the unseen Christ and their unspeakable joy in him who was "full of glory." He then expands on this last phrase, noting that when a believer is full of glory, the mind or the whole being is filled with a sight, a sense,

---

59. Chamberlain, "Self-Deception as a Theological Problem," 541–56; Edwards, *WJE* 2:86.

60. Edwards, *WJE* 2:93, 94.

and a power beyond nature—beyond the five senses. The believer has a supernatural sense, a divine consciousness, a new disposition, or "a supernatural principle of love." This enlivened sense, writes Edwards, is what he means by "holy affections." And so he proposes his thesis: "True religion, in great part, consists in holy affections." Admittedly, among Christians "religious affections are often mixed; all is not from grace, but much from nature." But the integrity of one's faith is judged by a "fixedness and strength of habit ... whereby holy affection is habitual" or steadfast during the expected trials of life.[61]

Religious Affections combines a critical examination of those signs that are indicative of true religion with the assumption that religion is, at the very least, a sense-oriented, experiential relationship with God. In part, Edwards's unique contribution lies in his insistence that genuine religion includes both the rational and experiential, the Word and the Spirit. Having a religious experience does not authenticate it; the mind must be used to access and clarify the nature of that experience.

Edwards divides his treatise into three parts. Part I addresses the nature of the affections and their centrality in the religious life. Part II describes what Edwards calls "negative signs" or unreliable criteria for judging whether or not the affections are truly gracious. Part III examines at length twelve positive signs of holy affections or the marks of the truly converted who are filled with the Spirit.

What, then, are the affections? Edwards addresses this question with a precise definition of terms and a careful examination of the operation of the mind. Although his analysis clearly rests on Puritan assumptions and a biblical framework (he draws from the Puritan traditions of practical divinity and scholasticism as well as copiously from Scripture), he integrates these into contemporary views of psychology.[62] Conversant with the writings of the English empirical philosopher John Locke (1632–1704), especially his *Essay Concerning Human Understanding* (1689), Edwards reiterates the view that God has created the soul or mind with two "faculties," intellect and will. Intellect is the knowing or perceiving faculty, that which Edwards variously calls "speculative knowledge" or "notional understanding."[63] With this faculty one observes

---

61. Edwards, *WJE* 2:94, 95, 118.

62. On Edwards's sources, see Smith, "Editor's Introduction," 53–73. By my count, Edwards makes 1,250 biblical references in this treatise.

63. For the influence of Locke on Edwards's notion of perception, see Lyttle, "Sixth Sense of Jonathan Edwards," 50–58; Laurence, "Jonathan Edwards, John Locke,"

or "beholds" the meaning of something, though with no inclination to approve or disapprove of it. Such knowledge is an assent to "words" or "signs," not the immediate object of consciousness. We may, for example, learn a mathematical formula, gain a new understanding of history, or memorize the Ten Commandments, but the mere knowledge of these has no influence upon our motives or actions.

On the other hand, the mind's faculty of will—variously called by Edwards the inclination or the sense of the heart—does not only "speculate and behold, but relishes and feels." The will chooses (accepts or rejects), values (likes or dislikes), and is the faculty that governs human actions or that enables one to act on acquired knowledge or understanding. In short, the exercise of the will—that which appears to us as the greatest apparent good—inclines us to take sides.[64]

At this point, we should note that, unlike seventeenth-century Protestant scholastics and others who embraced a mechanistic faculty psychology by which the mind was understood to operate by a number of faculties relatively independent of the others, Edwards affirmed the interconnectedness of the will and understanding. As he would note later in his discussion of the fourth sign of grace, "Spiritual understanding consists primarily in a sense of the heart of that spiritual beauty. I say, a sense of the heart; for it is not speculation merely that is concerned in this kind of understanding; nor can there be a clear distinction made between the two faculties of understanding and will as acting distinctly and separately, in this matter."[65] This sense of the heart—what Edwards will call the affections—is always informed by ideas. It is not unbridled passion or mere emotionalism but a synthesis of will and understanding. However, for purposes of clarity, and to demonstrate the priority of the heart in the true apprehension of religion, Edwards differentiated between the two.

Again, there is no neutral state of the will; it is either inclined for or against something; it approves or disapproves, is pleased or displeased. Moreover, the will expresses itself in varying degrees. The most lively and intense or the most "vigorous and sensible exercises" are those in a special category that Edwards calls the affections. Among those exercises so classified are love, hate, desire, joy, grief, and sorrow. There are, then, right affections and wrong affections. The point Edwards stresses is that right

---

107–23; Smith, *Jonathan Edwards*, chap. 2; Chai, *Jonathan Edwards*, chap. 2; McClymond, *Encounters with God*, chap. 1.

64. Edwards, *WJE* 2:272.
65. Edwards, *WJE* 2:272.

affections engage the heart; they incline the self away from self-interest and toward divine glory. Above all, heart religion is biblical: "The Holy Scriptures do everywhere place religion very much in the affections; such as fear, hope, love, hatred [of sin], desire, joy, sorrow, gratitude, compassion, and zeal." Among Christian virtues, "The Scriptures place religion very much in the affection of love, in love to God, and the Lord Jesus Christ, and love to the people of God, and to mankind."[66] As Edwards will later discuss, this love is not merely one of the affections, it is the chief of the affections; it is, in fact, the evidence of true religion.

Having defined the religious affections, Edwards proceeds to an analysis of religious appearances. What are the signs or indications of "truly gracious and holy affections"? Again, the Great Awakening unleashed a torrent of religious emotion, activity, and controversy. For a time, Edwards himself actively promoted the most radical dimensions of the evangelical new birth and supported itinerant ministers and lay exhorters and even embraced "Stoddardian" open Communion practices. But by around 1742, after fearing these practices would tear apart his congregation and the very fabric of society, he retreated from his earlier support of ecstatic visionary experiences and somatic manifestations as signs of the Holy Spirit. As is clear from the *Religious Affections*, Edwards's revival theology underwent a transformation.[67] Those radical dimensions of the revival that he earlier classified as "signs" of a genuine work of the Spirit he now classified, as we will see, as "no signs." He articulated a mediating position that was likely to make enemies on both sides of the revival: "'Tis a hard thing to be a hearty zealous friend of what has been *good* and glorious, in the late extraordinary appearances, and to rejoice much in it; and at the same time, to see the evil and pernicious tendency of what has been *bad*, and earnestly to oppose that."[68] *Religious Affections* thus represents an effort to avoid the Charybdis of emotional chaos and the Scylla of intolerant formalism and unite these in a biblically satisfying way.

It is to the superficial and often criticized aspects of the revival that Edwards initially turns in his analysis of religious appearances. Appealing to numerous biblical examples as well as general experience, he examines those signs that neither confirm nor disconfirm the presence of the Spirit. While they may, and often do, accompany gracious affections, they do

66. Edwards, *WJE* 2:102, 103.
67. Winiarski, "Jonathan Edwards, Enthusiast?," 683–739.
68. Edwards, *WJE* 2:85.

not validate their presence. As John E. Smith has observed, there is a difference between the Spirit *acting upon* the person and *dwelling within* the person.[69] The importance of Edwards's consideration of "no signs" is that many indiscriminate supporters of "experimental" religion believed that these signs corroborated the presence of true, heartfelt religion. Edwards argues that conversion is not an emotional free-for-all but takes place within a discrete, biblically informed spectrum of experience.

Briefly, what Edwards called "no signs" or negative signs include intense emotional experiences, "bodily manifestations," extensive and fervent religious conversations, devotion to religious practices, and even the frequent quoting of Scripture. These may accompany gracious affections but do not confirm their presence. Edwards also questioned the traditional Puritan preparationist model of conversion. He did not repudiate wholesale the morphology of conversion (his own *Faithful Narrative*—an authoritative text of American revivalism for over a century—offered a model of conversion),[70] but, as we have observed from his "Personal Narrative," his own conversion did not conform lock-step to this model, missing, among others, the important step of "humiliation" or "terror." In *Religious Affections* Edwards noted, "Some have gone too far towards directing the Spirit of the Lord, and marking out his footsteps for him, and limiting him to certain steps and methods." Because the Spirit of God is not limited to a certain prescribed order, one cannot judge salvation based on a certain method.[71] Finally, the approval of the congregation or even of the pastor is not in itself a reliable judge of the integrity of religion. Despite his conviction—which led to his ouster from Northampton—that one must give credible testimony to the work of God in one's soul as a condition of reception into church membership, Edwards admitted that these external judgments were only probable, not certain. Only God knew the heart. "The true saints have not such a spirit of discerning, that they can certainly determine who are godly, and who are not." While they know it in themselves, "They can neither feel, nor see, in the heart of another." God alone (along with the person affected) knows the condition of the heart (1 Sam 16:7).[72]

69. Smith, "Testing the Spirits," 31.

70. Goen, "Editor's Introduction," 29.

71. Edwards, "Personal Narrative," 283; Edwards, *WJE* 2:161, 162. See also Laurence, "Jonathan Edwards, Solomon Stoddard," 267–83.

72. Edwards, *WJE* 2:182, 181, 188–90.

One hundred pages into his treatise, Edwards turns to the distinguishing signs of a true Christian. Although it is difficult to know the exact criteria by which Edwards selected these signs, one thing is clear: all of them in one way or another point to the glory of God. Edwards's refrain throughout all of his writings is the answer to the first question of the Westminster Shorter Catechism ("What is the chief end of man?"): "To glorify God and enjoy him forever." Not only in *Religious Affections* but also in his "Resolutions" (1722), his autobiographical reflections, his sermons, and his formal (and formidable) theological treatises, Edwards made God and God's glory revealed in Jesus Christ and animated through the Holy Spirit the centerpiece of his thought. He took as his first resolution "that I will do whatsoever I think to be most to God's glory."[73] In his "Personal Narrative," as I have noted, he recorded his initial encounter with the "sweet delight in God and divine things." In rhapsodic language, Edwards introduces the notion of a "new sense" through which God's glory is apprehended. Finally, in his posthumous *The Nature of True Virtue* (1765), he recapitulates this theme: "'Tis evident that true virtue must chiefly consist in love to God; the Being of beings, infinitely the greatest and best of beings."[74] Edwards's theology—rooted in Scripture, affirmed in Reformed theology, and refined and defended in philosophical categories—is distilled to this: we exist for God rather than God for us; we are not made for ourselves, but for God and God's glory.

In his prefatory remarks to part III of *Religious Affections*, Edwards reminds the reader that these signs are intended primarily for private self-examination rather than for application by Christians, even ministers, as a yardstick to measure the spiritual condition of others. To make that judgment "is God's design" and "his prerogative" alone. He then returns to his basic argument in part I that gracious affections are made possible only by the supernatural work of the Holy Spirit. The Spirit gives a new disposition or taste or sense that enables the saint to discern and love the excellence of divine things. The Spirit is not only an external force influencing and moving upon natural principles—an operation Calvinists referred to as "common grace" or the common operations of the Spirit upon all people—but is also an indwelling principle as a "saving" operation whereby a new spiritual disposition is "infused" into the believer. This infused grace, observes Anri Morimoto, "is nothing but the

---

73. Edwards, "Resolutions," 274.
74. Edwards, *Nature of True Virtue*, 252.

Holy Spirit himself opening the eyes of the mind and enabling the person to see divine beauty and excellency."[75]

By such enablement, the convert loves God and Christ not exclusively or primarily for benefits gained from them (e.g., peace, comfort, eternal life) but for their intrinsic qualities. All people can detect God's "natural perfections," that is, God's power, might, and understanding, but only those with religious affections delight in God's "moral perfections," that is, God's goodness, mercy, faithfulness, and justice. This love is a "disinterested love." "The grace of God," Edwards writes, "may appear lovely in two ways; either as *bonum utile*, a profitable good to me, that which greatly serves my interest, and so suits my self-love; or as *bonum formosum*, a beautiful good in itself, and part of the moral and spiritual excellency of the divine nature."[76] We may observe that Edwards is arguing against the utilitarian philosophers of his day who rooted all love in self-love. There is a higher love, says Edwards, a love removed from the self or above the self, created by God and for God.

The holy affections expressed in love for God "are not heat without light." They are not all emotion without insight, knowledge, and certitude. "Knowledge is the key," he writes, "that first opens the hard heart and enlarges the affections." Here, Edwards stands in stark contrast to the subsequent anti-intellectual revivalist tradition in recognizing the role of the intellect in the Christian life. Such anti-intellectualism could not be further removed from Edwards's understanding of the nature of conversion. At the same time, though a basic knowledge of biblical truths is fundamental (for it must precede a holy affection), the "light" to which Edwards refers is not additional knowledge but a new understanding of existing knowledge found in Scripture. "Spiritually to understand the Scripture, is rightly to understand what *is in* the Scripture, and what *was in* it before it was understood: 'tis to understand rightly, what used to be contained in the meaning of it; and not the making a new meaning." Or, citing his favorite analogy, the difference between an unregenerate and a regenerate understanding of the Bible is the difference between being told *about* honey and actually tasting it. How do you know that you are numbered among the saved? You see life differently; you have a new frame of reference and a new quality of consciousness. You have a new sense experience—a taste so enhanced supernaturally that the Bible

---

75. Edwards, *WJE* 2:193; Morimoto, *Jonathan Edwards*, 23 (see also chap. 3).
76. Edwards, *WJE* 2:242, 262.

appears as a new book. This taste creates the "Aha, now I understand" experience. What was once a "dead letter, a dry, lifeless, tasteless thing" of words now takes on a life of its own.[77] Here, Edwards echoes the words of Luther, who recalled that "the whole of Scripture took on a new meaning" after his insight into justification by faith alone.

Arising from this supernaturally given illuminated understanding is an inner persuasion or certainty of divine things. Edwards does not want to overplay the role of knowledge. The fact is, learned scholars and apologists of the faith propose philosophical and historical arguments for the truth of the Christian faith, but "endless doubts and scruples remain." Moreover, the arguments of theologians make no sense to "at least nineteen in twenty, if not ninety-nine in an hundred, of those for whom the Scriptures were written." If the ground of assurance depended on knowledge, then heathens such as the Indians would have to become conversant in arguments supporting the faith, thus making "the propagation of the gospel among them, infinitely difficult."[78]

The remaining positive signs of conversion shift the focus from the divine source and divine goal of the affections to their manifestation in particular virtues and moral characteristics in the life of the believer. One tangible evidence of true religious affections is what Edwards designates (borrowing the term from Thomas Shepard) "evangelical humiliation." He deems this affection "one of the most essential things pertaining to true Christianity," for from it "all true holy affections do flow," and he contrasts it with "legal humiliation."[79] The former kind of humility originates in the special influence of the Spirit of God, whereas the latter is the common influence of the Spirit upon the conscience. Legal humiliation may admit that God is great and majestic and that humans are sinful and deserving of condemnation, but it is insufficient and consequently results in a false spiritual pride. Evangelical humiliation affects the core of one's being; it is expressed voluntarily in a "broken and contrite heart" (Ps 51:17), in self-denial and self-abasement. Evangelical humiliation is a view of oneself in relation to God, whereas legal humiliation is a view of one's relation to others ("Yes, I'm bad, but not as bad as Joan"). The result

---

77. Edwards, *WJE* 2:280, 274. See also Stein, "Quest for the Spiritual Sense," 108–10. For an earlier reference to the taste of honey analogy, see Edwards, "Divine and Supernatural Light," 127–28.

78. Edwards, *WJE* 2:304.

79. Edwards, *WJE* 2:311, 314, 339.

of evangelical humiliation is "true virtue," a love of God because of God's very nature.

Another sign of gracious affections is conversion. Obviously, *Religious Affections* is an extended treatise on this subject, but in just five pages (this sign is given the shortest space) Edwards provides a succinct definition of the term. He notes that conversion is a "change of nature" or "a great and universal change of man, turning him from sin to God."[80] The person with gracious affections has turned (or, more properly in Reformed thought, the person has been turned by God) from the lure of the world and toward the divine. Prior to conversion, persons may be restrained from sin, but when they are converted, they are not only restrained; their very heart and nature are turned toward holiness. There is an ontological alteration, a fundamental change. This transformation occurs not immediately and entirely but progressively throughout the course of one's life. Edwards is not so much concerned with an exact time or moment of conversion (which later revivalists would emphasize) but with its permanence.[81]

Moreover, there is a balance and consistency to the affections, a "beautiful symmetry and proportion."[82] Just as there is symmetry and

---

80. Edwards, *WJE* 2:340-41.

81. A clarification of Edwards's appropriation of the Reformed tradition's use of the terms "regeneration" and "conversion" is in order. As noted by Michael S. McClymond and Gerald R. McDermott, "The early Reformed tradition focused not on conversion but regeneration or the new birth, which it treated under the category of God's effectual calling. . . . Later Reformed thinkers began to distinguish regeneration from conversion, identifying the first as the passive reception of divine life and the second as active turning from sin to new life in Christ." Following the thought of Peter van Mastricht, Edwards developed the view that "sometimes there may be a lag between regeneration and conversion. . . . While for Edwards regeneration was immediate and instantaneous, he thought of conversion as an event that sometimes took place subsequent to regeneration" (McClymond and McDermott, *Theology of Jonathan Edwards*, 386). However, Edwards was not always consistent in making this distinction. At times, he spoke of regeneration as instantaneous, at others, as a lifelong process. And on still other occasions, he conflated the two. Despite the occasional inconsistency of usage, Edwards agreed with Mastricht that regeneration (the operation of the Holy Spirit) is that which makes conversion (turning to God) possible. See McClymond and McDermott, *Theology of Jonathan Edwards*, 387, 382n31.

82. Edwards, *WJE* 2:365. Here, Edwards expands on one of the fundamental insights he reached at an early age. In notes on "The Mind" (1723), written over two decades earlier, he proposed that "simple beauty" consisted of equality and "complex beauty" of proportionality. "All beauty," he mused, "consists in similarness, or identity of relation." He illustrated his point by first citing mathematical relations (shapes and numbers) and then observing the "millions of these equalities" in the world of nature: flowers, the bodies of humans and animals. See Edwards, "Mind," 23, 24, 25.

proportionality in the worlds of nature and mathematics, so in the spiritual realm humans were made in the image of God and were intended to reflect that image. Though sin distorted that image, the regenerate person can approximate that intended relationship. One of the surest signs of counterfeit Christianity is its disproportion or lack of uniformity. Hypocrites, notes Edwards, are like meteors that flare suddenly in a blaze of light but soon fall back to earth. True saints are like fixed stars that shine brightly through time and space.[83] A converted Christian not only loves God but extends that love to his neighbor; nor does he treat a neighbor with kindness and his wife with disdain; nor is he greatly engaged in Christian fellowship and spends little time in private devotion. There is a steady, abiding, universal application of the affections. The more true converts have of holy affections, the more they want them. They are never spiritually satiated but crave a deeper, richer relationship to God of continued growth.

Another positive sign of a true convert is conformity to the image of Christ (Rom 8:29; 2 Cor 3:18), consisting of love, meekness, quietness, forgiveness, mercy, and tenderness of spirit. Referring to the Beatitudes (Matt 5:3–12) as the best and most succinct description of the Christian character, Edwards mentions love, particularly love expressed toward the poor and unfortunate, as among the Christian virtues.

Edwards's last sign is "the chief of all the signs of grace," "the sign of signs, and evidence of evidences, that which seals and crowns all other signs." The previous signs described spiritual conditions and aesthetic perceptions, whereas the final sign describes holy action. Edwards goes to great lengths to affirm that the proof is in the practice; the power of true godliness culminates in habits of holiness. The natural result of setting one's affections on God is the performance of works of mercy and justice. "The motions of the body follow from the laws of union between the soul and body," and according to such laws "holy acts of mind" direct and govern the motions of the body. "Godliness in the heart has as direct a relation to practice, as a fountain has to a stream, or as the luminous nature of the sun has to beams sent forth, or as life has to breathing. . . . Regeneration, which is that work of God in which grace is infused, has a direct relation to practice."[84]

---

83. Edwards, *WJE* 2:373–74.
84. Edwards, *WJE* 2:406, 443, 423, 450, 398.

One of the primary reasons for judging the sincerity of oneself and others by the rule of holy practice is that "this evidence is above all others insisted in Scripture." In fact, holy action "is ten times more insisted on as a note of true piety, throughout the Scriptures . . . than anything else." Moreover, what Scripture teaches (e.g., see Jesus' words in Matt 5:16; 7:11), reason affirms: a person's actions give the clearest evidence of the state of their heart. Religious practice lived out consistently amid the trials one encounters throughout life is the most empirically verifiable religious affection and hence "is properly called by the name of experimental religion." In the laboratory of Christian life, "The saints have the opportunity to see, by actual *experience* and *trial*, whether they have a heart to do the will of God, and to forsake other things for Christ, or no." Edwards draws an analogy between spiritual and scientific methods: "As that is called experimental philosophy, which brings opinions and notions to the test of fact; so is that properly called experimental religion, which brings religious affections and intentions, to the like test."[85]

The Great Awakening that Edwards led, experienced, defended, and analyzed was not something to be seen as a spiritual condition or mental state divorced from the everyday expressions of love. A person can talk, listen, sing, and pray incessantly, he notes, but these will not promote religious renewal or give verifiable evidence of true conversion unless they are accompanied by works of love and mercy. "We should get into the way of appearing lively in religion, more by being lively in the service of God and our generation, than by the liveliness and forwardness of our tongues." If Christians' speech went "behind their hands and feet," the integrity of their religion would convince others "that there is a reality in religion." Edwards closes his treatise where he began—with a scriptural reference (Matt 5:16) ascribing glory to God: "Thus the light of professors would so shine before men, that others seeing their good works, would glorify their Father which is in heaven."[86]

CONCLUSION

In this brief analysis of Edwards's *Religious Affections*, I have discussed the new spiritual sense that comes to the truly converted while ignoring

---

85. Edwards, *WJE* 2:436, 409–10, 452.

86. Edwards, *WJE* 2:461. For a fitting example of this emphasis in Edwards's teaching, see Jonathan Edwards, "Much in Deeds of Charity" (1741), 197–211.

the rich body of scholarship that has explored the religious and philosophical sources from which Edwards drew to create his original synthesis.[87] Moreover, I have made only passing reference to the literary style of *Religious Affections*. Despite the vividness of Edwards's prose, the work is not an easy read. As one interpreter observes, *Religious Affections* is "a long, wordy, frequently cryptic, hyper-Calvinist defense of the spirituality of the colonial revival."[88] Given its sometimes obtuse, cumbersome presentation, how then did *Religious Affections* attain the status of a "classic" of Christian spirituality? Although the ministerial disciples of Edwards drank deeply from the original published version, the growing popularity of *Religious Affections* was tied directly to abbreviated versions that eliminated philosophical and theological themes and emphasized the work as a handbook of practical piety. John Wesley concluded that *Religious Affections* had "so many curious, subtle, metaphysical distinctions as are sufficient to puzzle the brain," but he gleaned enough spiritual substance from the work to produce an abridged version.[89] Likewise, in 1833 the American Tract Society printed a popular version of *Religious Affections* and by mid-century had distributed some 75,000 copies to a mostly lay audience. Those who read the Wesley or American Tract Society editions encountered a drastically altered text, one bereft of all but the skeleton—and even a few bones were missing in the abridged version (Wesley cut four of the twelve signs). Undoubtedly, outside of its value to scholars and educated ministers, *Religious Affections* would never have attained its popular status without wholesale revisions.[90] Yet, because of these abridgments, not to mention the promotional efforts of Edwards's culturally influential devotees, this work and others Edwards authored (especially *The Life of David Brainerd* [1749], his most popular and most reprinted work)[91] have had a profound influence on Protestant piety and understanding of conversion. Edwards, of course, was not the

---

87. For example, see Smith, "Editor's Introduction," 52–73; Hoopes, "Jonathan Edwards's Religious Psychology," 849–65; Morimoto, *Jonathan Edwards*, chaps. 2–3; Wainwright, *Reason and the Heart*, chap. 1; McClymond, "Spiritual Perception in Jonathan Edwards," 195–216.

88. Conforti, *Jonathan Edwards*, 33.

89. John Wesley, quoted in Smith, "Editor's Introduction," 80.

90. Conforti, *Jonathan Edwards*, 33–34; Steele, "Gracious Affection," 215–30.

91. Pettit, "Editor's Introduction," 1. Pettit observes that Edwards shaped Brainerd into a model of genuine conversion over against the excesses of the revival and that Brainerd's conversion bears a close resemblance to that of Edwards's wife, Sarah Pierpont (1, 8).

first to introduce the language of the affections, and he worked within a well-established tradition that placed the evangelical view of conversion at the center of the eighteenth-century transatlantic revivals, but his contribution to the rhetoric of the heart and his promotion of the revivals was unparalleled. His paradigm of conversion quickly became fixed in the popular mind and persists among evangelicals to this day. As for the supremacy Edwards attached to conversion, "If there be such a thing as conversion, 'tis the most important thing in the world."[92]

---

92. Edwards, "Reality of Conversion," 92.

2

Edwards, the Bible, and Conversion

A CONSIDERABLE AMOUNT OF scholarship has been dedicated to the philosophical and theological sources of Edwards's personal experience and views of conversion. We know how Edwards drew creatively from Puritan devotional writers, Cambridge Platonists, and the empiricist philosophy of John Locke in articulating a model of conversion based on a doctrine of a new spiritual sense or "sense of the heart."[1] We are thoroughly familiar with how Edwards distinguished between notional or speculative knowledge and spiritual knowledge or sensible apprehension of divine truths. And we are well informed about Edwards's theological interlocutors, both friends and foes, who shaped his views of conversion and religious experience.

However, considerably less attention has been given to ways in which the Bible—the fundamental textual source of conversion—informed Edwards's views. For the most part, Scripture's role has been assumed rather than examined; the Bible has appeared in the background and seldom made a front-and-center appearance. The editors of two of the most important volumes in the *Works of Jonathan Edwards* that focus on the subject of conversion, for example, give slight attention to Edwards's use of the Bible. In his lengthy introduction to Edwards's writings on the Great Awakening, C. C. Goen notes that Scripture shaped Edwards's views, but he says virtually nothing about how Edwards used the Bible.[2] Similarly, in an equally substantial introduction to *Religious Affections*,

---

1. The works are numerous, but see two recent articles published in *Jonathan Edwards Studies*: Stoever, "Godly Mind," 327–52; Helm, "Jonathan Edwards," 3–15.

2. Goen, "Editor's Introduction."

John E. Smith, apart from citing Edwards's biblical text (1 Pet 1:8), gives little attention to a work that is copious in biblical references and allusions.³ One reason for this oversight—and one that applies generally to all of Edwards's corpus—is that modern scholars have had little taste for Edwards's supernatural biblicism and penchant for "Scripture proofs."⁴ Consequently they have been drawn to more palatable subjects such as Edwards's ethics, metaphysics, aesthetics, theology, pastoral labors, and role in the Great Awakening.⁵ Given Edwards's biblical literalism, supercessionism, and typological views, America's "greatest theologian" comes across as a premodern fundamentalist whose views of the Bible stand far removed from contemporary critical approaches. And yet, Edwards the biblicist cannot be ignored; indeed, in recent years an increasing number of scholars have given greater attention to Edwards's biblically saturated world and his engagement with the critical issues of his day.⁶

To understand Edwards is to understand that Scripture informed the core of his being. As a teenager, Edwards "resolved, to study the Scriptures so steadily, constantly and frequently, as that I may find, and plainly perceive myself to grow in the knowledge of the same."⁷ To Edwards, the Old and New Testaments were a record of God's redemptive plan culminating in Christ, the center of God's purpose in the creation and redemption of the world. If redemption was the grand design of history, then conversion constituted the personal pieces of the design. As Edwards noted, God's plan of redemption was "to restore the soul of man in

---

3. Smith, "Editor's Introduction." Gerald R. McDermott offered a needed corrective in his popular, devotional-oriented work *Seeing God*.

4. On "Scripture proofs," see Kimnach, "General Introduction to the Sermons," 77–80.

5. Sweeney, *Edwards the Exegete*, 7.

6. Stein, "Editor's Introduction," *Apocalyptic Writings*, WJE 5:1–93; Stein, "Editor's Introduction," *Notes on Scripture*, WJE 15:1–46; Stein, "Editor's Introduction," "*Blank Bible*," WJE 24:1–117; Stein, "Jonathan Edwards and the Rainbow"; Stein, "Quest for the Spiritual Sense"; Stein, "Spirit and the Word"; Stein, "Edwards as Biblical Exegete"; Brown, "Edwards, Locke, and the Bible"; Brown, *Jonathan Edwards and the Bible*; Brown, "Bible"; Sweeney, "'Longing for More and More of It'?"; Sweeney, "Edwards and the Bible"; Sweeney, *Jonathan Edwards*; Sweeney, *Edwards the Exegete*; McClymond and McDermott, *Theology of Jonathan Edwards*, 17, 34–35, 116–48, 167–80, 717; Barshinger, *Jonathan Edwards and the Psalms*; Barshinger and Sweeney, *Jonathan Edwards and Scripture*.

7. Edwards, *WJE* 16:755.

conversion and restore life to it, and the image of God in conversion and to carry on the restoration in sanctification, and to perfect it in glory."[8]

This essay represents a modest and selective attempt to give Scripture the place it deserves in Edwards's understanding of conversion. Although his Calvinist theological presuppositions and Enlightenment-rooted philosophical insights supplied the framework for his understanding of conversion, the Bible provided the necessary foundation. Without the revealed Word, theologizing and philosophizing about conversion were inconsequential. Edwards had a lifetime preoccupation with conversion, and yet, as we will see, his attention to these matters of the heart appeared most prominent during periods of religious awakening.

EDWARDS AND THE IMPORTANCE OF CONVERSION

Edwards was consumed with conversion. According to George Claghorn, conversion was "the golden thread that runs through [his] letters from beginning to end."[9] Indeed, Edwards's written references to conversion abound. In the *WJE Online* database, a word search ("KWIC report") turns up 6,047 occurrences of "conversion" and related words ("converts," "converted," "conv" = "conversion" or "convert"), far exceeding occurrences of other associated terms such as "salvation" (4,933), "redemption" (3,274), "regeneration" (508), and "new birth" (147).[10] Not only did Edwards refer repeatedly to conversion, but he did so in effusive language. Conversion was "a glorious work, and a great change,"[11] "a great and wonderful mercy,"[12] "an evidence of the truth of religion,"[13] "the fruit of those things that are great,"[14] "a change of nature; such as being born again,"[15] and "a great and universal change of the man."[16] Indeed, it was "undoubt-

---

8. Edwards, *WJE* 9:124.
9. Claghorn, "Transcribing a Difficult Hand," 225–26.
10. *WJE Online*, Jonathan Edwards Center at Yale University, http://edwards.yale.edu/archive. It should be noted that "occurrences" include those mentioned by the editors of the printed volumes (vols. 1–26).
11. Edwards, *WJE* 8:335; *WJEO* 47, no. 255; see also *WJEO* 50, no. 358.
12. Edwards, *WJEO* 45, no. 154.
13. Edwards, *WJEO* 49, no. 324.
14. Edwards, *WJEO* 54, no. 519.
15. Edwards, *WJE* 2:340.
16. Edwards, *WJE* 2:340.

edly the most important thing in the world."[17] In fact, conversion "is one of the great and fundamental doctrines of the Christian religion.... It is a doctrine that 'tis of infinite importance ... because men's conversion ... is by Christ's express declaration absolutely necessary to their salvation."[18] In sum, "The whole of the Christian religion is evidenced by the conversion of one soul."[19]

Edwards offered one of his clearest explanations of conversion in 1729, several months after he replaced his grandfather Solomon Stoddard as the sole pastor in Northampton, Massachusetts. Conversion, he wrote, is "that which is first and the foundation of all." It "is the alteration of the temper and disposition and spirit of the mind; for what is done in conversion is nothing but conferring the Spirit of God, which dwells in the soul and becomes there a principle of life and action." Conversion brings about a "new nature" and a "divine nature" that changes one's very soul by admitting "divine light." It engenders a new spiritual understanding. "Divine things now appear excellent, beautiful, glorious, which did not when the soul was of another spirit." Finally, conversion enables the saint to distinguish "truth from falsehood."[20]

The doctrine of conversion, declared Edwards, was "abundantly taught by divine revelation."[21] If we deny the doctrine of conversion, "We do in effect renounce the Scriptures."[22] "If there be such [a thing as conversion], then Scripture is the Word of God. For 'tis by that word that this effect is wrought."[23] Because "God's Word comes as a conqueror: those that are not conquered by conversion," warned Edwards, "shall be conquered by destruction and execution of its threatenings."[24] From the Old Testament through the New, God's redemptive activity through conversion constituted its main theme. Moses taught conversion (see Deut 30:6); the prophets taught it (see Jer 31:32–33; Ezek 36:26–27); and, of course, Christ taught it (see John 3:3).[25] In July–August 1723, shortly

---

17. Edwards, *WJEO* 65, no. 859.
18. Edwards, "Reality of Conversion," 83.
19. Edwards, *WJEO* 49, no. 324.
20. Edwards, *WJE* 13:462–63.
21. Edwards, *WJEO* 49, no. 324.
22. Edwards, *WJEO* 65, no. 859.
23. Edwards, *WJEO* 49, no. 324.
24. Edwards, *WJE* 5:102.
25. Edwards, *WJEO* 65, no. 859.

after he left his pastorate in New York City, Edwards determined that conversion in the Old Testament was the same as conversion in the New:

> I am now convinced, that conversion under the old testament was not only the same in general with what it is commonly under the new, but much more like it as to the particular way and manner, than I used to think. Among the children of Israel, there was always without doubt two sorts of persons, wicked and godly, and there used to be as manifest a difference between these two as there is now. It appears that the wicked were the same as they are now: vain, profane, light, proud, scornful, hating the godly. The righteous, by the descriptions we have of them, were also the same: humble, meek and lowly, devout, full of fear, love and trust in God, just, righteous and charitable. And we can't question but that there were as frequent conversions from one to the other as there is now.
>
> This turning is very often spoken of in the Old Testament, frequently urged and encouraged; and we have no reason to believe that what was said had no effect. And undoubtedly the first motives of their turning were a sense of the dangerousness of sin, and of the dreadfulness of God's anger; and [they] were convinced so much of their wickedness, that they trusted to nothing but the mere mercy of God, and then bitterly lamented and mourned for their sins. Wherever turning is urged, such a turning as this is urged; and what instances we have were of this kind. And thus it doubtless was, not only amongst the Israelites but also among the antediluvians, and from the beginning of the world.[26]

Edwards later queried, "If faith justifies, or gives a right to divine benefits" that are secured by Christ, and if Old Testament saints "had no distinct respect to Christ in those acts of faith that are mentioned" in the New Testament, then how is it that they are saved? He concluded that "it was the Lord Jesus Christ, the second person of the Trinity, that was wont to appear and to reveal himself. . . . They closed with and cleaved to this their God, husband and Savior in a way agreeable to the dispensation they were under."[27] What mattered was the disposition of the saints, not their explicit justification by faith in Christ. In some sense, the Old Testament saints believed in Christ, just as Cornelius in the New believed in Christ of whom he had not heard. God created in both a clean heart and

---

26. Edwards, *WJE* 13:221–22.
27. Edwards, *WJE* 18:201.

renewed spirit (Ps 51:10). These are "the same kind of terms as are used to signify the first conversion of a sinner, both in the Old Testament and New."[28]

In keeping with traditional Reformed exegesis, Edwards interpreted the Bible both typologically and christologically. Of the former, through the Jews "God [might] shadow forth and teach as under a veil all future glorious things of the gospel."[29] So, in the Old Testament, conversion was signified by the cleansing of leprosy (Lev 14:8-9), the curing of Naaman (2 Kgs 5:14), the raising of the dead by the prophets Elijah and Elisha (1 Kgs 17:17-22; 2 Kgs 4:18-37), and Christ's miracles.[30] In addition, "The Chil. of Israel Passing through the Red Sea when they Came out of Egy & when they took their final Leave of the Egyptians seems to be a type of Conversion."[31]

Edwards interpreted the Song of Songs (which he called the Canticles), as had many commentators before him, through a christological grid.[32] Edwards likened "the saint's conversion" to that of "the betrothing of the intended bridegroom [Christ] before they come together."[33] During the "little revival" that spread rapidly through the Connecticut River Valley in 1734-35, Edwards chose Song 6:1 as his sermon text: "Whither is thy beloved gone, O thou fairest among women? whither is thy beloved turned aside? that we may seek him with thee." Edwards built his entire sermon on this last phrase. The "we" are the daughters of Jerusalem (Song 5:8) who are represented as being formerly "strangers to Christ" but now "are meant persons belonging to [the] visible church of Christ. Jerusalem is the church" and "they are persons living under means of grace." "My beloved" is Jesus Christ. "The fairest of women," states Edwards, "signifies the church or spouse of Christ, or those that are converted." The sermon centers on the example of conversion to others: "When some are converted, there is great encouragement in it for others, to seek to be converted." Edwards reiterates this theme in his concluding exhortation:

---

28. Edwards, *WJE* 20:56. See also McDermott, "Possibility of Reconciliation," 187-90.
29. Edwards, *WJE* 13:431.
30. Edwards, *WJE* 13:221-22.
31. Edwards, *WJEO* 50, no. 362; see also *WJEO* 52, no. 442. For Edwards's major works on typological exegesis, see *WJE* 11; see also Sweeney, *Edwards the Exegete*, chap. 3.
32. See Sweeney, *Edwards the Exegete*, chap. 6.
33. Jonathan Edwards, quoted in Sweeney, *Edwards the Exegete*, 132.

"When others have found the Lord Jesus Christ, let this stir you to seek him, that you may also obtain an interest in that glorious and lovely person. Inquire, as the daughters of Jerusalem do in the text."[34]

Edwards drew from other Old Testament texts (the Psalms and the Major Prophets were his favorites) and linked them to New Testament passages to illustrate the conversion process.[35] For example, he drew from the Psalms and Isaiah in observing that "the conversion of sinners . . . is several times represented in Scripture as the weaning of a child; as in Ps. 131 [v. 2, 'Surely I have behaved and quieted myself as a child that is weaned of his mother: my soul is even as a weaned child'] and Isa. 28:9 ['Whom shall he teach knowledge? and whom shall he make to understand doctrine? them that are weaned from the milk, and drawn from the breasts']."[36] Similarly,

> The ingenerating of a principle of grace in the soul, seems in Scripture to be compared to the conceiving of Christ in the womb (Gal. 4:19). . . . And the conception of Christ in the womb of the blessed Virgin, by the power of the Holy Ghost, seems to be a designed resemblance of the conception of Christ in the soul of a believer, by the power of the same Holy Ghost.

Yet a mystery remains: "we know not what is the way of the Spirit, nor how the bones do grow, either in the womb or heart that conceives this holy child" of God.[37] This mystery was reflected in Edwards's own experience of conversion and consequently led him to question the morphology of conversion that Puritans had so assiduously developed since the seventeenth century.

THE BIBLE AND EDWARDS'S CONVERSION

Suffice it to say, Edwards's work and legacy was shaped indelibly by his conversion, the most critical event in his life. Avihu Zakai contends that "perhaps no event can be compared, in terms of intensity of religious life and spiritual experience, to his conversion. . . . It led him to find his

---

34. Edwards, *WJEO* 49, no. 324.

35. On the psalms, see Barshinger, *Jonathan Edwards and the Psalms*. Barshinger argues that Edwards interpreted the psalms primarily through the lens of God's redemptive activity and only secondarily christologically.

36. Edwards, *WJE* 4:367.

37. Edwards, *WJE* 2:161.

vocation in life, and not least, it provided him with the form and content for his lifelong theological and philosophical undertakings"—and, we might add, his lifelong devotion to the Bible.[38] Sometime in May or June 1721, Edwards experienced a conversion, but not until nearly two decades later, in his "Personal Narrative" (ca. 1740), did he offer a written account of his spiritual pilgrimage from childhood to his mid-twenties. After eight years of spiritual struggles, he experienced a breakthrough. He embraced the "hard doctrines" of Calvinism; God's sovereignty appeared "exceedingly pleasant." After reading 1 Tim 1:17, an "inward, sweet delight" in the things of God and God's glory overcame him, so much so that he detected an ontological change, "a new sense," qualitatively different from anything he had ever experienced. He expressed this altered sense in words familiar to the Christian mystical tradition: he was "wrapt up to God in heaven" and "swallowed up in him." He prayed "in a manner . . . with a new sort of affection. But it never came into my thoughts," he said, "that there was anything spiritual, or of a saving nature in this." His attention turned to Christ's work of redemption: "I had an inward, sweet sense of these things." The words of Scripture, especially Song 2:1 ("I am the rose of Sharon, and the lily of the valleys"), reinforced this new sense. He envisioned "being alone in the mountains, or some solitary wilderness, far from all mankind, sweetly conversing with Christ, and wrapt and swallowed up in God."[39]

Two general comments are in order. First, as we have already observed, Edwards's view of reality was shaped by his thorough immersion in the biblical text. Of all books, the Bible gave him "the greatest delights." It disclosed the beauty of God, touched the soul, and nourished the spiritually hungry. Every word, every line, every sentence "seemed to be full of wonders."[40]

Second, Edwards's account of his conversion follows the conventional Puritan pattern of moving from despair and humiliation to hope and a state of grace. However, in other ways it diverges. The defined stages in the Puritan morphology of conversion are absent. Edwards was not beholden to the Puritan model of a predictable pattern to conversion. What mattered was the nature of the experience, not its order. God's sovereign and saving ways transcended human attempts to enumerate how the unsaved come to faith.

38. Zakai, *Jonathan Edwards's Philosophy of History*, 53.
39. Edwards, *WJE* 16:792–93.
40. Edwards, *WJE* 16:797.

Other aspects of the traditional Puritan conversion narrative are missing in Edwards's "Narrative." Edwards was neither overwhelmed with conviction of sin—deep penitence for sin came long after his conversion—nor did he dwell for any length of time on the condition of his soul. The typical Puritan preoccupation with the self is also absent. His spirituality, writes Michael McClymond, was "more outward- than inward-looking."[41] The persistent spiritual anxiety encouraged by the Puritan tradition is nowhere to be found; Edwards's gaze was Other-directed: "The sweetest joys and delights I have experienced," he wrote, "have not been those that have arisen from a hope of my own good estate; but in the glorious things of the gospel."[42]

As Edwards pondered his religious experience, one that departed from the ordinary Puritan way but, it should be noted, was not unique (e.g., Richard Baxter, the English Nonconformist of the seventeenth century, had a similar conversion experience), he looked both to the writings of Puritans and the authors of Scripture for clarity. In his "Diary" entry of May 25, 1723, Edwards resolved "to look into our old divines' opinions concerning conversion," and to that end, he kept a notebook, "Notes on Conversion from Various Authorities," in which he recorded the views of Giles Fermin, Henry Alline, William Ames, Peter van Mastricht, and Thomas Shepard.[43] Edwards also read the works of his grandfather Stoddard and knew firsthand the views of his father and minister, Timothy Edwards. These two commanding figures represented two schools in the preparationist scheme of conversion. According to Kenneth Minkema, "Whereas Stoddard had contended that individuals spend a nominal amount of time in each of the stages and trace their conversion to an epiphanic moment, an 'explicit act of faith,' Timothy Edwards did not insist on locating conversion at a particular time."[44]

From his own experience, his reading of Puritan authors, and the influences of his grandfather and father, Jonathan Edwards formulated a more expansive, organic view of the nature of conversion, one that focused more on the nature of the religious experience and less on hewing to a strict preparationist model. In the wake of the Great Awakening, Edwards wrote to Thomas Prince:

41. McClymond, *Encounters with God*, 47.
42. Edwards, *WJE* 16:800.
43. Edwards, *WJE* 16:771; Edwards, "Untitled Volume."
44. Minkema, "Preface to the Period," 41.

> There is nothing more manifest by what appears among us, than that the goodness of [a] person's state is not chiefly to be judged by the exactness of steps, and method of experiences, in what is supposed to be the first conversion; but that we must judge more by the spirit that breathes, the effect wrought on the temper of the soul, in the time of the work, and remaining afterwards.[45]

Ultimately, of course, Edwards knew that religious experience alone was not a sufficient refutation of a strict morphology of conversion. Scripture must be a necessary guide to confirm the experience by providing its own examples and insight. "'Tis abundantly safer," he noted, "to follow the light of Scripture, than to draw up rules from our own experiences."[46] In a "Miscellanies" entry probably written sometime in 1741, Edwards cited the womb imagery found in Old Testament texts, arguing that "the methods of grace are obscure, as those of nature":

> Ecclesiastes 11:5, "Thou knowest not what is the way of the Spirit, or how the bones do grow in the womb of her that is with child: even so thou knowest not the works of God who maketh all." The manner of the formation of Christ in the soul, is as indiscernible as the formation of a child, or the manner of Christ's conception in the womb of the Virgin, both which are fearful and wonderful. As it is said of the first, Psalms 139:14–15, "I am fearfully and wonderfully made: marvelous are thy works; and that my soul knoweth right well. My substance was not hid from thee, when I was made in secret, and curiously wrought in the lowest parts of the earth." Isaiah 53:8, "Who can declare his generation?"—that is, the generation of Christ, either in his person or in his people.[47]

Later, in *Religious Affections*, Edwards quoted the same texts and cited the same imagery in noting that

> sometimes the change made in the saint, at first work, is like a confused chaos; so that the saints know not what to make of it. The manner of the Spirit's proceeding in them that are born of the Spirit, is very often exceeding mysterious and unsearchable. . . . And 'tis oftentimes difficult to know the way of the Spirit in the new birth, as in the first birth.

---

45. Edwards, *WJE* 16:126.
46. Edwards, *WJE* 13:460.
47. Edwards, *WJE* 20:156.

Edwards appealed to other texts (Prov 25:2 and Isa 40:13) to prove his point, and then added,

> 'Tis to be feared that some have gone too far towards directing the Spirit of the Lord, and marking out his footsteps for him, and limiting him to certain steps and methods. Experience plainly shows, that God's Spirit is unsearchable and untraceable, in some of the best of Christians, in the method of his operations, in their conversion.[48]

Turning to the New Testament, Edwards noted that one of those "best of Christians" was the apostle Paul, a paradigmatic example of one who was given saving grace without first experiencing conviction of sin. Before Paul's "terrors of conscience were fully removed by Christ's gracious word by Ananias, Christ comforts him, in some measure declaring his favor and love to him, and his gracious purpose of making him an apostle and glorious instrument of multitudes of both Jews and Gentiles." The work of humiliation and conviction of sin came afterward, after grace was infused. It followed that

> it cannot reasonably be supposed that Christ would thus declare his love [to] him, and the great purposes of his grace concerning him, while he yet continued fully an enemy in his heart, without any mortification of that enmity, and while God held him under the guilt of sin and condemnation for it, and the wrath of God abode upon him.[49]

CONVERSION AND THE AWAKENINGS

If, as Edwards declared, conversion was "undoubtedly the most important thing in the world," we would expect that attention to conversion would be the primary focus of his sermons, just as it was for the other great preachers in the Connecticut River Valley (e.g., Edwards's father, Thomas Hooker, and his grandfather Solomon Stoddard). However, throughout nearly forty years of sermonizing, Edwards's emphasis on conversion was more prominent at certain times than others. To be sure, in the "Application" or "Use" section in many of his sermons, Edwards exhorted auditors to "close with Christ" and seek conversion, but there were times when the subject of conversion was preached more often and more explicitly. As

---

48. Edwards, *WJE* 2:160–61.
49. Edwards, *WJE* 23:86–87.

noted earlier, in his writings Edwards invoked the word "conversion" and associated terms thousands of times. However, if we limit these terms to his sermons and track Edwards's usage of them from 1720 to 1758, we find spikes during some years and a tailing off during others. As one might expect, the usage spiked during the "Little Awakening" of 1734–35 and the Great Awakening of 1740–41 (see figure 1).[50]

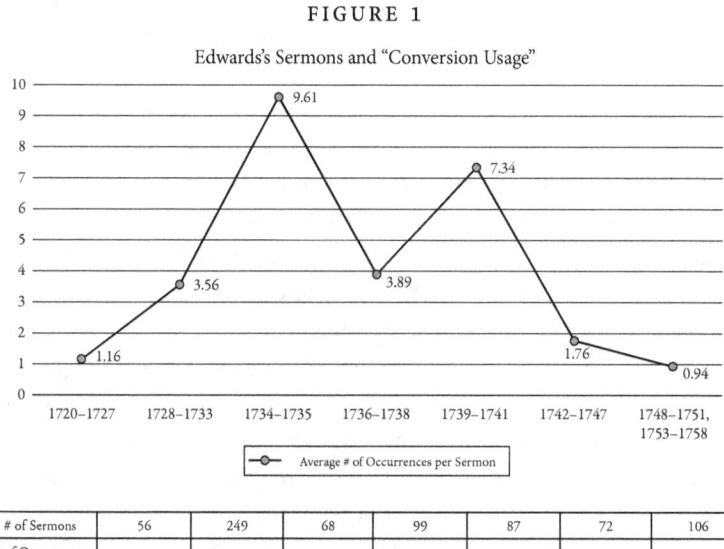

FIGURE 1

Edwards's Sermons and "Conversion Usage"

# of Sermons	56	249	68	99	87	72	106
# of Occurrences ("conversion," "convert," "converts," "converted," "conv")	65	887	654	386	639	127	100

Edwards's sermons and his usage of the term "conversion."

Both awakenings provided the laboratory wherein Edwards examined the nature of conversion and the excitement of the revivals. Three works written during or shortly after the revivals highlight Edwards's skills of observation as a religious psychologist and anticipate themes later extended in *Religious Affections*. In a letter titled *A Faithful Narrative of the*

50. Calculations are based on 737 (ca. 60 percent) of Edwards's nearly 1,200 extant sermons; the remaining 40 percent of Edwards's sermons have yet to be transcribed (ca. 10 percent) or are being prepared for posting online (ca. 30 percent). The author expresses his gratitude to Kenneth Minkema for his clarifying comments. Thanks also to Veronica Arce, former office manager in the Department of Religious Studies, University of Miami, for preparing the figure.

Surprising Work of God (1735; published 1737), Edwards chronicled the events leading up to the revival and then described the external behavioral and internal spiritual changes of the converted. Written shortly after the revival commenced, the narrative reflects the excitement of Edwards as both participant and observer. He described conversion as "a great and glorious work of God's power, at once changing the heart and infusing life into the dead soul."[51] Outwardly, the saved abandoned old vices and contentious ways for the bonds of love. Inwardly, they expressed a new or "lively" sense of the divine presence and a new "disposition" toward religious things.

From 1741 to 1746 Edwards gave extensive attention to revival, conversion, and religious experience. In *The Distinguishing Marks of a Work of the Spirit of God* (1741), he defended the revival as God's work by demonstrating the authenticity of the conversions. He admitted to irregularities and excesses but suggested heeding the advice of the writer of 1 John to "try the spirits whether they be of God" (4:1). To that end, he proposed "signs" (both positive and negative) by which the work of the Holy Spirit might be judged legitimate. Finally, in *Some Thoughts Concerning the Present Revival of Religion in New England* (1742), Edwards expanded his discussion of "signs," arguing for the identification of the "fruits of the Spirit" in Gal 5:22–23 with "religious affections." Holiness, Edwards argued, has its seat in the heart or will rather than in the understanding, and holy or religious affections are the substance of genuine religion. *A Treatise Concerning Religious Affections* (1746), published two years after Edwards declared that the revival was over, represented Edwards's definitive treatment of the subject of revival, for here he gave systematic attention to the nature of revival and, more broadly, to the nature of religious experience.

CONVERSION AND THE BIBLE IN THREE AWAKENING SERMONS

As critical as these works are to understanding Edwards's views of conversion and religious experience, I want to examine briefly three conversion-focused sermons preached in 1740—two in July and one in August. During the last six months of 1740, Edwards spoke more often about conversion than at any other time in his preaching career. His

---

51. Edwards, *WJE* 4:177.

"conversion usage" peaked at nearly fifteen occurrences per sermon during this period. We might view these three sermons as "warm-ups" in anticipation of the visit of George Whitefield, the "Grand Itinerant," who in October set New England aflame in revival. Each of these sermons represents a distillation of Edwards's use of the Bible in service of the "great and glorious" work of conversion.

Conversion Is Real

In "The Reality of Conversion," Edwards chose for his text John 3:10–11, Jesus' rebuke to the Pharisee Nicodemus that follows after he informs the Pharisee that he "must be born again": "Art thou a master of Israel, and knowest not these things? . . . We speak that we do know; and testify that we have seen; and ye receive not our witness." The choice of this text says something about Edwards's assessment of the spiritual condition of his congregation, one that he would describe several months later in a letter to Eleazar Wheelock on the eve of Whitefield's arrival, as "sorrowfully dull and dead."[52] Edwards thus set out to prove the doctrine "There is such a thing as conversion" and to urge his audience "earnestly to seek conversion." He argues that "the voice of reason, Scripture, and experience, and the testimony of the best of men" confirm this doctrine that is so fundamental to Scripture that "if we deny it, we do in effect renounce the Scriptures."[53] Edwards does little to exegete the passage, omitting his usual explication of the text. By modern standards—and this applies to his entire sermon corpus—Edwards is not an expositor or close reader of the text. Here, he uses the text as a point of departure, relating the spiritual blindness of Nicodemus to the people in the pews before him. The conversion of the apostle Paul is cited as proof that even those with a "notoriously vicious" nature can be "changed so as to make 'em holy." Moreover, "the faith, steadfastness and cheerfulness" of the persecuted, including Paul and the early martyrs in the church, testify to the reality of conversion. They endured with joy because of something beyond themselves—the "mighty work of God on their hearts, changing their natures."[54]

---

52. Edwards, *WJE* 16:85.
53. Edwards, *WJE* 16:89–90.
54. Edwards, *WJE* 16:86, 88–89.

In his lengthy application, Edwards goes out of his way to convince his hearers that "if there is such a thing as conversion, 'tis the most important thing in the world." Those who remain in an "undetermined state" should act and take full advantage of "the use of all appointed means." Edwards makes no mention of the standard means of grace—Bible reading, prayer, and attendance at corporate worship—but urges other spiritual practices, such as vigilant self-examination and especially the "duties of justice and charity to men." Of course, Edwards and his Calvinist colleagues argued that none are saved by their own righteousness and that God elects whom God wills to salvation. And yet they exhorted the people to good deeds and advised them, in Edwards's words, not to obsess "about the eternal decrees of God with respect to yourself." Edwards concluded, "If you follow these directions" (he gave seventeen!), "in all probability you will be converted." This was the pastoral side of Edwards, for he knew that conversion did not typically happen without moral exertion. He was also convinced that the Scripture taught as much: "These directions are agreeable to God's word . . . and, therefore, are his directions: so that, if you will follow them, you will be in God's own way."[55]

Conversion Transforms the Body

Not only was conversion real, but, as the Scriptures made clear, it changed all areas of life. Edwards addressed the totality of conversion a few weeks later when he argued that "in true conversion, men's bodies are in some respect changed as well as their soul."[56] His sermon text is 1 Thess 5:23, "And the very God of peace sanctify you wholly; and I pray God your whole spirit and soul and body be preserved blameless unto the coming of our Lord Jesus Christ." Although Edwards is more attentive to explicating this passage than the one previously examined, his major focus is on conversion's transformative effect on the body. Before turning to the body, however, Edwards defines what is meant by spirit and soul—those faculties of the mind that are naturally thought to be transformed in conversion. He identifies "spirit" with "the faculty of the will," including the

---

55. Edwards, *WJE* 16:92, 97, 102, 104; see also *WJEO* 49, no. 345: "Indeed tis more Probable that Persons . . . that are Earnestly striving for Conversion will obtain Conversion than . . . others that are negligent of means . . . because that is the way in which G. ordinarily bestows Conversion."

56. Edwards, *WJEO* 56, no. 561. This sermon has been transcribed but not published. For another mention of physical change in conversion, see *WJE* 17:187.

"disposition & affections of the mind," citing Eph 4:23, "And be renewed in the spirit of your mind." Edwards says little about "soul" other than that which "appertains to the other faculty of understanding including the apprehension [of] thought." The third part, the "temporal part," transformed in conversion is the body. It is evident, contends Edwards, that "not only the soul but also the body is in some Respect Changed in Conversion."

Not only did the Fall corrupt the soul and spirit, but Scripture also amply illustrates its pernicious effect on the body.[57] Edwards offers numerous "Scripture proofs." In Rom 3:13-15, Paul refers to the bodily parts of corrupted humanity: "Their throat is an open sepulchre; with their tongues they have used deceit; the point of asps is under their lips; Whose mouth is full of cursing and bitterness: Their feet are swift to shed blood." Second Pet 2:14 speaks of wicked men's eyes as full of sin. Proverbs 23:6 and 28:22 refer to the evil eye. First John 2:16 mentions "the lust of the flesh, and the lust of the eyes." In Acts 7:51 we read of an "uncircumcised ear." The apostle James speaks of the tongue as "a fire, a world of iniquity . . . that it defileth the whole body" (Jas 3:6). Paul also states that our bodies are the temple of God (1 Cor 6:19).[58] If the body as well as the soul "was changed by the fall & became corrupt," writes Edwards, "doubtless the whole is Renewed in Conversion for Conversion is a Restoring man from that corrupt state into which he fell or at Least it is the beginning of such a Restoration. [W]hen a man is Converted & the Renovation is begun of all that was corrupted by the fall." Christ died that the corrupted and damned body as well as the soul might be saved; union with Christ "is begun in Effectual calling or Conversion & then the body as well as the soul is united & theref[ore] the body is then sanctified as well as the soul."[59]

Scripture identifies particular members of the body that are renewed at conversion. The ear is circumcised (Jer 6:10); God gives clean hands and a pure heart (Ps 24:4); some of Christ's miracles are types of conversion, such as the restoration of withered hands and healings of diseases of the tongue and feet. Edwards is clear that these changes are

---

57. According to Edwards, the condition of Adam's and Eve's bodies before the Fall "appeared with such a beauty [and] had such a luster [and] Glory from head to foot that far more supplied the want of Garments." Quoted in Sweeney, *Edwards the Exegete*, 143. My thanks to the author for pointing me to this passage.

58. The transcription incorrectly cites 1 Cor 16:17 as the text.

59. Edwards, *WJEO* 56, no. 561.

neither immediate nor, more importantly, literally physical changes. There is no change to "the frame of the body, or"—and here Edwards assumes the prevailing scientific view of the body's "humors"—"changing the Temperament of the blood or other juices." Edwards also rejects the theory that the forbidden fruit that Adam ate was poisonous and so altered the body's appetites from a condition of moderate to inordinate desires, which consequently led to the body's infection of the soul. If that were the case, then conversion would be the work of God upon the body, "rectifying the depravity & expelling the poison." But the opposite is true: humanity's corruption begins in the soul and proceeds to infect the body. Thus, "The renovation of the body in Conversion dont at all Consist in being the ... w. of G. on the flesh or blood or constituent parts of the body to make them to be alteration in the body" but "begins with the Heart & proceeds from thence to members of the body." The bodily change is the result of a new disposition infused by the Spirit of God, so that, in Paul's words, the body is brought under subjection (2 Cor 9:27). Higher appetites displace lower appetites; "the soul employs the body in a new manner in a new work & service" (see Rom 6:11–13). The body is presented as "a living sacrifice" (Rom 12:1). New tongues are given to praise; new hands serve the needy; new eyes read the Bible; new ears listen to things of great importance; and new feet follow in the footsteps of Christ.[60]

Edwards's primary sermonic purpose is to jolt his hearers out of their halfhearted spiritual commitment or false sense of spiritual security. He felt that "hypocrisy" (a false confidence in one's spiritual status) was a long-standing problem in his Northampton congregation—one that his grandfather had not given sufficient attention.[61] He exhorted both "those that never have been truly Converted" and those "who are Converted" to examine their controlling bodily appetites. In the conversion process, the body cannot be separated from the soul. We are embodied people; what we think, believe, and say is expressed socially in physical or bodily movements—talking, walking, seeing, hearing, and so forth. Conversion is a totality, a transformation of body, soul, and spirit. Scripture's instructions are clear: put off the old man and put on the new (Col 3:9–10); mortify your bodies and forsake the wicked use of its members (Matt 5:29–30). The progressive sanctification of body and soul "will be a Certain sign &

---

60. Edwards, *WJEO* 56, no. 561.
61. On "hypocrisy," see Chamberlain, "Self-Deception as a Theological Problem," 541–56.

a kind of a pledge of your more literal & Glorious Resurrection hereafter, when your body that is now sanctified shall be glorified."[62]

Conversion Is an Ongoing Process

In his July sermons, Edwards preached that conversion was real and changed all areas of life; in August he declared that it was an ongoing process. "The Subjects of a First Work of Grace May Need a New Conversion" was based on Jesus' words to Peter in Luke 22:32, "But I have prayed for thee, that thy faith fail not: and when thou art converted, strengthen thy brethren." Peter was "truly savingly converted before now," but in light of Satan's activity, Jesus prays for Peter, anticipating his failure. Thus, notes Edwards, "We may observe something in the text that implies that Peter would yet need to be converted."[63] Or, as he remarked in another sermon, "True converts themselves need to be converted."[64]

Throughout his writings Edwards made repeated references to "first conversion" and the necessity of continuous conversion.[65] In making this distinction, Edwards drew from a long tradition in Puritan thought and, more immediately, from the works of Thomas Shepard.[66] Edwards described first conversion as the instantaneous work of God's Spirit. In opposition to Arminian views, Edwards argued that conversion was neither gradual nor of human effort nor of human habit. His favorite image to describe immediate conversion was that of light (as expressed in his famous sermon "A Divine and Supernatural Light"). The "seeing" that comes from the divine light, declared Edwards, "is produced by God immediately."[67] Elsewhere, Edwards appealed to other biblical images, metaphors, and examples to support the doctrine of immediate

62. Edwards, *WJEO* 56, no. 561.
63. Edwards, *WJE* 22:183–84.
64. Edwards, *WJE* 10:575.
65. A search of "first conversion" in *WJEO* turns up the following references: 2:267, 341, 347, 380, 418, 443; 7:503, 508, 545; 11:115; 13:456; 14:269; 15:66, 331; 16:119, 126, 127; 18:38, 403; 20:56, 74, 207; 22 (eleven in the sermon previously discussed); 24:833, 1058; 25:246, 493 (two times); 43, no. 84; 47, no. 255; 51, no. 375; 52, no. 442; 53, nos. 470, 498c (three times). Edwards also applied the term to his own experience. *WJE* 16:803.
66. On Shepard's "first conversion," see Pettit, *Heart Prepared*, 106–7. On Shepard's use of this term in preaching, see Shepard, *Parable of the Ten Virgins*, 233. For Shepard's influence on Edwards, see Ramsey, "Editor's Introduction," 53–57.
67. Edwards, *WJE* 17:416.

conversion. He likened conversion to the instantaneity of a "resurrection" (John 5:25), a "calling" (Christ "does but speak the powerful word, and it is done"), the work of God in creation, and miracles. Moreover, "a pattern to all future ages" was providentially given by the instant conversion of the apostle Paul and other early Christians.[68]

To Edwards, "first conversion" is just that—a beginning. In two "Miscellanies," written about the same time as his August sermon, Edwards observes that first conversions are found in both testaments: "We often read of conversion in the Old Testament under such terms of giving a new heart and a right spirit, etc.," he writes, "yet this was long after the Psalmist was first converted." In the New Testament, the apostle Paul informs Timothy that to be "faithful in his ministry, he should save himself as well as those that heard him" (1 Tim 4:16). Similarly, Paul himself, long after his conversion, pronounced a self-maledictory oath should he not preach the gospel (1 Cor 9:16), and he disciplined his body lest he should become a "castaway" (1 Cor 9:27). So Cornelius, who already believed in Christ as did Old Testament saints, requested that Peter "should tell him words whereby he and his house should be saved" (Acts 11:13–14)."[69] "Miscellanies" number 847—probably a textual parallel to Edwards's sermon on Luke 22:32—drives home the point that conversion may still be necessary even after one has become a saint.[70] "Christ's words seem to intimate that if Peter should not be converted after his fall, in answer to his prayer for him, Satan would have had him."[71]

Edwards's sermon draws out the doctrine that "those who have true grace in their hearts may yet stand in great need of being converted." As in his two earlier sermons, Edwards sought to rouse his people from their spiritual slumber and reliance on their previous experiences of grace. At the initial infusion of grace, the convert "thirsts" after Jesus Christ but is not yet enabled "to rejoice" in him as Savior and Redeemer. Conversion is an ongoing spiritual restoration that often resembles the ordering of the Spirit's work in the first conversion: fear, awakening, conviction of sin, and so forth. Edwards reminds his hearers that all "godly persons . . . stand in great need of being converted." Indeed, he concludes, "'tis pity

---

68. Edwards, *WJE* 21:161–63, 297; 18:230–33.

69. Edwards, *WJE* 20:56.

70. Pauw, "Editor's Introduction," 35. Regarding Edwards's use of "regeneration" and "conversion," see 33n81 in chapter 1 of this volume.

71. Edwards, *WJE* 20:74.

there is no more said of godly persons' conversion."⁷² The work of God in the soul is not a momentary but a lifetime journey.

CONCLUSION

In many respects, Edwards's sermons had their desired effect. Like John the Baptist's message that prepared the way of the Lord, so Edwards's sermons prepared the way for George Whitefield's coming in mid-October. Almost immediately after Whitefield arrived, a spiritual awakening erupted throughout the Connecticut River Valley. Hundreds were converted. Edwards was overjoyed; the millennium appeared to be on the horizon. For a time he actively promoted the most radical dimensions of the Awakening—ecstatic visionary experiences and bodily manifestations (weeping and writhing)—as signs of the Holy Spirit. And yet he tempered his enthusiasm with caution. In November 1740, he preached a sermon, "Sudden Conversions Are Very Often False" (Matt 13:5–7), warning those who had been suddenly converted in the contagion of revival to count the cost. The gate is straight, and the way is narrow; a new life in Christ entails self-denial, suffering, and persevering obedience.⁷³

Edwards would later extend the theme of genuine conversion in his *Treatise Concerning Religious Affections*, clarifying the "signs" and "no signs" of authentic conversion (see chapter 1). Drawing his sermon text from 1 Pet 1:8, Edwards contended that the test of true religion comes amid trials and persecution. In that context, "True faith appears more precious than gold."⁷⁴ Trials of faith, which every Christian faces, test the integrity of the believer's conversion. For Edwards, a biblically rooted, true conversion, from the first infusion of divine life to the end of mortal existence, is built on persevering in Christlike word, thought, and deed, to the everlasting glory of God.

---

72. Edwards, *WJE* 22:184, 186, 192–94, 199.
73. Edwards, *WJEO* 56, no. 577.
74. Edwards, *WJE* 2:93.

3

Edwards, Petitionary Prayer, and the Cognitive Science of Religion

IN THIS ESSAY, I extend the findings of cognitive science to one kind of religious practice—prayer, and more particularly petitionary prayer—in the life and writings of Jonathan Edwards, arguably America's greatest theologian. My intent is to address some of the conclusions of cognitive scientists regarding human nature. In retrieving the past, I hope to speak to present theological and pastoral challenges.

A word of caution. I am aware of the danger of the historical fallacy of anachronism—of interpreting the past though the lens of the present—but I am convinced that applying cognitive science to a fundamental aspect of spiritual life offers a conceptual tool for gaining insight into the prayers of Jonathan Edwards and his Northampton, Massachusetts, congregation.[1]

COGNITIVE SCIENCE: SOME BASICS

According to Justin Barrett, one of the leading scholars in the field, cognitive scientists "bring scientific evidence to bear on claims and predictions about how humans think and the character of the human mind, and attempt to discover naturalistic explanations for the phenomena the data reveal."[2] Cognitive scientists study domains of human thought, includ-

---

1. In a somewhat similar vein, Richard Bushman applied the findings of psychoanalysis to Edwards. See Bushman, "Jonathan Edwards as Great Man," 15–46.
2. Barrett, *Cognitive Science, Religion, and Theology*, 12.

ing perception, attention, memory, conceptualization, communication, decision-making, imagination, feelings or emotions, general tendencies, natural limitations, and biases. One of the theoretical problems pursued by cognitive scientists considers a fundamental question: Are there certain behaviors, personality dispositions, or ways of thinking that reflect the operation of evolved cognitive systems? Is there intuitive knowledge that all people share as part of our natural or inborn (not practiced) cognitive development?

In the last thirty years, the interdisciplinary field of cognitive science has expanded into the realm of religion, examining the ways the human mind works and thinks in matters related to religious beliefs and practices.[3] Psychologists and anthropologists in particular have used the tools of cognitive science to study religion, researching and conducting experiments into the ways in which our mental tools plus the surrounding environment resist, contest, or encourage the spread of particular religious ideas, beliefs, and practices. I want to focus on two important discoveries by cognitive scientists that relate to the study of religion: first, religion is "natural"; second, humans employ a dual-process or two-system model of reasoning.

RELIGION IS NATURAL

According to cognitive scientists, the mind is not a tabula rasa or blank slate; it is not a passive receptor or a sponge, waiting to be influenced by the surrounding environment. Yes, nurture does influence the trajectory of our lives in important ways, but so does nature. One of the basic conclusions of cognitive scientists is that people seem naturally receptive or predisposed to religious concepts. They have a God-awareness, developed as a by-product of evolutionary processes.[4]

Religious thinking and experiencing, like all human thought and experience, is neurologically and cognitively mediated.[5] For one group of cognitive scientists, the militant atheists including the likes of Richard Dawkins, Daniel Dennett, Paul Bloom, Pascal Boyer, and Jesse Bering (to name a few of the most prominent), the fact of the presence of the idea of God does not prove that this God actually exists. From their perspective,

---

3. For a succinct overview, see Visala, *Naturalism*, 1–12.
4. Clark and Barrett, "Reformed Epistemology," 174.
5. Jones, *Can Science Explain Religion?*, 5, 27.

religion is a mere by-product of human evolution, or a spillover of childish thinking, or a remnant of "folk psychology," or an adaptive illusion that we would be better off without. For them, religion is "nothing more" than a natural phenomenon—a cultural trait that evolved to increase its own transmission (like a disease organism such as a virus or parasite)—without benefitting human individuals or groups.

To be sure, religion is a natural phenomenon. "Regardless of metaphysical claims," states Justin Barrett (who is a Christian), "what we observe as religion is still a constellation of human phenomena communicated and regulated by natural human perception and cognition."[6] Natural, human processes are at work in religion—something few Christians would deny. In a sense, cognitive science confirms the apostle Paul's contention in Rom 1:19–20 and Calvin's *sensus divinitatis*—although without acknowledging that God is the source of this predisposition.[7]

Cognitive science demonstrates that a belief in a divine source behind the world and its events is actually quite natural. Religious belief comes naturally to children, who are, as Barrett titled his book, "born believers."[8] Preschoolers are inclined to see purpose and design everywhere—what the developmental psychologist Deborah Kelemen calls "promiscuous teleology." Young children, perhaps as young as one year old, acknowledge that it takes some*one* to create order or purpose, not just some*thing*. And that someone is not human. Children spontaneously interpret events in the world as the product of intelligent, intentional agents or other beings—and in fact of a god or spirits who has caused the natural world. Children are, contends Kelemen, "intuitive theists."[9] These conclusions apply even to children raised in militantly atheistic homes.

The belief in God or gods extends into adulthood and is amplified by our survival mechanisms. In fact, the survival of our ancestors depended upon what Barrett calls a "hyperactive agency detection device."

---

6. Barrett, "Exploring the Natural Foundations of Religion," 29.

7. Edwards similarly argues: "We first ascend, and prove a posteriori, or from effects, that there must be an eternal cause; and then second, prove by argumentation, not intuition, that this being must be necessarily existent; and then thirdly, from the proved necessity of his existence, we may descend, and prove many of his perfections a priori." See Edwards, *Freedom of the Will*, 182.

8. Barrett, *Born Believers*.

9. Kelemen, "Are Children 'Intuitive Theists'?," 297. Kelemen clarifies by noting that the term "embodies no claims regarding children's emotional or metaphysical commitments"; all that she claims is that children "make sense of the world in a manner superficially approximating adult theism" (297).

For example, when walking in the woods and hearing a twig break or seeing movement in the bushes, humans immediately detect some agent—a predator threatening their life. Of course, the sound or the movement may not be a predator (false positives drastically outnumber the true positives), but our ancestors adapted to the menacing environment and survived by attributing agency to any potential threat. Better to be safe than sorry. Better to assume the rustling in the bush is a hungry bear or malicious human than to make a potentially fatal mistake by ignoring it.

This natural propensity by children and adults to detect non-human agency around us is part of why humans so easily sense the presence of supernatural agents in their environment. When there are experiences where agency is unclear (for example, unusual fortune or misfortune), there is a tendency to regard these experiences as evidence of the activity of a god or gods. Adults do not outgrow this inclination to see the world in teleo-functional terms. In one study, even atheists implicitly admitted that "everything happens for a reason."[10] Random events in life have causes. "Attributing the cause (or blame) for a great many events or conditions to gods or a God strikes many adults as reasonable."[11] If anything, adults have to unlearn this natural proclivity, override it, or suppress it. Their default setting is to trust in the existence of super-agents, gods, or God, working behind the scenes and making things happen.[12]

According to the evolutionary biologist Dominic Johnson, we live as if we are being watched, whether by spirits, ancestors, or God, or some other ordering principle of the universe. And because we are being watched, we are being judged for our actions by a supernatural agent (God) or supernatural agency (karma). What goes around, comes around. This belief in supernatural reward and punishment is cross-cultural, a ubiquitous phenomenon of human nature.[13] No matter how scientifically informed we might be, people continue to believe that events have supernatural meaning. Religious beliefs come creeping back into one's consciousness despite one's best efforts to get rid of them. "Atheism," Johnson asserts, "is not a battle just against culture, but against human nature."[14] Or, in the words of Jesse Bering, to remove God or supernatural

---

10. Bering, *Belief Instinct*, 161–62.
11. Barrett, *Born Believers*, 57.
12. Barrett, *Born Believers*, 79.
13. Johnson, *God Is Watching You*, 7. See also Bering, *Belief Instinct*, 191–94.
14. Johnson, *God Is Watching You*, 11.

THE TWO-SYSTEM MODEL OF REASONING

As fascinating and controversial as the "naturalness" of religion is from a cognitive science perspective, I want to turn to a second (and related) finding that, as we will see shortly, has direct implications for the study of prayer. This is the proposed dual-processing or two-system model of reasoning. According to cognitive scientists, the brain is like a book. Nature provides the first draft, while experiences contribute to ongoing revisions.[16] The initial draft, written by our genes in fetal development, reflects built-in "cognitive biases"; that is, aspects of reasoning (or thinking mechanisms) that are considered basic, intuitive, tacit, quick, effortless, or nonreflective. They come naturally. They do not have to be learned in any conscious way (cognitive scientists call these "folk beliefs," "folk psychology," or "folk physics"). Subsequent revisions to the first draft—a higher level of reasoning that comes through lived experience—are the result of reflective, conscious, deliberate, or explicit thought. For example, first language acquisition comes naturally, or effortlessly, whereas learning to read the language requires deliberate instruction.

This two-tier model has implications for religion. The features of the first mode of reasoning—belief in God, gods, or spirits—are subsequently elaborated theologically or particularized in the second mode of reasoning. Yet this mental move from natural religion to the thoughtful, deliberative second mode of reasoning is not easy. The anthropologist T. M. Luhrmann has studied the difficulty of making sense of the supernatural among U.S. evangelicals, observing that they

> often believe in some abstract, absolute sense that God exists but struggle to experience God as real in the everyday world around them. For many who believe intuitively that the supernatural

---

15. Bering, *Belief Instinct*, 200. Bering continues: "Knowing what we now know, is it wise to trust our evolved, subjective, mental intuitions to be reliable gauges of the reality outside our heads, or do we instead accept the possibility that such intuitions in fact arise through cognitive biases that—perhaps for biologically adaptive reasons—lead our thinking fundamentally away from objective reality? Do we keep blindly serving our genes and continue falling for this spectacularly evolutionary ruse of a caring God, or do we peek behind the curtain and say, 'Aha, That's not God, that's just Nature up to her dirty little tricks!'" (200–201).

16. Haidt, *Righteous Mind*, 152–53, citing the work of Gary Marcus.

exists, it takes effort to accept that a particular interpretation of the supernatural is correct, and it takes effort to live in accordance with the interpretation—to live as if they really do believe that their understanding is correct.[17]

This transition from natural religion to theology is not only difficult but can also lead to a tension, if not a contradiction, in our way of thinking. As Barrett notes, "There seems to be a difference between what people tend to believe in an automatic, day-to-day sort of way and what they believe when they stop to reflect and systematically figure out what they do and do not believe."[18] "Adults," he continues, "may actually have two or more different sets of ideas about God." The results from a number of experiments conducted by Barrett and others indicate that "ideas that deviate too far from our natural conceptual tendencies are difficult to use."[19] Put another way, in catechism, sermons, and other forms of theological instruction, we learn theologically correct notions, whereas in everyday settings, an incorrect (though natural) theological understanding may simply crop up directly from the depths of the human mind. Christians play a perpetual game of theological "whack-a-mole."

For example, there is the natural tendency to anthropomorphize God.[20] Some of this inclination is, of course, drawn from the Bible itself, although the theologically correct way of interpreting anthropomorphisms is to understand them in a metaphorical sense. Yet the data suggest that in real-life activities, God is automatically treated anthropomorphically. God is made into the image of ourselves, as a super-human. Thus, Christians (as does the Bible) often speak of "the hand of God," ("He's got the whole world in his hands"); or they declare, "God sees" ("His eye is on the sparrow"), or more crudely, they may refer to the "Big Guy in the Sky."[21] Why so? This conception of God is more easily comprehended, related to, etc. The theological God is radically different from the "intuitive" God described in everyday discourse. "The ontological chasm between humans and God," conclude the authors of one study, "is solved by ignoring the difference."[22]

17. Luhrmann et al., "Absorption Hypothesis," 67. Luhrmann extended this theme in *When God Talks Back*.
18. Barrett, *Born Believers*, 152.
19. Barrett, *Born Believers*, 163.
20. Barrett and Keil, "Conceptualizing a Nonnatural Entity," 219–47.
21. Barrett, *Born Believers*, 166.
22. Barrett and Keil, "Conceptualizing a Nonnatural Entity," 244. See also Barrett, "Theological Correctness," 325–39.

In some cases, nonreflective beliefs contradict or challenge religious beliefs. For example, you may be a Calvinist who is a theological determinist when it comes to conversion, yet you may be involved in an evangelical ministry, trying to persuade people to follow Jesus, assuming—even representing to those you are trying to convert—that they have the freedom to become a Christian. Although there are ways to reconcile limited election and God's predestining decrees with active evangelism (Jonathan Edwards certainly thought so), it does take some reflective, higher-level thinking to square these apparent contradictions. What theory of mind research indicates is that at the natural, basic level there exists a strong nonreflective belief that people possess the freedom to act on the basis of their own desires.[23]

Consider another example, the Christian doctrine of grace. Intuitively, it is not a natural idea. People across cultures seem to have a deeply ingrained sense of fair exchange practices and the need to reciprocate. No one wants to be in someone's debt; we try to settle accounts. Accordingly, no matter how many times we are told "It's all about grace" or "God doesn't need anything from you," we just cannot seem to shake the nagging feeling that God wants something from us in exchange for salvation. We must do something to placate God. We must balance the ledger. A sort of quid pro quo or "if . . . then" formula injects itself into our understanding of our relationship with God.[24] Martin Luther was well aware of this inclination. Making the correct doctrinal distinction between a human-centered "active" righteousness and a "passive" Christ-centered righteousness, he wrote, "must be diligently taught and continually practised."[25]

---

23. Barrett, *Why Would Anyone Believe in God?*, 10.

24. See two contemporary books addressed to a popular audience: Yancey, *What's So Amazing about Grace?*; McCullough, *If Grace Is So Amazing*. Drawing from a variety of sources, these quotes from Yancey are especially pertinent: "We read, we hear, we believe a good theology of grace. But that's not the way we live" (15). Jesus was "aware of our inbuilt resistance to grace" (45). "From nursery school onward we are taught how to succeed in the world of ungrace. The early bird gets the worm. No pain, no gain. There is no such thing as a free lunch. Demand your rights. Get what you pay for" (64). "By instinct I feel I must do something in order to be accepted. Grace sounds a startling note of contradiction, of liberation, and every day I must pray anew for the ability to hear its message" (71). And, quoting Simone Weil: "All the natural movements of the soul are controlled by laws analogous to those of physical gravity. Grace is the only exception" (271).

25. Luther, *Galatians*, 101.

These kinds of considerations have led some cognitive scientists of religion to conclude that the concept of God's radical and complete grace is counterintuitive to the way people think. How then is the unnatural and counterintuitive concept of God's radical grace theologically corrected? Grace may change everything, but not without constant teaching, preaching, reminding, and the influence of a nurturing community.[26] The point to all this is that religious concepts involving reflective thought often have intuitive violations and thus are difficult to maintain consistently. In real-time situations, argue cognitive scientists, we often default to basic, intuitive reasoning.

COGNITIVE SCIENCE AND PETITIONARY PRAYER: PRESENT AND PAST

From these general findings, I want to examine how cognition informs one particular class of religious phenomena, that of petitionary prayer. Specifically, I interrogate Jonathan Edwards's views of petitionary prayer and those of his congregation, both from "theologically correct" and "theologically incorrect" perspectives. In this regard, cognitive science helps to clarify religious doctrine from the inside. First, however, some general comments about the focus and nature of petitionary prayer.

One reason for petitionary prayer in the contemporary context stands out above all others: seeking God's help in matters of health.[27] Throughout the centuries, prayers related to physical health have been the staple of Christian piety. I became especially aware of this in two contexts—both of which coincided to spark my interest in pursuing the subject of this essay. First, as an elder in a Presbyterian church, I have been privy to weekly prayer requests and praises from the congregation.[28] By far, there are more requests than praises, and among the requests, the plurality address health concerns—mostly physical but also emotional.

---

26. Edman, "Applying the Science of Faith," 245. According to Barrett, children do not have the same problems with grace and gratitude that adults have. They have no such sense of obligation and reciprocation and thus may be better able to accept grace from God than adults—feeling the need neither to earn salvation nor to add stipulations and conditions. See Barrett, *Born Believers*, 144–47.

27. Spilka and Ladd, *Psychology of Prayer*, 109.

28. For a brief overview of prayer requests for the sick in a Presbyterian ministerial setting, see Winter, "Presbyterians and Prayers for the Sick," 141–55.

The other context for my attention to petitionary prayer is historical. As a student of Jonathan Edwards, I became aware of prayer requests made by his Northampton congregation. Called prayer bids or prayer bills, these requests were delivered weekly to the pastor on small clips of paper. Given the scarcity of paper, Edwards saved the parishioners' notes for scrap paper, in some cases sewing them into booklets used for sermons, in others inserting them into his private notebooks.[29] Of the ninety-nine prayer bids culled from Edwards's manuscripts by Stephen Stein, nearly all were directed toward illnesses, accidents, and deaths. Ironically, as much as Jonathan Edwards promoted prayer for revival, his congregants had less spiritual matters on their minds. Perhaps by their very intent, prayer bids were to address this-worldly concerns, or perhaps the content of the requests reflected what most preoccupied the minds of the colonists. Whatever the case, the prayer bids echoed the constant theme that God would "sanctify his holy and afflicting hand" in taking away infants, children, parents, spouses, and siblings, and that some "spiritual good" would come of this loss.

Sickness and accidents were an everyday occurrence in colonial life: pleurisy, cancer, "long fever" (typhoid), "throat distemper" (diphtheria), and the "bloody flux" (dysentery) were commonly referenced by petitioners. Fatal accidents from burns, drowning, and other mishaps were also mentioned.[30] On four occasions, prayers for safety in the military expedition against the French at Cape Breton were noted (which I will say more about later). In a few instances, parishioners submitted prayer bids of praise, giving thanks for the safe delivery of a baby and the continued health of the mother or for sparing a man's life from a falling tree.[31]

---

29. Stein, "'For Their Spiritual Good,'" 261. See also Winiarski, *Darkness Falls*, 67–69.

30. Though generally confined to coastal areas, colonial epidemics also affected inland towns such as Northampton, but with less severity. See Duffy, *Epidemics in Colonial America*; Grob, *Deadly Truth*, chaps. 3–4. For a general overview of health-related issues in the colonial period, see Tannenbaum, *Health and Wellness*.

31. See these prayer bids in Stein, "For Their Spiritual Good": "Thos Wells and his Wife Desires Thanks may be given to God In the Congregation for his Goodness to her in Childbed in making her the Living Mother of a Living Child. they also ask Prayers that God would perfect his Goodness to her In Raising her up to perfect Health and strength again" (270). Another: "Noah pixley & his wife Do desier that Thanks may be Returned to god in this Congregation for the preservation of his Life when it was grately Exposd by the fall of a Tree upon him & likewise They desier prayers that God would heel him of his Broken Boons & that he may be Restor'd To perfit soundness againe" (272).

Prayers were offered for recovery from illness, often with the addendum "that God would fit" the petitioner "for his sovereign will and pleasure," "whether it be in life or by death."

Now, in both congregations (my own and Edwards's), the ecclesiastical settings are (and were) firmly situated in the Reformed tradition. In both churches, leaders and members subscribed to the Westminster Confession and would affirm the following answer to Q 98, What is Prayer?: A. "Prayer is an offering up of our desires unto God, for things agreeable to his will, in the name of Christ, with confession of our sins, and thankful acknowledgement of his mercies." Despite the time gap of two-and-a-half centuries, one might expect that shared doctrine would result in a theologically consistent view of petitionary prayer—i.e., that both my church and Edwards's would agree on the nature of petitionary prayer regarding what the petitioners hope will result from their prayer requests and the manner in which God answers prayer. This expectation, however, does not hold.

First, there was nothing distinctively Reformed in the petitions at my Presbyterian church. There was no mention of praying "for things agreeable to his will." There may have even been a hint that prayers could move God to act. Despite its Reformed roots and the denomination's attention to correct doctrine, most of the church attenders were generic evangelicals, not particularly well informed regarding the nature of Reformed doctrine and prayer. Second, the provincials of Edwards's day were much more likely than the moderns of ours to interpret bad things that happened as acts of divine chastisement. In the past, people cried out to God. Today, we call an ambulance or phone the doctor. Illnesses and accidents fit within the Puritans' providential theology of affliction.[32] As Cotton Mather noted, those who suffered from toothache should recall that the original sin had been committed with the teeth, when Adam and Eve bit into the forbidden fruit.[33]

In the Northampton prayer bids, the theological language of the Reformed tradition permeates the requests. As Stein observes,

> It is striking how well the townspeople speak that language, well enough and with sufficient consistency to imply considerable familiarity and understanding—perhaps a measure of the impact of the preaching in Northampton, an evidence of the continuing

---

32. Winiarski, *Darkness Falls*, 62–63.
33. Cotton Mather, quoted in Tannenbaum, *Health and Wellness*, 7.

influence of Puritan theology in the middle of the eighteenth century, and a reflection of the staying power of local religious practices solidified by years of experience in the community.[34]

Viewing Stein's comments from a cognitive science perspective, we have a case where natural religion is overridden by theological correctness. For that to happen, a great deal of "cultural scaffolding" or constant theological self-correcting must occur.[35] The natural tendency is to foreground private, pragmatic interests, to engage God in an instrumental way, to coax God to act. As we will see, Edwards's sermons on prayer exposed this tendency among his parishioners; however, in their prayer bids, the Northampton inhabitants, as children of the Puritans and more immediately recipients of the ministrations of Jonathan Edwards, exhibited a theologically correct understanding of prayer.

How might the congregations in Edwards's day and in my own think about the manner in which God responded to their prayers? As research indicates, more often than not, the return on petitionary prayers (i.e., the outcome desired by the petitioner) is pretty bleak. "There is no convincing evidence for the efficacy of petitionary prayer or other forms of supernatural intervention in the natural world. The most extensive and careful studies of petitionary prayer have not shown statistically significant" results.[36] People pray, but the wife dies in childbirth, the grandfather doesn't survive the surgery, the son is killed in war, the friend succumbs to the ravages of cancer, the wayward child continues to reject the faith, the prayed-for job doesn't come through, the hurricane doesn't spare your community, etc. As C. S. Lewis remarked, "Every war, every famine, almost every death-bed, is the monument to a petition that was not granted."[37]

Why do not failed petitions shake the faith of believers? Because, contends Barrett, the religious system has a large degree of "conceptual control"; that is, it has the ability to withstand alleged evidence of failure. How does the religious community accommodate the possibility of failure? What answers are given? In the case of Edwards's parishioners, they responded with a theology of dependence in recognition of the

---

34. Stein, "'For Their Spiritual Good,'" 268.

35. The term "cultural scaffolding" is discussed in Barrett, *Cognitive Science, Religion, and Theology*, 141–42, and referenced throughout his other writings.

36. Boudry and De Smedt, "In Mysterious Ways," 455.

37. Lewis, *Letters to Malcolm*, 58.

sovereignty of God. They had no interest whatsoever in interrogating evidence for or against their beliefs in this domain. Writes Stein,

> In requests arising from situations of distress, the petitioners regarded themselves as deficient in capacity and therefore in need of assistance. Powerless to help themselves, they turned to God whose goodness, wisdom, and power were acknowledged by the very act of the request. Prayer in distress served as an affirmation of faith as well as a cry of alarm. The stated hope, "that God would be pleased" to act on their behalf, and the conventional refrain, "if it be his will," were public declarations of dependence on his sovereign decision. If God did not choose to answer the request for aid, the petitioners affirmed, then they desired assistance in accepting his pleasure. No questions were raised concerning divine prerogatives. Total submission informs the frequent refrain, "but if he has otherwise determined, that he would prepare them for his will."[38]

In prayer requests arising from situations of good fortune, the parishioners acknowledged that the source of their happiness was God's action in "raising, giving, and preserving." I will say more about the contents of this theology shortly when I discuss Edwards's views of prayer, but note the general emphasis on submission to the divine will. Moreover, there is in play what psychological research identifies as "confirmation bias." That is, people pay attention to and remember confirmations of direct answers to prayer (however few they may be) but offer other explanations as to why their prayers may go answered. For example, God may have a different timetable, or God may deny the request for God's own good reason, or God's ways are past finding out, or God cannot be coerced through prayer. Or, in what has been expressed through the centuries, prayers function as a form of spiritual self-help. As Augustine put it, "The purpose of prayer is to construct the soul, not to instruct God."[39] Calvin affirmed the same: God ordained prayer "not so much for his own sake as for ours."[40] Or, as voiced in the Northampton prayer bids, prayer is offered that God would "fit" the petitioner "for his sovereign will and pleasure."

What these responses suggest is that believers are able to transcend the basic level of reasoning that conceives of God in instrumental, transactional, or pragmatic terms and offer more theologically correct

38. Stein, "For Their Spiritual Good," 267.
39. Augustine, quoted in Boudry and De Smedt, "In Mysterious Ways," 460.
40. Calvin, *Institutes*, 3.30.2 (2:852).

answers that are expressed in relational terms. God always *responds* but only sometimes *answers* prayer in the sense of God bringing about that which was requested by the petitioner. An updated version of these views is the "Serenity Prayer" by Reinhold Niebuhr: "God grant me the serenity to accept the things I cannot change, courage to change the things I can, and wisdom to know the difference." This is a "hedge-all-bets" prayer. Instead of asking God to intervene directly, we request God to influence our psychological attitude regarding a certain condition—that we will rely upon a God who, in Calvin's words, "will never forsake us, who cannot disappoint . . . since all good things are contained in him."[41]

These responses to petitionary prayer have been the church's staple responses throughout the centuries, and certainly they reflect the Puritans' perspective. According to Rick Ostrander, the "Puritans recognized certain conditions on prayer that had to be met, such as having faith, praying from a godly motive and with God's glory in mind, and praying in submission to God's will."[42] Edwards cited similar reasons for prayers that went unanswered: God may see that what people ask for is not best for them; some people pray for the wrong things, such as temporal goods; God doesn't hear insincere and unbelieving prayers ("The mouth seems to pray, but the heart don't pray"); or God exercises God's own wisdom as to the time and manner of answering prayer.[43] Note the difficulty of measuring these necessary spiritual/psychological attitudes. By being structured to accommodate a certain amount of failure, traditional Christian theological conceptions of petitionary prayer enable believers to transcend a basic level of reasoning. Here, prayer is effective in helping people cope spiritually and psychologically. This is especially so in the context of health-related problems, where God is seen as providing comfort, nurturance, and a source of personal strength in dire circumstances.[44]

EDWARDS AND THE LIFE OF PRAYER

Although Edwards's waking moments were bathed in prayer, we know little about the actual content of his prayer life.[45] According to Samuel

41. Calvin, *Institutes*, 3.30.52 (2:919).
42. Ostrander, *Life of Prayer*, 5.
43. Edwards, *WJE* 19:786–88; *WJE* 22:220; *WPE* 6:508–10; *WJEO* 54, no. 507.
44. Kirkpatrick, *Attachment*, 63–64.
45. The single major work on Edwards and prayer is Beck, *Voice of Faith*. A devotionally centered work is Najapfour, *Jonathan Edwards*. The following articles focus

Hopkins, Edwards's first biographer and a boarder in the Edwards household, Edwards kept his personal devotions secret.[46] However, there are enough glimpses to know that his prayer life conformed to Puritan devotional practices, especially "secret" or private prayer, of which there were two types: "ordinary prayers at set times" and "ejaculatory" or "extraordinary" prayer.[47]

In his "Personal Narrative," Edwards noted that as a boy (eight or nine years old) during a spiritual awakening in his father's congregation in East Windsor, Connecticut, in 1712, he was so affected that he "used to pray five times a day in secret" and that he met with other boys to pray together. They "built a booth in a swamp, in a very secret and retired place, for a place of prayer," and Jonathan also created a secret praying place of his own. Nearly a decade later he described his conversion experience (May/June 1721) as one where he had a "sense of glory," of "being swallowed up" in God, to the extent that he "went to prayer, to pray to God that I might enjoy him; and prayed in a manner quite different from what I used to do; with a new sort of affection." A year or two later, Edwards wrote that he was "almost constantly in ejaculatory prayer, wherever I was. Prayer seemed natural to me; as the breath, by which the inward burnings of my heart had vent."[48] In 1722, he began composing his "Resolutions," number 29 of which reads, "Resolved, never to count that a prayer, nor let that pass as a prayer, nor that as a petition of a prayer, which is so made, that I cannot hope that God will answer it."[49] At about the same time, he recorded in his diary that he applied himself "to the duty of secret prayer," and yet he resolved some months later, "when I am lifeless in secret prayer, to force myself to expatiate, as if I were praying before others more than I used to."[50] To that end, he set aside personal prayer time at least twice a day. Following his marriage to Sarah Pierpont in 1727, he prayed with her at least once a day; and when children

---

on one of Edwards's sermons or treatises: Kreider, "Jonathan Edwards's Theology of Prayer," 434–56; Ehrat, "Jonathan Edwards' Treatise," 11–16. A brief summary on Edwards and prayer is van Vlastuin, "Prayer," 455–57. On the role of prayer in the Great Awakening, see Kidd, "'Very Vital Breath of Christianity,'" 19–33.

46. Hopkins, *Life and Character*, 39.
47. Hambrick-Stowe, *Practice of Piety*, 180.
48. Edwards, *WJE* 16:792–94.
49. Edwards, *WJE* 16:755.
50. Edwards, *WJE* 16:766, 782.

followed, so did family prayer.[51] Among Edwards's recent biographers, Iain Murray has commented most extensively about Edwards's prayer life:

> Prayer was not a compartment in his daily routine, an exercise which possessed little connection with the remainder of his hours alone. Rather he sought to make his study itself a sanctuary, and whether wrestling with Scripture, preparing sermons or writing in his notebooks, he worked as a worshiper. Thought, prayer and writing were all woven together.[52]

In keeping with Puritan tradition and biblical precedent, Edwards's prayers from the pulpit were "free" or "conceived." True prayers of the heart were spoken spontaneously; Puritan ministers, as exemplars of true religion, were not to be tied to the "stinted Liturgie" of Anglican and Catholic churches.[53] According to Hopkins, Edwards "was the farthest from any appearance of a Form, as to his Words & manner of Expression, of almost any Man. He was singular and inimitable in this.... He appeared to have much of the Grace and Spirit of Prayer."[54] Because Edwards and other giants of his day such as Cotton Mather and George Whitefield thought it improper to use written prayers of any kind, we have no record of their practice of this vital Christian devotional activity.[55]

Despite the absence of personally written prayers, Edwards has left us with extensive commentary on prayer in his sermons and other writings. Perhaps the best known is his *Humble Attempt* (1747), wherein, following similar efforts to promote revival in Scotland, he called for a "Concert of Prayer" throughout the colonies.[56] A close second is Edwards's *Life of David Brainerd* (1749), an edited version of the diary kept by David Brainerd, in which Edwards extolled Brainerd's prayer life as a model to follow. "His sweetest joys," wrote Edwards of this abstemious missionary to the Native Americans, "were in his closet devotions and solitary transactions between God and his own soul.... He delighted greatly in sacred retirements; and loved to get away from all the world to converse with God alone in secret duties."[57]

51. Hopkins, *Life and Character*, 43–44.
52. Murray, *Jonathan Edwards*, 143.
53. Quoted in Hambrick-Stowe, *Practice of Piety*, 105.
54. Hopkins, *Life and Character*, 49.
55. Rice and Williamson, *Book of Reformed Prayers*, 49. For views of prayer within the Reformed and Puritan traditions, see Beeke and Najapfour, *Taking Hold of God*.
56. Edwards, *Humble Attempt*, WJE 5. See esp. 288–89, 320–28, 444–47, 460.
57. Edwards, WJE 7:509.

Edwards enjoined all Christians, whatever their age or status, to engage in fervent, constant prayer for revival. Amid the Great Awakening in 1741, he advised a recent convert, the eighteen-year-old Deborah Hatheway, to "set aside a day of secret fasting and prayer alone . . . searching your heart, and looking over your past life, and confessing your sins before God."[58] In ordination sermons, he urged ministers to "imitate their great Master in his fervent prayers for the good of the souls of men."[59] During times of spiritual awakening, he recommended praying societies, where men, women, young men and young women, and boys and girls prayed in separate groups "to promote the work of God, and advance the kingdom of Christ."[60] This was the highest priority of prayer: "Pray for the time when the light will enlighten the whole world."[61] "The prayers of the saints," he wrote in *Some Thoughts Concerning the Present Revival of Religion in New England* (1742),

> should be the one great and principle means of carrying on the designs of Christ's kingdom in the world. When God has something very great to accomplish for his church, 'tis his will that there should precede it the extraordinary prayers of his people.[62]

We may ask, however, if "extraordinary prayers" preceded the spiritual awakening in Edwards's congregation. Were the "Little Awakening" of 1734–35 and the Great Awakening of 1740–41 the result of the extraordinary prayers of God's people? Were they praying with greater fervor than at other times? Did they pray with greater faith? Were more people praying than before? If so, why then did Edwards term the awakening a "surprising work of God"?[63] Does the quality and/or quantity of prayer make a difference?

Edwards's own prayer requests and concerns in his correspondence reflected his advice to others. He desired "the fervent prayers" of George Whitefield that God "would more and more pour out his Spirit upon us" and that in particular he would "be filled with his Spirit, and may become fervent, as a flame of fire in my work." He asked his colleague, the Reverend Joseph Bellamy, to pray that God would continue to revive

---

58. Edwards, *WJE* 16:94.
59. Edwards, *WJE* 25:337.
60. Edwards, *WJE* 4:518. See also *WJE* 19:403–4; *WJEO* 67, no. 922.
61. Edwards, *WJE* 19:722.
62. Edwards, *WJE* 4:516.
63. See Edwards, *Faithful Narrative* (1737), *WJE* 4.

New England, and especially that God would "fill me with his own fullness" and "improve me as an instrument to revive his work." He wrote to his daughter Mary, "My desire and daily prayer is that you may . . . meet with God . . . and have much of his divine influences on your heart." And he expressed a similar prayer to his fourteen-year-old son Timothy "that God would make you wise to salvation."[64]

Whether on a personal or cosmic scale, Edwards considered his lofty vision of millennial glory to be the primary purpose of not only theologically correct but also biblically correct prayer. Prayers in the New Testament minimize personal wants, desires, or predicaments; they are aimed primarily at the success of the apostolic mission, the coming kingdom of God, personal and corporate sanctification, the work of the Holy Spirit, and perseverance on judgment day.[65]

Edwards's people, however, often had more earthly, mundane concerns on their minds. In a Fast Day sermon ("Praying for the Spirit") in November 1740, Edwards berated his congregation for not being sincere in their prayers for the outpouring of the Spirit. Temporal affairs—a measles epidemic and unseasonably cold, rainy weather—undoubtedly preoccupied the minds of his people, but Edwards thought their minds should be elsewhere. In his sermon he addressed weather conditions, although to make his point he discussed not rain but drought, observing that if there is natural drought, Christians engage in serious prayer, but if there is spiritual drought, God is not earnestly sought.[66] Yet the Holy Spirit "is the greatest blessing that can be asked."[67] "We have seen," noted Edwards, "that God is to hear prayer for such a blessing as rain. But God is much more ready to bestow spiritual showers; he is more ready to shower down of his Holy Spirit than he is rain."[68] During the ensuing eighteen months, the Great Awakening swept through the Connecticut River Valley, yet in April 1741 Edwards again admonished his congregation for their short-sighted concerns: "They insist much in their prayers on petition for personal favors, spiritual blessings to be bestowed on themselves. . . . But the state of God's church in general is commonly

---

64. Edwards, *WJE* 16:87, 99, 289, 580.
65. Crump, "Are Practical Prayers Pagan Prayers?," 231.
66. Edwards, *WJE* 22:218.
67. Edwards, *WJE* 22:214.
68. Edwards, *WJE* 22:220.

too much neglected."⁶⁹ Without the prayers of the people, the glorious millennium would be forestalled.

Did Edwards have no interest in praying for temporal affairs? Clearly this was not the case. He asked for prayers for his three-year old daughter, Elizabeth, who was "in a very languishing, dangerous state."⁷⁰ He preached a Fast Day sermon imploring his congregation to pray that God would spare them from the 1735 epidemic in Boston; a year later, he preached a sermon "to pray for rain"; and in 1745, on the eve of American English attack on the French citadel at Louisburg he preached "that God is ready . . . to hear the prayers of his people and give 'em success, when they offer up their prayer in the manner that he has appointed."⁷¹ Subsequently, in *An Humble Attempt to Promote Explicit Agreement and Visible Union of God's People in Extraordinary Prayer*, he acknowledged the role of prayer in "God's preserving and delivering the nation" from the Jacobite rebellion in England and by defeating the French at Cape Breton in 1745, and then two years later in the miraculous defeat of the French armada.⁷²

EDWARDS AND THEOLOGICALLY CORRECT PETITIONARY PRAYER

To what extent did Edwards's people grasp their minister's teaching on prayer? How much of Edwards's theological correctness sank into the hearts and minds of the people? To address these questions, we need to examine more closely other questions related to Edwards's own understanding of prayer. First, what is prayer? Second, why should Christians pray? Third, in what sense do the prayers of the saints make a difference?

"True prayer," Edwards observed in words nearly identical to that of Calvin, "is nothing but faith expressed" or "the voice of faith"; it is a communicative act, "the voice of faith to God through Christ."⁷³ Christians' "faith in God is expressed in praying to God. Faith in the Lord Jesus Christ is expressed in praying to Christ and praying in the name of

---

69. Edwards, *WJE* 22:375.
70. Edwards, *WJE* 16:323.
71. Edwards, *WJEO* 51, no. 500; Edwards, *WJE* 25:135–36.
72. Edwards, *Humble Attempt*, *WJE* 5:358, 361.
73. Edwards, *WPE* 7:434; *WJE* 19:204, 787; *WJE* 21:437. In his *Institutes*, Calvin titles the section on prayer, "Prayer, Which is the Chief Exercise of Faith," 3.20 (2:850).

Christ, and the promises are made to asking in Christ's name in the same manner as they are to believing in Christ."[74] Its source is holy affections; it is God's sovereignly ordained means of blessing. "The Spirit of God, the chief subject matter of prayer, [is] the great purchase and promise of Christ."[75] It is through the Spirit's regenerating work that we are able to pray. This trinitarian dimension to prayer is summarized by Peter Beck: "As God the Father stands at the headwaters of Edwards's theology of prayer and the Son of God bridges the gap between creature and creator, the Spirit of God bathes the entire process in the grace of God."[76]

Second, why should Christians pray? What is the purpose of prayer? I have already noted that, according to Edwards, "Prayer should be the one great and principle means of carrying on the designs of Christ's kingdom in the world."[77] To that end, Edwards repeatedly emphasized that prayer is a duty enjoined upon all, saints and sinners alike.[78] It is, after all, a precept from Jesus himself. Christians pray for "the blessing of the Spirit . . . so that the Spirit of God may not leave us."[79] One communes with God in prayer, fulfilling the purpose for which one was created: to enjoy and glorify God.[80]

Edwards was clear and adamant about what was *not* the purpose of prayer. In fact, the content of many of his sermons on prayer focus on correcting what he considered theologically flawed prayers. Consider the titles of these sermons: "God Doesn't Thank Men for Doing Those Things He Commands Them" (1727); "There is no Goodness in Praying, Though It Be Never so Earnestly, Merely Out of Fear of Misery" (1728); "God's Manner is First to Prepare Men's Hearts and Then to Answer Their Prayers" (1735); "'Tis in Vain for Any to Expect to Have Their Prayers Heard as Long as They Continue in the Allowance of Sin" (1739); and "Hypocrites Deficient in the Duty of Prayer" (1740). In these and other sermons, Edwards challenged the commonly held notion that we pray to

---

74. Edwards, *WJE* 21:439.
75. Edwards, *WJE* 25:203.
76. Beck, *Voice of Faith*, 273.
77. Edwards, *WJE* 4:516.
78. Edwards, *WJE* 16:766; *WJE* 22:165; *WPE* 7:429–48 ("duty" mentioned eleven times); *WJE* 25:101; Edwards, *Glory and Honor of God*, 85, 90, 91, 95; *WJE* 4:516; *WJEO* 64, no. 809; *WJE* 25:726, no. 809; *WJE* 5:201; *WJEO* 51, no. 400; *WJEO* 68, no. 958 (six times); *WJE* 25:752, no. 1143.
79. Edwards, *WJE* 22:214; *WJE* 19:403.
80. Edwards, *WJEO* 68, no. 958; *WJE* 10:381.

tell God about our circumstances, our needs, and our desires or that God is in some way obliged to hear the prayers of obedient people. No, says Edwards, God knows your needs. Moreover, just because Christians are "careful and conscientious in doing their duty" by praying, God is under no obligation to hear their prayers (i.e., to answer their prayers as they wish). In fact, no religious act—seeking God, praying to God, or living a moral life—obliges God in any way to convert sinners.[81]

No doubt Edwards would have blanched at the lyrics of the nineteenth-century hymn "Tell It to Jesus": "Are you weary, are you heavy hearted? / Tell it to Jesus, / . . . Are you grieving over joys departed? / Tell it to Jesus alone. / . . . Are you anxious what shall be tomorrow? / Tell it to Jesus alone."[82] All bad theology for Edwards. Why do we need to "tell it to Jesus"? He already knows. Prayer, Edwards asserted, has a different purpose: it is required as a means to prepare us for the mercies we need.[83] "We don't cause God's ear to hear, but he causes it. The mercy of God towards his people is not moved or drawn by them, but 'tis self moved." Although the Bible speaks anthropomorphically of God being moved or persuaded by the prayers of his people, "yet it is not to be thought that God is properly moved or made willing by our prayers." Instead, God bestows mercy "*as though* he were prevailed upon by prayer" (emphasis added). It is not the prayers of God's people that is the cause of God's mercy toward them, but "from his own sovereign pleasure he always shows mercy according to the pleasure of his will. . . . The whole affair in its beginning and end is from free grace."[84]

If, then, prayer is the voice of faith, if prayer is communing with God, if true prayer begins with God's initiating grace, then in what sense do the prayers of the saints make a difference? And if they do make a difference, how do we know? Edwards repeatedly assured his people that they should pray because "God is a prayer-hearing God."[85] For example, "God won't begrudge his people anything that they ask as being too good for them. God stands ready to fulfill all their petitions in anything that they ask that is for their own good. . . . God is ready to bestow the blessings on his people that they need or desire." God delights in bestowing

81. Edwards, *Containing 16 Sermons*, 41–42, 45–46.
82. Rankin, "Tell It to Jesus."
83. Edwards, *Glory and Honor of God*, 85–86.
84. Edwards, *Glory and Honor of God*, 78–79; Edwards, WPE 6:505.
85. This is the theme of "Most High a Prayer-Hearing God," WPE 6:498–511. See also "Continuing God's Presence," WJE 19:403; and "Keeping the Presence of God," WJE 22:528.

and waits for us to ask, and yet the asking is "not to move him to bestow the blessing, but that we may be prepared to receive it.... God is so ready at all times to hear and grant you whatever you desire that tends to your happiness."[86]

Here, we confront a conundrum. On the one hand, Edwards insisted that God hears and responds to petitionary prayer. On the other, his high view of God's sovereignty, his conviction that God not only sustains the universe from moment to moment but always acts according to rational and fixed laws in the realm of nature, led Norman Fiering to conclude that, for Edwards, "God does not capriciously intervene in particular cases." More to the point, argues Fiering, "Edwards explicitly denied the efficacy of petitionary prayer to bring about external change in the world. The value of prayer lies primarily in its effects upon the souls of the prayerful."[87] As Edwards stated in his *Treatise Concerning Religious Affections* (1746)—a work in which he wrote far more about insincere prayer than genuine prayer—the purpose of prayer is "to affect our own hearts with the things we express, and so to prepare us to receive the blessings we ask."[88]

Prayer has no effect on God (who is self-moved) but rather affects the person who prays. Since God cannot change in either purposes or knowledge, God's "answer" to prayer is not a response to people's prayer as much as their prayers are a response to God's predetermined answer. God has ordained that certain things will come to pass only as a result of offered prayers, which are themselves ordained by God to be offered. "Perhaps the most that humans can affirm," concludes Glenn Kreider in his analysis of Edwards's sermon "God Is a Prayer-Hearing God," "is that God hears and responds to prayer and He also remains the Sovereign of the universe."[89]

I will return to these matters shortly by examining a counterexample in Edwards's view of petitionary prayer—one that appears to affirm causation—but I conclude this section by returning to the relationship between Edwards and his parishioners. Edwards's sermons were not

---

86. Edwards, *WJE* 19:783, 785.

87. Fiering, *Jonathan Edwards's Moral Thought*, 97. See also Moody, *Jonathan Edwards and the Enlightenment*. Moody disagrees with Fiering's apparent critique of predestinarian theology (although he mistakenly attributes Fiering's quote to Henry May) yet reaches the same conclusion that "prayer's distinguishing significance as a means is the effect it has on the person who prays[,] not the effect that it has on God" (27).

88. Edwards, *WJE* 2:115; Lucas, *God's Grand Design*, 164.

89. Kreider, "Jonathan Edwards's Theology of Prayer," 455.

composed in a vacuum. As a "watchman on the walls of Zion," he observed the attitudes of his congregation, ever alert to the external threat of Arminianism and the internal threat of hypocrisy.[90] His sermons on prayer, many of which focused on theologically incorrect forms of prayer, addressed these threats. Why did he direct so much energy preaching against false understandings of prayer if they were not a real problem in his congregation? According to cognitive scientists, "The more complex that theological ideas are—the more they deviate from the ordinary cognition that undergirds natural religion—the more effort will be required to teach them and maintain them."[91] Edwards expended great effort because his theology deviated from an ordinary, natural way of thinking about petitionary prayer—that humans as free, moral agents can in some way influence God.

To what extent did Edwards's sermons on petitionary prayer have their desired effect? How did persons in the pew respond to their pastor who assured them that God heard their prayers yet at the same time told them that God's response to their petitionary prayers was only "apparent"?[92] Did they believe that this personal God could be moved by their prayers? Did they believe that every individual event always

---

90. See esp. Edwards, "Hypocrites Deficient in the Duty of Prayer," *WPE* 7:429–48.

91. Barrett, *Cognitive Science, Religion, and Theology*, 134.

92. According to David Crump, Edwards "attempts to construct a theological solution that not only reaches well beyond the contours of the biblical passages, but leaves significant textual wreckage behind. It is very difficult to read the Lord's Prayer—not to mention the rest of Jesus's prayer teaching—as anything but misleading, even deceptive, if God's responses to petition are only 'apparent.' From this perspective, an informed surface reading of the prayer is inexplicably replaced by a dogmatic paradigm that leaves the text no longer meaning what it straightforwardly appears to mean." Crump, *Knocking on Heaven's Door*, 129–30. Crump, a professor of religion and theology at Calvin College, is convinced that a personal God is willing to be moved. God cannot be coerced, but God can be influenced by our prayers. "There can be no doubt about the Creator's sovereignty over the growth of his church and the course of salvation-history." Yet, "The New Testament makes it equally clear that the sovereign Lord does some things precisely because we pray for them; furthermore, had we not prayed as we did, God would not have acted as he did. Some possibilities remained unrealized because they are never requested. The Father's unfolding plans for the world, and our part in those plans, may develop in more than one direction depending, in part, on how we pray.... The future has options. The New Testament insists that God is sovereign in the sense that the 'game' of history never spins outside his control, never veering from its final goal, but he makes no claim to sovereignty in the sense that every individual event (or every play in the game) always occurs exactly as he willed or foreordained. This is so, not because God's foreordination is subject to human sabotage, but because he has decided not to micromanage human history" (289–91).

occurred exactly as God willed or foreordained? Or did they see themselves as moral agents who could affect the outcome of events? We cannot answer these questions with certainty, but we can be certain that Edwards was convinced that his parishioners needed theological correction.

In his 2004 book *Theological Incorrectness: Why Religious People Believe What They Shouldn't*, the cognitive scientist Jason Slone argued that theology does not determine people's actual thoughts and behaviors. "Sorry, clergy," he writes, "but theological ideas simply do not determine, per se, how or what people think."[93] Rather, religious ideas and behaviors are constrained by the ordinary cognitive mechanisms involved in everyday nonreligious behavior. He points to the work of Justin Barrett who, while a professor at Calvin College, conducted several experiments with students who presumably believed that God controls every event in the world, including their eternal destiny. Yet his task-specific experiments revealed that, when faced with tasks requiring what Barrett called "online" thinking—quick and immediate—the students did not believe this dogma. When asked questions that allowed them to reflect on their beliefs, however, they answered in a theologically correct way.[94] According to Slone, "Absolute sovereignty is a maximally counterintuitive concept and thus inherently unstable because of its cognitive burden. Simply put, if God controls everything, then humans control nothing—and that is hard to believe."[95] The doctrine goes against the grain of natural cognition, namely, that we are actors who can freely and willfully choose to act.[96] Slone speculates that because of this hard-to-believe doctrine, Calvinism has had a short shelf life. Historically, he is off the mark, but he does point to a trend that gained momentum in the Great Awakening—the emphasis on the role of self-agency. He concludes, "Calvinism proves to be less likely to survive over the long run because it is a burdensome idea that precludes the role of human agency."[97] So much for Collin Hansen's *Young, Restless, Reformed* (2008)—a book about the recent Calvinist renaissance in America.[98]

---

93. Slone, *Theological Incorrectness*, 66.
94. See Barrett, "Dumb Gods," 93–109.
95. Slone, *Theological Incorrectness*, 4–5.
96. Barrett, *Cognitive Science, Religion, and Theology*, 77.
97. Slone, *Theological Incorrectness*, 97.
98. In a similar genre, see the rejoinder by Austin Fischer in *Young, Restless, No Longer Reformed*. Fischer appeals to the first-step model of reasoning (intuitive, spontaneous, tacit); he states, "But we certainly experience ourselves as free if nothing else,

Within the context of petitionary prayer, we can see why Edwards's views were a challenge to his congregation—as Slone puts it, "hard to believe." On the one hand, their prayer bids exhibited theological correctness. On the other, the natural human proclivity to resort to natural inferences about psychological agency led them to believe that their prayers in some way could influence God's actions toward them and toward the world. Edwards was passionate about prayer being God's appointed means of salvation, yet the lost were told that their prayers were not acceptable to God: "All that a natural man does in seeking salvation is wrong."[99] Why, then, pray? Again, because God commands it. The most that Edwards can say is that "the prayers of sinners, though they have no goodness in them, yet are made a means of preparation for mercy."[100]

EDWARDS, THE NATIONAL COVENANT, AND SUBTLE FORMS OF DIVINE CAUSATION

In other contexts, Edwards and his fellow Calvinists appeared to recognize a greater role for human agency. Two modes of thought—that God controls and directs everything and that humans can in some way influence God—existed side by side (and perhaps these exist in the minds of all Christians who affirm both God's sovereignty and human agency). The Puritan notion of the national covenant best exemplifies the view that prayer can influence God's actions. An extension of the "covenant of works," which demanded that people regulate their own lives and others' by the keeping of God's law, the national covenant envisioned the Puritans as Israel of old; individuals, communities, and nations were blessed or punished according to their obedience to God.[101] Days of communal fasting and prayer and covenant renewal addressed the need to reset one's relationship to God or to petition God for God's blessings—even God's intervention.

Perhaps the most explicit example of national covenantal theology in Edwards's writings is found in his sermons and correspondence

---

which is why no one starts out a Calvinist" (7), notes that Calvinist compatibilism is "counter-intuitive" (74), and questions "whether the emphases of Calvinism *naturally* produce disciples" (96).

99. Edwards, *WJE* 19:529.

100. Edwards, *WPE* 6:511.

101. On Edwards and the national covenant, see Stout, "Puritans and Edwards," chap. 9; McDermott, *One Holy and Happy Society*, chap. 1.

dealing with King George's War (1744–48), a war that extended the larger European conflict between England and France to America. Edwards was a loyal British subject and patriot who viewed military warfare as necessary to ensure not only the safety and independence of English colonists but also as a form of spiritual warfare against the depredations of the Catholic Church (aka the Antichrist). On April 4, 1745, Edwards preached a Fast Day sermon for success in the expedition against Cape Breton, a key military outpost in the French-fortified town of Louisburg. The odds did not favor the English. They had assembled forty-three hundred inexperienced troops (including twenty from Edwards's congregation) and set out from Boston on March 24 for a six hundred–mile journey (they would not land on the island until April 30). They faced a French regiment of four thousand regulars, in addition to French naval forces. "The Gibraltar of the New World"—a fort set in high cliffs—appeared impregnable.

Edwards called upon his people to pray. He assured them that God alone "determines the event of war and gives the victory," but he also impressed upon his hearers of the duty, "by prayer and supplication, to look to God for help to maintain their cause." Should the people "offer up their prayers in the manner that he has appointed," God is ready to hear their prayers "and give 'em success."[102] What is striking is the last comment—"give 'em success." Edwards could never be so sure about the efficacy of prayers in matters of salvation, but here he boldly states that God will bring about that which was requested by the petitioners—success in battle—if the people humbly and fervently seek God's help. As James Byrd notes, "Prayer was pragmatic. Nothing could determine the outcome of a battle more decisively than prayer, because prayer enabled people to unleash God's aid on the battlefield."[103] In support of his contention that God vanquishes his enemies, Edwards cited the "many remarkable instances" in the Bible of "the success of faith and prayer in warlike undertakings": Joshua taking the city of Jericho, Gideon's victory in battle, David slaying Goliath, the Israelites defeating the Amalekites and Philistines, the Jews emerging victorious against their enemies in Esther's time, etc.[104] All of these demonstrated how God delighted in "subduing mighty enemies and strong cities, and breaking the greatest

---

102. Edwards, *WJE* 25:134–36.
103. Byrd, "Jonathan Edwards, War, and the Bible," 200.
104. Edwards, *WJE* 25:139–40.

power of the enemy, in answer to the believing prayers of his people that walk in his ways."[105]

Others shared neither Edwards's interpretive framework nor his optimism. In a letter to his brother, Benjamin Franklin pointed out the inexperience of the colonial forces and the daunting task of capturing the fort at Cape Breton. He then turned to calculating the potential effectiveness of prayer: "You have a fast and prayer day in which I compute five hundred thousand petitions were offered up to the same effect in New England." If each New England family had prayed twice a day since the day the General Court approved the military plan, he noted, another "forty-five millions of prayers" would be offered up to God. On the Catholic side, "a few priests in the garrison" prayed "to the Virgin Mary." If one measures potential success by the quantity of prayers, then the New Englanders should win the battle hands down. Yet, continued Franklin, "if you do not succeed, I fear I shall have but an indifferent opinion of Presbyterian prayers in such cases, as long as I live. Indeed in attacking strong towns I should have more dependence on works, than on faith."[106]

Remarkably—through God's special providence, even miraculous intervention, declared Edwards—the English defeated the French at Cape Breton. In a lengthy letter to a correspondent in Scotland, Edwards announced that the victory was "the most remarkable of its kind, that has been in many ages, and a great evidence of God's being one that hears prayer ... and a great argument ... that we live in an age, wherein divine wonders are to be expected."[107]

He offered details of the expedition, noting God's specific providential ordering of circumstances: the favorable vote by the Assembly

105. Edwards, *WJE* 25:141.

106. Benjamin Franklin, quoted in Byrd, "Jonathan Edwards, War, and the Bible," 200.

107. Edwards, *WJE* 16:197. On Edwards's view of miracles, see Sweeney, "Evangelical Supernatural." Protestants generally made a careful distinction between miracles and acts of providence. According to Robert Bruce Mullen, "Providential acts were actions of God through the natural order. Some were acts of general providence. The beauty, harmony, and fruitfulness of nature were all seen as gifts of a loving God.... But there were other blessings—known as 'special providences'—that were reserved for the faithful" (such as the British victory at Cape Breton). "The difference between a 'miracle' and 'special providence' was in the interconnection between God's will and the physical action. In a miracle the divine intervention was dramatic and immediate; in a special providence the divine action was remote and comparatively hidden in the regular course of nature.... A miracle possessed an 'objective' witness; a special providence was unrecognizable without the eyes of faith." See Mullen, "Science, Miracles, and the Prayer-Gauge Debate," 206.

(carried by a majority of a single vote), "moderate and fair weather," the kept secrecy of the mission, the preservation of the soldiers from smallpox (during an epidemic in Boston), the support of an English man-of-war, the advantageous timing of the attack, the French desertion of the fort, the discovery of abandoned cannon, etc.[108] "Thus," declared Edwards,

> God gave into our hands the place of greatest importance of any that the French have in North America, the principal fountain of the king of France's wealth, from these parts of the world, and the key to all his northern colonies, and the chief annoyance of the British colonies.[109]

What George Marsden has called Edwards's "providentialist patriotism" continued in full display as Edwards subsequently interpreted the quashing of the rebellion of the Young Pretender, British victories in Europe, and especially the failed effort of the French fleet to retake Louisburg as "the wonderful and immediate hand of heaven against these enemies of God's people." Indeed, "consider how ready God has shown himself to appear [on] our side."[110] Yet two years later, Edwards's guaranteed success of the prayers of the people met the realities of international diplomacy. On October 18, 1748, in the peace of Aix-la-Chapelle, the English handed Louisburg back to the French. What became of the provincials' prayers? Had they not been answered? Or was the setback only temporary, a postponement of an inevitable battle between the forces of a covenant people and the Antichrist—a prelude to God's great work of cosmic redemption?

Edwards's pleas for petitionary prayer against the French and his later account of English victory lends itself to analysis from the perspective of cognitive science. In a recent article on petitionary prayer, Maarten Boudry and Johan De Smedt discuss "the implicit belief patterns about the causal mechanism by which God effects changes in the world." They review various experiments and studies of petitionary prayer, concluding that religious believers "prefer" modes of divine action that are subtle and indistinguishable from the natural course of events. Why? Because

---

108. Edwards, *WJE* 16:185–94. A number of Edwards's facts about the military expedition were selective, if not wrong. See Marshall, "Taking Louisbourg by Prayer," 9.

109. Edwards, 16:195. Edwards would extend these views of providential history in *A History of the Work of Redemption*, *WJE* 9.

110. Marsden, *Jonathan Edwards*, 313; Edwards, "God's People in Danger"; Edwards, "Walking Righteously, Speaking Uprightly," Sermons 846, 843, *WJEO* (my thanks to Ken Minkema for making the edited transcript of these sermons available).

believers "will have a better chance of finding themselves in a situation in which they can attribute the events in question to God answering their prayers" compared to those who expect full-blown miracles.[111] The fact is, people will not keep praying for undeniable supernatural acts if the results are invariably disappointing. Instead, they will engage in a process of self-correction (again, what Barrett calls "conceptual control") and favor subtle divine intervention, especially in situations of high ambiguity and high threat—such as the Cape Breton military expedition.

The authors note three settings "in which divine causality is rendered subtle and unascertainable": first, God may intervene in situations where causal relations are practically impossible to assess (e.g., weather phenomena, natural disasters, success in sports, victory on the battlefield, changes in government); second, God may intervene in natural processes that are invisible or difficult to observe directly (e.g., being protected from, or cured from, or stricken with a disease); and third, God may act as a partial agent in combination with natural causes in a way that makes it difficult to separate the respective contributions (e.g., giving strength to win a game, emboldening soldiers to fight, successfully completing an exam, supporting a bridge on the verge of collapse).[112]

As is apparent from his account of the Louisburg battle, Edwards calls to mind all three forms of subtle divine intervention, something he also did in *Humble Attempt* and in his earlier *Redemption Discourses*, a sermon series delivered in 1739 (published posthumously as *A History of the Work of Redemption*). Boudry and De Smedt remark,

> Given that the causal structure of the world is partly inscrutable, beliefs in subtle and unascertainable modes of supernatural causation will be compelling and cognitively appealing because they are more susceptible to occasional confirmation and less vulnerable to repeated disconfirmation.[113]

Under the interpretive gaze of Edwards, the many circumstances contributing to the English victory at Louisburg confirmed supernatural causation that, after the fact, was neither inscrutable, subtle, nor unascertainable. This was a case where the prayers of the saints were susceptible to confirmation. A prayer-hearing God responded according to their desires.

111. Boudry and De Smedt, "In Mysterious Ways," 459.
112. Boudry and De Smedt, "In Mysterious Ways," 457.
113. Boudry and De Smedt, "In Mysterious Ways," 466.

Although many Protestants in colonial America, including theological liberals such as Charles Chauncy, shared Edwards's views of providentialist patriotism, devout Catholics and skeptics such as Franklin would have been hard pressed to interpret the specific details of the English victory from this perspective. Later critics of *History of the Work of Redemption* shared a similar perspective, deriding Edwards's interpretation of history as work of "the most unbridled imagination" and of "an intoxicated visionary presuming to see the will of God."[114] Yet, for Edwards, not only does all of human history participate in the drama of Christian redemption, but he could identify precisely those events that gave proof of this drama.

CONCLUSION

I have tried to show how cognitive science can offer insight into religious belief and practice, and in particular into petitionary prayer. I noted how two strands of reasoning—the natural or intuitive and the reflective or deliberative—exist side by side, often in tension, sometimes in contradiction. There exists a chasm between basic religious concepts and the scaffolding of theological concepts.

Within Calvinism, and particularly in Edwards, this tension was exacerbated by an emphasis on God's absolute sovereignty. Here, the focus of petitionary prayer shifted from its effect on God to its effect on the petitioner. And yet this theological move could not be maintained consistently—neither by Edwards's congregation nor, as I have suggested, even by Edwards himself. When faced with the very real threat of extermination by the French, Edwards did not pray for a renewed spiritual attitude; he prayed for God to answer his prayers by intervening directly and "giving success." However one might interpret this request within the larger purposes of God (i.e., that God alone "determines the event of war and gives the victory"), Edwards linked cause (asking God to bring about a certain state of affairs) with effect (victory at Cape Breton). Did this petition contradict Edwards's contention that "the mercy of God towards his people is not moved or drawn by them, but 'tis self-moved"? Is this a case where, according to cognitive scientists, an inference generated during religious thought comes from the activation of ordinary cognitive resources?

---

114. Quoted in Wilson, "Editor's Introduction."

We may view these findings not simply as an exercise of historical retrieval but from the perspective of challenges facing every Christian. Aside from one's specific theological outlook (e.g., Arminian or Calvinist or something in between), cognitive science directs our attention to the proclivity to "theological incorrectness." While belief in God may be a natural product of our common cognitive faculties, we are continually faced with the challenge of maintaining theological correctness (in whatever form that may be). In cognitive science terms, this is realized only by a process of cultural scaffolding, that is, by deliberate attention to preaching, teaching, prayer, and worship.

Pastors and theologians would do well to consider the contributions of cognitive science, particularly in reassessing humans' "natural" condition. If we really are born with natural ideas about God and prayer that are theologically incorrect, do we want to call them "natural" without any qualification? Has God made us with a theologically incorrect sense of the divine? Is this natural condition a result of the Fall? Must pastors and theologians revise their theology in the light of the cognitive science of religion, or does cognitive science merely illuminate or confirm their theology? While these questions are beyond the scope of this essay, they point to the necessity of ongoing dialogue between cognitive scientists and the work of constructive theologians.

4

Edwards in the Context of International Revivals and Missions

Have not in time past in my prayers, enough insisted upon the glorifying God in the world, and the advancement of the kingdom of Christ.
—Jonathan Edwards, *Diary*, 5 February 1723–24 (*WJE* 16:784)

My heart has been much on the advancement of Christ's kingdom in the world. The histories of the past advancement of Christ's kingdom, have been sweet to me. When I have read histories of past ages, the pleasantest thing in all my reading has been, to read of the kingdom of Christ being promoted.
—Jonathan Edwards, "Personal Narrative," ca. 1740 (*WJE* 16:800)

It is evident from the Scripture, that there is yet remaining a great advancement in the interest of religion and the kingdom of Christ in this world.
—Jonathan Edwards, *Humble Attempt*, 1747 (*WJE* 5:329)

From the beginning to the end of his pastoral career, Jonathan Edwards was consumed with the mission of God in the redemption of humankind. In private written entries, correspondence, sermons, occasional writings, miscellanies, and theological treatises, Edwards repeatedly focused on what he termed "the advancement of the kingdom of Christ" or "the propagation of the gospel." In the aftermath of the "Little Awakening" in

Northampton, Massachusetts (1734-35), Edwards increasingly insisted that revivals of religion were the primary means by which the gospel would spread to the ends of the earth. Following the Great Awakening in New England (1740-42), and after reading accounts of divine renewal in parts of Britain and Europe, he wrote in *Humble Attempt* (1747), "The late remarkable religious awakenings, that have been in many parts of the Christian world, are another thing that may justly encourage us in prayer for the promised glorious and universal outpouring of the Spirit of God."[1] For Edwards, revival, with its accompanying conversions, was the engine that drove redemptive history and prayer was the fuel that ignited it.

Edwards came on the scene during the early stages of a transatlantic evangelical awakening. On the Continent and in Britain, Halle Pietists and mission-minded Moravians had been actively spreading the gospel before the turn of the eighteenth century. The conversions and early gospel ministries of renowned evangelicals such as George Whitefield and John and Charles Wesley in England, Howell Harris, Griffith Jones, and Daniel Rowland in Wales, and Ebenezer Erskine and William McCulloch in Scotland preceded Edwards's wide-ranging literary impact. In North America, the Middle Colonies experienced revivals beginning in the 1720s under the preaching of the East Frisian Pietist Theodore Frelinghuysen and the Scots-Irish Presbyterians William and Gilbert Tennent. In Edwards's own Puritan New England backyard, perhaps as many as twenty religious stirrings occurred between 1712 and 1732, including spiritual "harvests" led by his grandfather, Solomon Stoddard, and his father, Timothy. Revival, as Harry Stout has noted, was in Edwards's genes.[2] And, of course, Whitefield epitomized the Anglo-American make-up of the Great Awakening by traversing the Atlantic seven times. Thousands responded to his message of the new birth, including Edwards's Northampton parishioners, when the "Grand Itinerant" toured New England in the fall of 1740.

Within this context of transatlantic evangelicalism, Edwards's efforts to advance the gospel were both immediate and delayed: immediate insofar as his writings, particularly *A Faithful Narrative of the Surprising Work of God*, inspired his Scottish Presbyterian and German and Dutch Pietist evangelical contemporaries to promote revival; delayed insofar as

---

1. Edwards, *WJE* 5:363.
2. Stout, "Edwards as Revivalist," 125.

his impact on foreign missions was not felt until the end of the eighteenth and well into the nineteenth century. Of the latter, Edwards is best understood as a transitional figure in international missions. He lived during an interlude after the establishment of Roman Catholic, Anglican, Pietist, and Moravian missions in the sixteenth through mid-eighteenth centuries and before the beginnings of the modern Anglo-American Protestant missionary movement in the late eighteenth century. As Andrew Walls observed, Edwards "operated before the movement emerged in the English-speaking world as a distinct element of Protestant consciousness."[3] Edwards awakened that consciousness by providing the theological and inspirational motivation for the *possibility* of foreign missions. He fulfilled a critical, intermediate role. Genealogically speaking, if William Carey is recognized as the father of modern Protestant missions, then Edwards may be rightly acknowledged as its grandfather.[4]

Edwards's international influence in revivals and missions is entirely dependent on the reception of his writings. The key to this reception was an already well-established transatlantic network of correspondence, shared literature, and printed sermons. On both sides of the Atlantic, pastors and theologians had exchanged writings since the early seventeenth century. During the first decades of the eighteenth century, however, a more integrated market enhanced the continuous transatlantic flow of letters and printed material,[5] especially among evangelically minded Protestants in the British world and Continental Europe. Edwards's own aspirations to communicate to a wider audience beyond the provincial world of New England would also help to boost his reputation among the Reformed and Lutheran communities across the Atlantic.

During the Great Awakening the Anglophone, German, and Dutch evangelical network expanded. News of revivals in America, England, Scotland, Wales, and on the Continent convinced the evangelical community that the scattered local revivals were greater than the sum of their parts. An international movement, to be crowned in millennial glory, materialized. Edwards, ever eager to receive the news of revival, conveyed a vision that encompassed the world. In a 1739 sermon, "God's Grace Carried on in Other Places," he referenced the work of revival in parts of the British dominion and the raising up of young ministers such as John Wesley, George Whitefield, and Howell Harris. The news

3. Walls, "Missions and Historical Memory," 257.
4. Davies, "Jonathan Edwards."
5. O'Brien, "Eighteenth-Century Publishing Networks."

of revivals in Britain and in other places, claimed Edwards, "should stir all up" with "thoughts of the near approach of the day of Christ's coming in his kingdom."[6] In spring 1743, six years after his own account of the Northampton awakening had exerted a guiding influence on the Scottish revival, Edwards joined an epistolary exchange initiated by his Scottish brethren that persisted for nearly fifteen years. In his first letter, written to the Reverend William McCulloch, Edwards extolled the revivals as a "forerunner of something vastly greater . . . and more extensive."[7] Two years later he wrote to one of these correspondents that "the church of God, in all parts of the world, is but one; the distant members are closely united in one glorious head. This union is very much her beauty."[8]

Edwards consistently expressed "great interest of religion in the world," citing revivals at home and abroad as heightened motivation to pray for the coming of Christ's kingdom.[9] Even as Edwards served as a critical exchange point for information among evangelicals in America and abroad, the transmission of news was serialized in periodicals on both sides of the Atlantic. Anglo-American evangelicals and European Pietists participated enthusiastically in a multifaceted network of reading communities. For example, New Englanders read *The* [Glasgow] *Weekly History* (April 1741) and its successor, *The Christian Monthly History* (November 1743–January 1746); the Scots read the works of Edwards and the broader coverage contained in Thomas Prince Jr.'s weekly pro-revivalist periodical *Christian History* (March 1743–February 1745); and Germans read about the Great Awakening in America and missionary activities around the world in the journals (*Sammlung* or "Collection" in various titles, 1735–61) of the Magdeburg Pietist Johann Adam Steinmetz, who translated pieces from the *Weekly History* and *Christian History*.

INTERNATIONAL REVIVALS: EDWARDS'S IMMEDIATE IMPACT

The earliest of Edwards's writings to gain international popularity and contribute directly to spiritual awakening was his *Faithful Narrative of the Surprising Work of God* (1737), an account of revival in Edwards's

6. Edwards, *WJE* 22:109.
7. Edwards, *WJE* 16:106.
8. Edwards, *WJE* 16:180.
9. Edwards, *WJE* 16:272.

Northampton village and the surrounding area. As the first text of a genre of revival narratives, it became the most significant book to precede the transatlantic evangelical awakenings of the 1740s, as well as Edwards's most widely read book throughout the eighteenth century. What was truly "surprising" about Edwards's account was that its impact occurred outside of the colonies themselves and became a catalyst for awakenings in other places. The work proved to be a publishing blockbuster, printed in at least sixty editions—ten editions in five countries, including Britain—and in three languages.[10] Its widespread popularity and acceptance as a benchmark of authentic awakenings prompted the historian W. R. Ward to comment, "If ever revival seemed to flag, someone somewhere would reprint *Faithful Narrative*."[11]

In their preface to the first London edition (1737), the Dissenting ministers Isaac Watts and John Guyse took inspiration from Edwards's narrative, noting, "It gives us further encouragement to pray, and wait, and hope for the like display of his power in the midst of us."[12] The revival, unprecedented "since the first ages of Christianity . . . ought not to be concealed from the world. . . . May a plentiful effusion of the blessed Spirit also descend on the British Isles and all their American plantations, to renew the face of religion there!"[13] A year later, while reading the *Faithful Narrative* as he walked from London to Oxford, John Wesley confided in his journal (quoting Ps 118:23), "Surely, 'this is the Lord's doing, and it is marvelous in our eyes.'"[14] Edwards's account may have opened the eyes of Wesley and other evangelicals in the Church of England to the possibility of mass conversions. Subsequently, Wesley provided his preachers and members of his societies with his own abridged version of Edwards's narrative (as he did with Edwards's four other writings about revival and their implications). In Wales, the Methodist revivalists Howell Harris and Daniel Rowland discussed *Faithful Narrative* in 1738, eighteen months after the Welsh revival had begun. Rowland was so taken by Edwards's treatise that he declared, "Sure the time here now is like New England." Edwards's description and analysis of the colonial awakening confirmed in Rowland's mind that the Welsh revival was indeed a work of the Spirit. According to a historian of the Welsh revival, the *Faithful Narrative* had

10. Simonson, "Jonathan Edwards," 366.
11. Ward, *Early Evangelicalism*, 140.
12. Watts and Guyse, "Preface," 132.
13. Edwards, *WJE* 4:130, 137.
14. Ward and Heizenrater, *Works of John Wesley*, 19:16.

"a disproportionately significant impact on the development of the revival in Wales."[15]

News of the revival in Northampton and the publication of *Faithful Narrative* soon spread to the Continent, where revival-minded German and Dutch Pietists released translations of Edwards's account as early as 1738. In his lengthy preface to the German translation (1739), Johann Steinmetz downplayed the confessional differences between Lutherans and Calvinists and expressed the ecumenical hope that the narrative would spark conversions and revive the Protestant churches from their spiritual slumber.[16] A few years after the Dutch translation (1740), revival broke out in the town of Nijkerk in the Dutch Republic. From there, revival spread to the surrounding areas in the Netherlands and German border countries. In 1750, one of the promoters of revival, Gerardus Kuypers, published his own "Faithful Narrative," linking the religious stir in Nijkerk to the broader transatlantic movement in play since the mid-1730s. Thanks to Edwards's *Faithful Narrative*, the English, the Germans, the Dutch, and the Americans shared in the work of the Holy Spirit on both sides of the Atlantic.[17]

Unlike in Wales, where it is difficult to trace the exact ways in which Edwards's extensive influence was felt,[18] the revival in Scotland unmistakably owed its genesis to Edwards's works. In Wales, *Faithful Narrative* authenticated what had already taken place; in Scotland, Edwards's work facilitated the revival to come. Indeed, the most direct and profound impact of *Faithful Narrative* was felt in Scotland, where a spiritual stir broke out in Kilsyth in 1740, and then a "plentiful effusion" descended on Cambuslang (a suburb of Glasgow) and the surrounding area, including Kilsyth again, in 1742. *Faithful Narrative* became a veritable handbook—an urtext—for Scottish evangelicals. Inspired by the possibility of replicating the American awakening, they adopted Edwards's vision of the pivotal role of revivals in God's grand scheme of salvation and assiduously followed Edwards's account in conducting, documenting, and interpreting the revival. According to Michael Crawford, "The character and timing of the Scottish religious revivals of 1742 . . . were all

---

15. Jones, *Welsh Methodism*, 137.
16. Stievermann, "Faithful Translations," 339.
17. Yeager, *Jonathan Edwards*, 88–91.
18. Jones, *Welsh Methodism*, 291–94.

influenced in a high degree by events external to Scotland, especially the Great Awakening in New England."[19]

In his earliest communication with Scotland's ministers (May 12, 1743), Edwards rejoiced at the news of the Cambuslang revival and its "glorious work."[20] William McCulloch, one of Edwards's primary Scottish correspondents, modeled his preaching after Edwards, going so far in one sermon as to describe the plight of the sinner in words strikingly similar to Edwards's *Sinners in the Hands of an Angry God*: "How can ye allow yourselves quietly to eat or sleep when ye know Nothing of the new birth, and where there is nothing but the frail thread of life between you and everlasting burnings." Should the thread break, "It may be this night you instantly drop down into the pit of hell."[21]

As was common among Anglo-American evangelicals, printed reports of revivals were often read by ministers to their congregants as a primary means of promoting the work of the Spirit. After a worship service, McCulloch's reading from Edwards's *Faithful Narrative* so inspired one woman that she considered moving to America! Another woman remarked that she "was very glad to hear that there was such a work of conversion in those far distant places."[22] Such preparatory work by McCulloch and other ministers, including James Robe in nearby Kilsyth, heightened spiritual expectations among the people. Robe was so taken with *Faithful Narrative* that, following the 1740 revival in Kilsyth, he published his own *Faithful Narrative of the Extraordinary Work of the Spirit of God* (1742), whose contents and organization mirrored Edwards's work. Edwards's *Faithful Narrative* was not only a catalyst that prepared the way for the Scottish revivals; it also introduced a new genre of revival literature replicated by Scottish revivalists and others.

As in the American revival, controversy erupted in Scotland over the heightened religious emotions and disregard for social conventions. In answering their critics, the Scottish evangelicals once again had recourse to Edwards, relying upon *Distinguishing Marks of a Work of the Spirit of God* (1741) to defend the scriptural basis of experimental religion. (I should note as well that William Williams, the leader of the Welsh Methodist movement in the 1750s, relied upon the criteria set forth in *Distinguishing Marks* to judge the bizarre somatic manifestations during

19. Crawford, "New England," 23.
20. Edwards, *WJE* 16:105.
21. Crawford, "New England," 26.
22. Fawcett, *Cambuslang Revival*, 92.

an outbreak of revival in 1762.)[23] Edwards was not only the architect of revival but also its defender. In his analysis of religious conversion in *Distinguishing Marks*, Edwards proposed authentic signs of true conversion that offered a sense of assurance of one's salvation through empirical tests. By melding Enlightenment rationality with religious experience, Edwards shifted the previous Puritan emphasis on continual introspection and soul-searching to a new confidence, security, and outward-looking evangelistic concern that spurred Christians to proclaim the message of the Gospels to others.

An outward-focused missionary-mindedness was thus one of the major consequences of the revival. Although there had been mounting interest in missionary activity in Scotland before the actual awakenings of 1742, the revivals accelerated overseas missionary outreach. The Scottish Society for Promoting Christian Knowledge (organized in 1709) became the sending organization of evangelistic outreach, and in appointing David Brainerd as one of its missionaries, the society lay claim to the most famous Protestant missionary as its own.

In sum, by his exemplary writings, Edwards inspired and emboldened the Scots to preach the message of the new birth, to defend the revivals as a genuine work of God's Spirit, and to declare that the revivals heralded the great advance of religion around the world.

INTERNATIONAL MISSIONS: EDWARDS'S LATER IMPACT

Edwards's most important contributions to international missions are derived from his conception of cosmic redemption (*Humble Attempt*, *History of the Work of Redemption*), his distinction between moral and natural ability (*Freedom of the Will*), and his presentation of an archetypical missionary model (*Life of David Brainerd*). In examining Edwards's works, I will treat each separately, but their impact on international missions should be seen as mutually reinforcing. Some works had a greater influence than others, and certain works attracted different audiences. Some works had an immediate effect, others a long-term impact. Taken together, they constitute a major force in advancing the modern Protestant missionary movement. Edwards, observed David Bebbington, "created an intellectual framework within which his successors in the

---

23. Jones, "'Sure the Time Here Now,'" 55.

English-speaking (and Welsh-speaking) world did their thinking and their mission."[24]

Although Edwards was at the vanguard of global missiological thinking in his own day, the full impact of his writings did not come to fruition until well after his death, at the end of the eighteenth century. Since the Reformation, Protestants had made only a few concerted efforts to engage in worldwide evangelization, certainly nothing on the scale of Catholic missions. There were a number of reasons for this neglect, but one of the main theological reasons was the widespread view that the Great Commission of Matt 28:19–20 was restricted to the apostles who fulfilled Jesus' command to "go and make disciples" when they took the gospel to the then circumscribed known world. The task of successive generations of Christians was to maintain the purity of the gospel witness. Mainline reformers such as Calvin contended that "the pastor does not have the mandate to preach the Gospel all the world over, but to look after the church, that has been committed to his charge."[25] To be sure, there were exceptions to the general consensus. Anabaptists (influenced by Erasmus) affirmed the present-day applicability of the text, as did Richard Baxter (1615–91) a century later. Within a decade on either side of 1700, three new missionary societies were created whose focus was primarily on colonists in America: the Society for Promoting Christian Knowledge (1698), the Society for the Propagation of the Gospel (1701), and the aforementioned Scottish Society for Promoting Christian Knowledge (1709). Successive generations of New England Puritans (including Edwards) engaged in outreach to Native Americans, and the Halle-Danish-English Mission in Tranquebar, India, and Moravian Brethren Pietist efforts were notable in extending the gospel to the "uttermost part of the earth." A nascent global consciousness among Anglo-American and Continental Protestants was emerging, yet there was little in the way of large-scale evangelistic efforts.

Edwards's interest in international missions and his enlarged view of the Great Commission were influenced by a variety of sources. There was, first, his grandfather, Solomon Stoddard, who argued in a published report that Christ commanded that the gospel should be preached to the Indians. He cited Matt 28:19 and commented, "This Command was not given to the Apostles alone, but to their Successors also throughout all

---

24. Bebbington, "Remembered around the World," 187.
25. Davies, "Great Commission," 44.

generations.²⁶ Once Edwards became Stoddard's assistant, he no doubt had access to this work.²⁷ Perhaps a more significant influence on Edwards was Robert Millar's two-volume *History of the Propagation of Christianity* (1731), which Edwards owned.²⁸ In a letter (June 1, 1740) to Josiah Willard, the secretary of the Province of Massachusetts, Edwards referenced Millar's work. After expressing hope that Willard's extensive knowledge of European affairs could provide more details about Lutheran Pietist revivals in Prussia, he cited an account in Millar's *History* of the spiritual stir in the East Indies led by Danish missionaries. In reading this work, Edwards would have encountered not only a history of missionary expansion but also a rationale for its continuance. The Scottish Presbyterian minister from Paisley cited Matt 28:19-20 as a proof text for the duty of pastors to convert nations: "We are obliged to propagate the saving knowledge of Christ among all men so far as we can, and as orderly called by the very words of that commission from which we derive our office." He further declared that every Christian "should act with zeal in this manner."²⁹

Millar's *History* (as well as a host of other authors writing on the apocalypse) shaped Edwards's perspective on the timing of the expansion of the gospel. In his *History of the Work of Redemption*, Edwards cited Christ's commission to his disciples as a critical component of the redemptive process in proclaiming the gospel to the world.³⁰ Unlike Calvin, he mentioned nothing about what a post-apostolic pastor might or might not do in this regard. In *The "Blank Bible"* commentary, Edwards took a somewhat different tack. Here he connected Jesus' words to his disciples with the worldwide expansion of the gospel preceding the millennium. Edwards averred that when Jesus commissioned his disciples, his intention was to bring "all nations into his kingdom." But since "this has never been accomplished, we may suppose that there is a day remaining in which it will be accomplished."³¹

Although Edwards's brief exposition never appeared in print, his mindset demonstrated an enlarged vision of the scope and timing of God's work of redemption, as well as an understanding that advancing

26. Stoddard, *Question*, 7.
27. Davies, "Jonathan Edwards," 60.
28. Edwards, *WJEO* 26:71.
29. Millar, *History of the Propagation of Christianity*, 2:394, 395.
30. Edwards, *WJE* 9:363-64.
31. Edwards, *WJE* 24:878; see also *WJE* 18:366.

the kingdom of Christ required that all Christians play their part. He explicitly transmitted this vision in his published works *Humble Attempt* and *History of the Work of Redemption*.

The Great Designs of God in the World

The half century from the 1740s to the 1790s, Stuart Piggin writes, "is threaded through with many cords connecting Edwards with the founders of modern Protestant missions."[32] To unravel these cords is to trace the profound influence of Edwards's writings upon the awakening of the missionary spirit in Britain and America. In *A History of the Work of Redemption* (originally a sermon series in 1739; published posthumously in 1774) and *Humble Attempt*, Edwards proposed that the eighteenth-century revivals in Europe, England, Scotland, Wales, America, and elsewhere signaled the dawn of the millennium. Beginning in the late 1730s and extending through the Great Awakening, Edwards predicted that the world was on the cusp of a massive religious revival. According to Edwards, this new age would come not through cataclysmic means (as earlier interpreters had suggested) but through natural means, through the outpouring of God's Spirit manifested in Christian teaching, preaching, praying, and other religious activity. Because the world was gradually improving in anticipation of Christ's return, a guarded optimism attended this view. Christian activity was a precondition of the coming new age, for Christians who engaged in benevolent activities, prayer, and missionary outreach actually played a divinely ordained role in ushering in the kingdom of Christ. Edwards's millennialism thus joined revivalism and missions in a redemptive scheme.

Prayer: *Humble Attempt*

Edwards enjoined all Christians, whatever their age or status, to engage in constant prayer for promoting revival. He urged fellow ministers to "imitate their great Master in his fervent prayers for the good of the souls of men."[33] During times of spiritual awakening, he recommended praying societies where men, women, young men and young women, and boys and girls organized themselves in separate groups "to promote the

---

32. Piggin, "Expanding Knowledge of God," 269.
33. Edwards, *WJE* 25:337.

work of God, and advance the kingdom of Christ."[34] Entreating God in prayer was the highest of Christian priorities: "Pray for the time when the light will enlighten the whole world."[35] "The prayers of the saints," he wrote in *Some Thoughts Concerning the Present Revival of Religion in New England*, "should be one great and principle means of carrying on the designs of Christ's kingdom in the world. When God has something very great to accomplish for his church, 'tis his will that there should precede it the extraordinary prayers of his people."[36]

In 1745, Edwards's pleas for united prayer were taken up on the other side of the Atlantic when Scottish and English ministers, inspired by *Some Thoughts* and already cognizant of existing praying societies in Britain, organized their own "concert of prayer." Writing to a correspondent in Scotland later in the year, Edwards enthusiastically endorsed the praying societies. He called them "exceeding beautiful" and expressed hope that a concert would spread throughout America, extend into other British dominions, and "all over the visible church of Christ."[37] Edwards was at once thrilled at the initiative taken overseas and yet troubled at the waning of spiritual interest at home in the aftermath of the Great Awakening. Compounding the "withdrawal of God's Spirit" in New England was an unstable international political climate created by European wars that spread to America. Yet all was not spiritually lost. Edwards, ever alert to the news, tracked signs of renewal elsewhere—reports of revivals in Maryland and Virginia, Brainerd's success among the Indians, Britain's miraculous defeat of the (Catholic) French at Cape Breton, and showers of divine blessing in various parts of Europe.

In *Humble Attempt* Edwards proposed a concert of prayer as a remedy for the spiritual ills in the evangelical world, the disquieting international situation, and the hastening of the millennium. His larger objective was to place past and present events within a biblical apocalyptic timetable. Edwards sought, as the lengthy title of this work attests, "to promote explicit agreement and visible union of God's people in extraordinary prayer for the revival of religion and the advancement of Christ's kingdom on earth" but also, as the subtitle clarified, "*pursuant to Scripture-promises and prophecies concerning the last time*" (emphasis added). According to Edwards's prophetic scheme, constant, united

34. Edwards, *WJE* 4:519.
35. Edwards, *WJE* 19:722.
36. Edwards, *WJE* 4:516.
37. Edwards, *WJE* 16:181, 183.

prayer was the primary means that God gave to God's people to prepare the way for revival, the spread of the gospel worldwide, and the coming millennium. The revivals in New England and Europe were a foretaste of what was to come. "There is *yet remaining*," Edwards wrote, "a great advancement of the interest of religion and the kingdom of Christ in this world, by an abundant outpouring of the Spirit of God, far greater and more extensive than ever yet has been."[38] *Humble Attempt* offered a grand vision of the progressive unfolding of the plan of redemption in history, with united prayer and revival as its centerpiece.

During Edwards's lifetime, his treatise and efforts to promote the concert of prayer were integral to the rise of the Scottish overseas missionary movement. But beyond Scotland and until the end of the eighteenth century, *Humble Attempt* generally lay dormant. How this work became one of the most important sources in awakening Anglo-American evangelicals to their missionary calling is the stuff of legend. It began with John Erskine, one of Edwards's frequent Scottish Presbyterian correspondents and a key transmitter of Edwards's evangelical Calvinism. In 1784 Erskine sent a parcel of books, including *Humble Attempt*, to the Northampton Baptist leader John Ryland Jr.—already a devotee of Edwards.[39] Reading Edwards's treatises had convinced Ryland that the gospel was to be preached to all people and not, as other Particular Baptist theologians argued, to the elect only. After reading *Humble Attempt*, Ryland passed it on John Sutcliff in Olney, England, who then shared it with Andrew Fuller in Kettering. Deeply affected by Edwards's treatise, the trio agreed to meet with others on a monthly basis "to seek the revival of religion, and the extension of Christ's kingdom in the world." Soon thereafter, at the annual meeting of the (Baptist) Northamptonshire Association, *Humble Attempt* became the focus of attention. At Sutcliff's recommendation, the association issued a prayer call: One hour on the first Monday of each month was to be set aside for corporate prayer. The concert of prayer continued through the 1780s and soon spread to other countries, including the United States.

As the number of praying societies grew, Sutcliff reissued *Humble Attempt* in 1789. In his preface, he enjoined all Christians, regardless of their denominational affiliation or theological differences, however slight, to gather for united prayer. This edition influenced William Carey,

38. Edwards, *WJE* 5:329.
39. Yeager, *Jonathan Edwards*, 124.

who three years later published his clarion call to missionary service, *An Inquiry into Obligations of Christians to Use Means for the Conversion of the Heathens*. Carey, an active participant in the concert of prayer since the 1780s, claimed that the Great Commission was as binding in the present day as in apostolic times. Christians were responsible for using the means at their disposal (e.g., preaching, praying) and going to the unreached "heathen." Moreover, he relied on *Humble Attempt* to discount the contention that certain prophecies had yet to be fulfilled before the heathen could be converted. *Humble Attempt* injected eschatological optimism, calling upon all Christians to pray for revival and assuring them that they could play an active part in advancing the kingdom of Christ.

With Carey's manifesto and the English publication of many of Edwards's works, the modern Protestant missionary movement was "born in a world awash with Edwards."[40] The Baptist Missionary Society was formed in 1792, the London Missionary Society in 1795, the Scottish Missionary Society in 1796, the Glasgow Missionary Society in 1798, and the Church Missionary Society in 1799, and others followed, including in the United States. What also followed was a cascade of reprints of *Humble Attempt* well into the second half of the nineteenth century. As Protestant missionaries traveled to foreign counties, so did *Humble Attempt*. The treatise continued to be published in English; translations were issued in French, German, and Arabic; and in 1859 *Humble Attempt* was printed in Calcutta. Andrew Walls deftly summarized the connective links from Edwards's *Humble Attempt* to the modern Protestant missionary movement: "The chain that led to William Carey's pioneering missionary initiative of 1792 was forged by a gift from a Scottish Presbyterian to an English Baptist of a book by a New England Congregationalist."[41]

History: *The Work of Redemption*

In the annals of missionary history, Edwards's *A History of the Work of Redemption* cannot claim the same pedigree as *Humble Attempt*, and yet throughout the nineteenth century the treatise was one of the most popular missionary reference books, attracting a wide readership on both sides of the Atlantic. Preached originally as a sermon series with the aim of awakening his Northampton congregation, Edwards's *History of*

---

40. Piggin, "Expanding Knowledge of God," 274.
41. Walls, "Evangelical Revival," 310.

the *Work of Redemption* was not published in Edinburgh until thirty-five years later in 1774. The impact of this sermon series cum treatise can be charted by its publication history. Relevant here is that throughout the nineteenth century its major disseminators were evangelical and mission-focused organizations. For example, between 1838 and 1875 the American Tract Society distributed over sixty thousand copies. The British-based Religious Tract Society reprinted *History of the Work of Redemption* four times in the 1830s alone. A French copy made its way to Basutoland (now Lesotho) Africa via the Paris Evangelical Mission Society. Edwards's historical dispensations in *History of the Work of Redemption* became the organizational structure for the French missionary Adolph Mabille's systematic theology *Dogmatique* (1856) and for his catechism in the vernacular Basuto language.⁴² The reception and especially the translations of *History of the Work of Redemption* "were intimately connected to the rise of the worldwide Protestant evangelical mission movement of the early nineteenth century."⁴³

Whereas *Humble Attempt* cleared away scriptural and theological objections to human participation in the advancement of the kingdom of Christ, *History of the Work of Redemption* offered historical "proof" of its advance, placing revivals at the center of redemptive history. In his treatise, Edwards divided history into three distinct eras, the third being the period from Christ's death until his millennial return or the "last days," which ostensibly were on the horizon. To nineteenth-century missionary-minded evangelicals in America, Europe, and beyond, *History of the Work of Redemption* reinforced their convictions that the revivals they were witnessing and promoting were a part of the grand divine scheme of redemptive history. This reading of history sustained them in the dark days of resistance to the gospel and inspired them to extend the gospel throughout the world. "[God's] Spirit shall be gloriously poured out," wrote Edwards, "for the wonderful revival and propagation of religion." God's Spirit will enable "men to be glorious instruments of carrying on his work," filling them "with knowledge and wisdom and a fervent zeal for promoting the kingdom of Christ."⁴⁴ Edwards's bold historical optimism, fervent expectation of imminent revival, and global interest in the progress of the gospel (he referenced China, the East Indies, South America, and Africa in *History of the Work of Redemption*) inspired generations of

42. Neele, "Reception," 78–82.
43. Neele, "Reception," 71–72.
44. Edwards, *WJE* 9:460.

missionaries. Generally neglected or undervalued by earlier scholars of missions, *History of the Work of Redemption* may rightly claim the status of *primus inter pares* with *Humble Attempt* and *Life of Brainerd* among Edwards's most important works on international missions.

The Human Condition: *Freedom of the Will* and *Original Sin*

Two of Edwards's works written during his Stockbridge years (1751–58) had implications for the international spread of the gospel. *The Freedom of the Will* (1754) and *Original Sin* (1758, published posthumously), penned while Edwards served as missionary to the Native Americans, made possible the offer of salvation to all peoples, whatever their status, race, or ethnicity. *Freedom of the Will* was aimed primarily at defending Calvinist views of the will against the Arminian threat, but its argument enabled the Kettering Baptist Andrew Fuller (1754–1815) and his Particular Baptist brethren to liberate themselves from the constricting views of divine election that removed any responsibility for preaching the gospel to the non-elect. According to some hyper-Calvinist Baptist theologians, no ministers had a warrant to call on the unregenerate to repent and believe the gospel. They needed to first identify those who had an inner warrant (a text of Scripture in their minds) as confirmation of their elect status. Fuller and others, in wrestling with the implications of this theological fatalism, discovered in *Freedom of the Will* a way out of this quandary. Edwards distinguished between non-elect sinners' natural inability to repent and their moral inability to do so. There were no natural, physical, external factors that hindered unbelievers from choosing or rejecting the gospel. In this sense, they were "free" to accept the gospel (even though that freedom always led to wrong choices and sinful behavior) and were thus morally responsible for their choices. If they rejected the gospel, they did so according to their desires. God's sovereign election and the obligation to accept the gospel were consistent.

Not until he encountered Edwards's *Freedom of the Will* in 1775 did Andrew Fuller find a way to reconcile his High Calvinism with the offer of salvation to all people. In 1785 he published *The Gospel Worthy of All Acceptation*, citing the Great Commission in Mark (16:15–16) as his text. In his preface, he named those sources that convinced him to alter his views. The first was people: John Eliot and David Brainerd, missionaries to the Native Americans, appeared "to have none of the shackles with which I felt myself encumbered."[45] Second, and more important, were ideas. Fuller read Edwards's *Freedom of the Will* "on the distinction of *natural and moral ability, and inability.*" He concluded that men's inability to come to Christ "was of a voluntary kind—that they will not come to Christ that they may have life—will not hearken to the voice of the charmer, charm he never so wisely—will not seek after God."[46] Edwards gave Fuller and the Baptists theological permission to preach revival and evangelize beyond their own churches. *The Gospel Worthy of All Acceptation* enabled Baptists to become evangelical Calvinists. "This evangelical development," writes Chris Chun, "then became an important source for revival among English Baptists, which ultimately gave birth to the Modern Missionary Movement."[47] Fuller's Edwardsean theological reconstructions so enlightened William Carey that in his *Inquiry* Carey urged Christians to abandon fatalistic notions of God's sovereignty and use the means at their disposal to preach the gospel to all people. Taking the lead in the formation of the Baptist Missionary Society, Fuller became its first secretary and the society's greatest promoter of missions. The publishing history of *Freedom of the Will* indicates that its popularity and stimulus to missions was not restricted to Baptists. From 1774 to 1830, the work was printed in Utrecht (1774), Glasgow (1790), Edinburgh (1818, 1830), and London (seven times from 1762 to 1816).[48]

Although *Original Sin*, another work of Edwards's written during his Stockbridge years, did not have the kind of game-changing impact on international missions as did *Freedom of the Will*, it nevertheless created (to extend the analogy) a level playing field in affirming the depraved common constitution of all humanity, be they the presumed heathen, backward Native American or the supposed morally upright, civilized European. Edwards "found the unity of the human race in the depths of sin."[49] If not for the grace of God, all would perish. Challenging prevailing views about the moral superiority of Europeans, Edwards maintained that the Fall had rendered all humanity equally helpless and in need of God's regenerating grace. Although Edwards made no direct connection between original sin and the need for missions, Rachel Wheeler has drawn out the implications of Edwards's emphasis on the universal human

45. Fuller, *Gospel Worthy of All Acceptation*, iii.
46. Fuller, *Gospel Worthy of All Acceptation*, v–vi.
47. Chun, *Legacy of Jonathan Edwards*, 32.
48. Lesser, "Honor Too Great," 304–5.
49. Edwards, *WJE* 3:101.

condition: "In the Calvinist doctrine of human depravity, Edwards found grounds to affirm the equality of Indian and English. It was the related doctrine of the necessity of divine grace through Christ's salvific work that fostered the missionary impulse in Edwards and other Christians."[50]

Spirituality: *Life of David Brainerd*

Edwards's *Life of the Late Reverend Mr. David Brainerd* (1749) was Edwards's most influential writing; it touched the personal and spiritual lives of laity, clergy, revivalists, and missionaries. *Life of David Brainerd* was to the spiritual lives of missionaries what *Faithful Narrative* was to the implementation of revival—a paradigmatic text. What Edwards analyzed as true religion in *Religious Affections*, the companion text of *Life of David Brainerd* authenticated. More editions and reprints of *Life of David Brainerd* have been issued than of any of Edwards's other books. It was the first of Edwards's works to reach a foreign audience and, as with his other works, the initial impact of *Life of David Brainerd* was stronger abroad than in America. Multiple editions were issued by English Baptists and Methodists, Scottish Presbyterians, and German Pietists. Evangelical leaders urged every preacher to model his life after Brainerd, emphasizing the necessity of converted and committed pastors.

Life of David Brainerd succeeded in raising the missionary consciousness among Anglo-American and German evangelicals and shaping their views of spirituality. Every Protestant English-speaking mission library featured a copy of *Life of David Brainerd*. The abstemious, devout missionary to the Native Americans was a personal inspiration and subject of study in missionary training schools. Brainerd achieved a heroic, saintly status, becoming "the principal model of early British missionary spirituality."[51] The first generation of modern missionaries (and successive ones beyond the scope of this chapter) who testified to the inspiration of *Life of David Brainerd* represents a veritable hall of fame of renowned evangelists. In his *Inquiry*, Carey cited Brainerd three times; he urged his missionary band, "Let us often look at Brainerd"; and he so treasured *Life of David Brainerd* that, according to John Ryland Jr., it became "a second Bible to him." Henry Martyn, chaplain for the East India Company,

---

50. Wheeler, "Edwards as Missionary," 207; but see also Van Andel, "Geography of Sinfulness."

51. Walls, "Evangelical Revival," 310.

testified after reading the biography, "No uninspired writer ever did me so much good. . . . Let me burn out for God."[52] Others attesting to the influence of Brainerd included Melville Horne, English missionary to Africa; Robert Morrison, Scottish missionary to China; Christian Frederick Schwartz, German missionary to India; Samuel Marsden, English missionary to New Zealand; and Adoniram Judson and his wife, Ann "Nancy" Judson, American missionaries to Burma.

Redux: American International Missions

In a letter to Andrew Fuller in 1799, Samuel Hopkins wrote, "I am pleased to hear that Edwardean principles are gaining ground and spreading . . . and that all or most of the late remarkable exertions to send missionaries among the heathen, and propagate the gospel among others in Europe and America, have originated in a *poor shoemaker* [William Carey], from having imbibed these principles." He then recognized that the recent missionary societies formed in America owed "their rise to those formed in England" and that four out of five of these American societies embraced Edwardsean theology.[53] Hopkins's letter encapsulates the organizational and theological progression of Anglo-American missions. In its theology of missions, England owed a debt to Edwards; in its organizational structure of missions, America owed a debt to England. As we have noted above, Edwards's *Life of David Brainerd*, *Humble Attempt*, *History of the Work of Redemption*, and other writings inspired England's and Scotland's foray into overseas missions. For their part, American evangelicals adopted British organizational models, borrowed freely and extensively from their missionary publications, incorporated British eschatological speculations into their writings, and circulated sermons of their British counterparts.

Although Hopkins never lived to see the reality of the missionary movement in America, a succeeding generation of Edwardseans (called the New Divinity) extended and applied the implicit missionary theology of Edwards (and Hopkins's modifications) into an explicit theological justification for missionary endeavor. Following the British example, in 1810 Edwards's New Divinity heirs created the American Board of Commissioners for Foreign Missions (ABCFM), the great sponsoring

---

52. Grigg, *Lives of David Brainerd*, 165.
53. Hopkins, *Works of Samuel Hopkins*, 1:236.

body for hundreds of Edwardsean missionaries around the world. The ABCFM would soon outdistance all other evangelical foreign missionary organizations in both numbers of missionaries and geographical scope. Complementing the ABCFM and Andover Theological Seminary—its educational feeder and a virtual New Divinity missionary training school—was Mary Lyon's Mount Holyoke Female Seminary, whose Edwardsean religious culture supplied nearly forty female students and missionaries to foreign missions by the middle of the nineteenth century.[54]

While inspired by the British example of foreign missions, America's first foray into overseas missions must be seen as a continuation and extension of New Divinity revivals (the Second Great Awakening) and frontier missions. Amid religious stirs at home, the New Divinity clergy advanced the missionary cause under the Edwardsean banner, though not without their own theological modifications.[55] Of these revisions, perhaps the most distinctive American contribution to missionary motivation was the refinement of Edwards's notion of "disinterested benevolence." The phrase was not unique to Edwards but was in currency among British moral philosophers and employed in a wider discussion of the nature of "true virtue." Edwards equated true virtue with the condition of the regenerate and defined it as a love or "benevolence to Being in general." True Christians are given a new disposition (or "taste" or "relish") for God and all things that God has brought into existence, and consequently, they have a love of "being in general."[56] There is no private or selfish interest involved; rather, God is loved, adored, and worshipped for who and what God is.

Edwards proposed this concept as an aesthetic, beatific vision; his followers, especially Samuel Hopkins, transposed the concept into an ethic. Whereas Edwards saw true virtue culminating in holy consciousness, Hopkins viewed it as culminating in holy action. True Christians, such as David Brainerd, expressed themselves in unselfish acts of love and mercy in order to bring glory to God and further God's kingdom. And what could be more unselfish than leaving the comforts of civilization for the hardships of missionary service? Whether expressed as duty, benevolence, or a "pure and holy love," the concept of disinterested benevolence acted as a motivational missionary detonator. When wired to the dynamite of revival, it set off an explosion of vast human energy,

54. Conforti, *Jonathan Edwards*, 105.
55. See chap. 6 in this volume.
56. Edwards, *WJE* 8: 540.

both at home and abroad. Thus, *Life of David Brainerd* coupled with the concept of disinterested benevolence inspired the first generation of American Protestant missionaries. Personalizing *Life of David Brainerd*, Levi Parsons, the ABCFM's first missionary to Palestine, epitomized the Hopkinsian model of disinterested benevolence. Prior to his departure, he declared, "Every devoted Christian will enquire, not where he can enjoy the most ease . . . but where he can most successfully labor in the cause of Christ & promote the salvation of men." It was far better to "wear out and die in three years, than live forty years in slothfulness."[57]

CONCLUSION

Historians have long recognized Edwards's writings as a major stimulus to the beginnings of the modern missionary movement. Recent scholarship has made an even more convincing case, highlighting not only the dissemination of Edwards's works that inspired missionary outreach but also those that had a direct bearing on international revivals. To be sure, as crucial as Edwards was in these developments, he was never directly involved in orchestrating international revivals or promoting missionary outreach. He lived as a provincial colonial in the backwoods of the British Empire, far removed from the center of the Protestant world. Yet, as has been made clear throughout this chapter, his reach was global. Indeed, in the half century following his death, Edwards's publications were by far more influential abroad than at home. American evangelicals eventually reclaimed Edwards as their own, and, due in no small part to Edwards's New Divinity heirs, their contributions to international revivals and missions would far exceed those of their peers in England and Europe. Had he lived to witness the "great century" of missionary expansion and the continued global growth of Christianity in the twentieth and twenty-first centuries, Edwards no doubt would have enlarged and revised what he called "a great work"—his *History of the Work of Redemption*. What he saw only through a glass dimly but envisioned expectantly—the spread of the gospel around the world—was fulfilled in his hope for the advancement of the kingdom of Christ.

---

57. See chap. 6 in this volume.

PART TWO

The Edwardseans

5

Jonathan Edwards in the Second Great Awakening

The New Divinity Contributions of Edward Dorr Griffin and Asahel Nettleton

THE PULSATING HEART OF Jonathan Edwards's theology was God's great work of redemption, in which revival was the lifeblood. In his lifetime Edwards experienced, promoted, and wrote extensively about revival. The core of his writings from 1734 to 1746 concerned revival. In letters, treatises, and sermons, Edwards explained, defended, promoted, and tracked revivals. He viewed revivals as the means to corporate renewal and moral reform—indeed, the means by which the millennium would come. Edwards conceded that the events of history "might appear like confusion," but if viewed through the lens of providential design, if alert to the work of the Holy Spirit, the divine pattern was discernible.[1] God's work of redemption, "the great subject of the whole Bible" and subsequent history, would not be accomplished "by authority of princes, nor by the wisdom of learned men, but by the Holy Spirit" that "shall be gloriously poured out for the wonderful revival and propagation of religion."[2] The key to human history, then, was "glorious," "wonderful," "blessed,"

---

1. Edwards, *WJE* 9:121.
2. Edwards, *WJE* 9:514, 460.

"great," "remarkable," and "happy" revivals.³ And the key to personal human destiny was conversion—"the most important thing in the world."⁴

If Edwards lived and breathed revival, and if by his estimation revivals were the center stage of God's work of redemption, then any consideration of "after Edwards" must take into account his influence on the revivalist tradition.⁵ As Avihu Zakai and others have pointed out, "By placing revival at the center of salvation history, Edwards conditioned many generations of Protestants in America to see religious awakenings as the essence of sacred, providential history."⁶ In the past three decades a growing body of scholarship has addressed this legacy. Of particular interest and the focus of this essay is the way in which Edwards was appropriated in promoting revival (and by extension, missions) by his third-generation New Divinity disciples associated with the Second Great Awakening.

Edwards's immediate disciples certainly shared his vision for God's work of redemption being accomplished through revivals, and in a number of cases (e.g., in Joseph Bellamy's Bethlehem, Connecticut, congregation) that vision became a local reality, though not until the post-Revolutionary era did another "great" revival take place. Harry Stout has observed that, thanks to the influence of Edwards's father Timothy and his maternal grandfather Solomon Stoddard, "Revivals were in [his] genes."⁷ What Jonathan passed on to his Edwardsean progeny, however, was a recessive gene, for not until a third generation of Edwardseans (which included Edwards's grandson Timothy Dwight) did revival erupt in any numerically significant and widespread way.

The circumstances surrounding the origins and duration of the Edwardsean Second Great Awakening have been examined elsewhere, although a synthesis of New Divinity revivals in New England, the Middle Atlantic States, and the frontier awaits historical investigation.⁸ Suffice

---

3. A cursory review of "revivals" in *WJEO* reveals Edwards's use of these adjectives.

4. Edwards, "Reality of Conversion," 92.

5. For a sampling of articles on Edwards and revival, see Eversley, "Pastor as Revivalist," 113–30; Westra, "Divinity's Design," 131–57; Pauw, "Edwards as American Theologian," 14–24; Stout, "Edwards as Revivalist," 125–43; Sweeney, "Evangelical Tradition in America," 217–38; Stout, "Edwards and Revival," 37–52; van Vlastuin, "Alternative Viewpoint, 53–61.

6. Zakai, *Jonathan Edwards's Philosophy of History*, 330; see also Conforti, *Jonathan Edwards*, 47–48.

7. Stout, "Edwards and Revival," 38.

8. Studies include Kling, *Field of Divine Wonders*; Rohrer, *Keepers of the Covenant*;

it to say that by the 1790s proponents of the New Divinity movement were in a position to push their agenda for an outpouring of divine grace. This they did by recourse to Edwards, who, in his extensive writings on revival, recommended preparatory "concerts of prayer" or "praying societies," conference meetings or lectures, clerical visitation teams, evangelistic preaching aimed at the heart, and the circulation of published accounts of revival.

Theologically, the New Divinity uplifted two of Edwards's fundamental convictions. First, they defended his distinction between natural and moral ability to obey God. In *Freedom of the Will* (1754), Edwards claimed that original sin did not obliterate the human capacity to obey divine commands; it only disoriented the human will and affections so that the sinner no longer desired what is right. Humans had freedom, but that freedom always led to wrong choices and sinful behavior. Second, the New Divinity echoed Edwards's insistence on immediate repentance. No one, of course, could pass through heaven's portals except by grace alone, but God nonetheless called sinners to forsake spiritual passivity posthaste and take the kingdom by violence (Matt 11:12). Working from these dual theological concerns, Edwards and his disciples defended revivals and heartfelt, "affectionate," or "experimental" religion as an authentic expression of the Spirit and insisted that only the regenerate or truly saved qualified for church membership. These "pure church" principles prompted the Edwardseans to repudiate the Half-Way Covenant and to conceive of the church as a radical new kind of community at odds with the world.

The New Divinity also embraced Edwards's view of providential history. In *A History of the Work of Redemption* (1782 in America) and *An Humble Attempt to Promote . . . Union Among God's People* (1747), Edwards proposed that the eighteenth-century revivals in Europe, England, Scotland, Wales, America, and elsewhere signaled the dawn of the millennium.[9] According to Edwards, this new age would come not through cataclysmic means (as earlier interpreters had suggested) but through natural means, interposed by the outpouring of God's Spirit manifested in Christian teaching, preaching, and religious activity. Because the world was gradually, though haltingly, improving in anticipation of

---

Conforti, *Jonathan Edwards*, chap. 2; Sassi, *Republic of Righteousness*, esp. 133–35; Sweeney, *Nathaniel Taylor*, esp. 39–42; Sweeney, "Evangelical Tradition in America," 219–25.

9. Edwards, *WJE* 9:433–36; *WJE* 5:363–64.

Christ's return, guarded optimism attended this view. Christian activity was a precondition of the coming new age, for Christians who engaged in benevolent activities, social reform, and missionary outreach actually played a divinely ordained role in ushering in the kingdom of Christ. Edwards's millennialism thus joined revivalism and missions in a providential scheme.[10]

TWO NEW DIVINITY REVIVALISTS

It is these two areas—revivals in established congregations and missions to the unchurched frontier regions, Native Americans, and non-Christian "pagans" abroad—that captured the imagination of the New Divinity.[11] And it is in the work and writings of two of the New Divinity's premier revivalists, Edward Dorr Griffin (1770–1837) and Asahel Nettleton (1783–1844), that these developments are most clearly embodied. Both confirmed Edwards's conviction that "the deliverance of the Christian church will be preceded by God's raising up a number of eminent ministers that shall more plainly and fervently and effectually preach the gospel than it had been before."[12] Both expressed their fidelity to Edwards by promoting revivals as the means of God's great work of redemption. Their success vindicated Edwards's view of salvation history and substantiated his conviction that "there is *yet remaining* a great advancement of ... the kingdom of Christ in this world, by an abundant outpouring of the Spirit of God, far greater and more extensive than ever yet had been."[13]

Neither Griffin nor Nettleton achieved the status of a great theologian or revivalist comparable to an Edwards, a Whitefield, or a Finney. Considered minor figures by scholars of the Second Great Awakening, neither has been the subject of a scholarly article or monograph.[14] How-

---

10. For a more expansive treatment of the relationship between Edwards's millennialism and missions, see Rooy, *Theology of Missions*, 294–309; De Jong, *As the Waters Cover the Sea*, 120–37; Chaney, *Birth of Missions in America*, 65–70.

11. The Connecticut Missionary Society (1797–98) and the Massachusetts Missionary Society (1798)—merged later into the American Home Missionary Society (1826)—were primarily New Divinity creations.

12. Edwards, *"Miscellanies,"* no. 810, WJE 18:518, quoted in Pauw, "Edwards as American Theologian," 15; see also WJE 4:374.

13. Edwards, *Humble Attempt*, WJE 5:329.

14. Since this essay was originally published, Mark Rogers has written a dissertation on Griffin titled "Edward Dorr Griffin and the Edwardsian Second Great Awakening." The most extensive published treatment of Griffin is found in Kling, *Field of Divine*

ever, both were well-known figures within the New Divinity movement and were hailed as outstanding revivalists in their day. One of Griffin's eulogists called him "unequal as a preacher" and elevated him to the rank of a Great Awakener: "I doubt whether the minister can be named since the days of Edwards and Whitfield [sic]," wrote Gardiner Spring, "to whom God has given more seals of his ministry. God had eminently fitted him for usefulness in revivals."[15] Nettleton, by far the more successful revivalist, was accorded Wesley-like status by Lyman Beecher, who concluded that Nettleton had "been the means of plucking thousands as brands from the burning and bringing them into the kingdom of God."[16]

Both Griffin and Nettleton remained firmly tethered to New Divinity theology yet exhibited an ecumenical Reformed evangelicalism insofar as they, like Edwards, developed mutual and lasting relationships with other Reformed pastor-theologians. Both ministered beyond the New Divinity stronghold of New England, including in New York among the Dutch Reformed community and in the mid-Atlantic region among Presbyterians. In this respect, both (especially Griffin) were part of the larger "united evangelical front," a coalition of evangelicals bent on advancing the gospel, defeating the forces of godlessness, and promoting a "republic of righteousness."[17]

Griffin and Nettleton offer an instructive contrast in career paths and preaching styles, illustrating the variety within the New Divinity movement as well as the overlapping connection of people, places, and events that gave the movement its particular character. Griffin could be confrontational, exceedingly formal, and autocratic (as president of

---

Wonders; and chap. 8 in this volume. Nettleton has been the subject of two dissertations: Birney, "Life and Letters of Asahel Nettleton"; May, "Asahel Nettleton." Several recent dissertations from Southwestern Baptist Seminary deal with Nettleton and Charles G. Finney: Nelson, "Relationship between Soteriology and Evangelistic Methodologies"; Kang, "Evangelistic Preaching of Asahel Nettleton"; Hwang, "Bible and Christian Experience." A solid though somewhat uncritical biography is Thornbury, *God Sent Revival*. Other semi-scholarly articles on Nettleton include Ehrhard, "Asahel Nettleton," 67–93; and Thornbury, "Asahel Nettleton's Conflict," 103–19.

15. Spring, *Death and Heaven*, 31, 32–33.

16. Beecher, *Autobiography of Lyman Beecher*, 2:363. For a similar estimate by Francis Wayland, the Baptist president of Brown, see Thornbury, *God Sent Revival*, 55.

17. See Sassi, *Republic of Righteousness*. Griffin held official positions in or delivered sermons to the African School (Synod of New York and New Jersey), American Bible Society, American Board of Commissioners for Foreign Missions, American Education Society, American Society for Meliorating the Condition of the Jews, American Sunday School Union, Marine Missionary Society, Portsmouth Female Asylum, Presbyterian Education Society, and the United Foreign Missionary Society.

Williams College, he insisted that students doff their hats to him when passing).[18] Nettleton was reserved, somewhat enigmatic, and publicly irenic (his private correspondence reveals another side). Whereas Griffin excelled in rhetorical skills before large audiences, Nettleton mastered pastoral techniques of personal counsel in small groups. Griffin chased fame in the cities of Newark, New Jersey, and Boston, whereas Nettleton itinerated in the villages of New England and New York. Griffin's ambition got him into salary troubles at Boston's Park Street Church, whereas Nettleton never demanded or accepted a salary.[19] Griffin spent the last years of his life preserving his legacy by revising sermons for publication; Nettleton never published a sermon. Occasionally, their paths crossed, but not until later in their careers when they united in their opposition to Charles Finney's "new measures" in the 1820s and Nathaniel William Taylor's "improvements" to Edwards's theology in the 1830s.[20]

EDWARDS IN GRIFFIN: MISSIONS ABROAD

His sympathizers called him the greatest revivalist and missionary spokesman of his day; his detractors deemed him vain, pompous, a man of "great ambition." Edward Dorr Griffin was that and then some. A man whose ego matched his stature—no small feat considering he stood six feet three inches and weighed 260 pounds—he was, as a colleague put it, "one of the most eloquent, pungent, and useful preachers" he had ever

---

18. Peterson, *Divine Discontent*, 106.

19. Ironically, Nettleton became wealthier than Griffin, thanks to profits from his *Village Hymns* (1824), but he gave away the proceeds to various New Divinity–inspired organizations such as the American Board of Commissioners for Foreign Missions and the Theological Institute of Connecticut. See Tyler, *Nettleton and His Labours*, 422–23.

20. Griffin communicated with Nettleton regarding an 1827 Finney revival in Troy, New York (Tyler, *Nettleton and His Labours*, 343). When Griffin was informed about the founding of the Theological Institute of Connecticut—a foil to Taylor's New Haven Theology at Yale and an institution to which Nettleton gave time and money—he responded: "I rejoice exceedingly in the firm stand which the brethren of Connecticut have taken against the New Haven school . . . I vote for the new school with all my heart" (quoted in Birney, "Life and Letters of Asahel Nettleton," 363). Nettleton also asked Griffin to send Williams students to the Theological Institute of Connecticut. Asahel Nettleton to Edward Dorr Griffin, July 29, 1836, Gratz Collection. In his correspondence, Nettleton thanked Griffin for his anti-Taylor theological work, *The Doctrine of Divine Efficiency* (1833), and recommended it to others. Asahel Nettleton to Edward Dorr Griffin, September 30, 1833, Gratz Collection; Asahel Nettleton to William Swan Plumer, January 29, 1836, Plumer Papers.

heard.[21] Throughout Griffin's forty-year career, in all but one of his pastoral appointments, be they rural or urban settings in Connecticut, New Jersey, or Massachusetts or as president of Williams College (1821–36), numerous conversions followed. Nearing the end of his life, he observed, "I wish to live long enough to promote revivals of religion by preaching and the kingdom of Christ by any other means in my power. These are the only two objects for which I wish to live."[22]

Griffin's revivalist successes have been documented elsewhere;[23] what has been overlooked is his crucial role in promoting "the kingdom of Christ" in foreign missions and his dependence on Edwards to that end. Although Edwards and his closest disciple, Samuel Hopkins, never provided an explicit theological rationale for foreign missions, their writings profoundly influenced the modern American missionary movement. Edwards proposed a metahistory of cosmic redemption and supplied the exemplary missionary model in *Life of David Brainerd* (1749), his most popular and most frequently reprinted work. Hopkins then furnished the theological underpinnings for missions by revising Edwards's aesthetic concept of "disinterested benevolence" into a practical one of self-denial for the greater glory of God's kingdom and the betterment of humankind.[24] Drawing from these concepts, proponents of the New Divinity such as Griffin made explicit what was implicit. Inspired by evangelicals in England, who themselves were influenced by Edwards's writings, New Divinity men promoted the cause of missions and became the dominant force in creating what would become the largest U.S. missionary society in the first half of the nineteenth century, the American Board of Commissioners for Foreign Missions.[25]

Influenced by Edwards and subsequent evangelicals, Griffin linked revival to the extension of God's kingdom throughout the world. Since the 1790s, continuous revivals and expanding missions raised expectations of the millennium to a fever pitch. In Edwards's view, the revivals of the 1730s and 1740s signaled the imminence of Christ's second coming and possibly the beginning of the new age; with the Second Great Awakening, millennial prognostications were validated in the minds of

21. Griffin, *Sermons of the late Rev. Edward D. Griffin*, 1:242–43.
22. Edward D. Griffin to Mark Tucker, August 29, 1837, Gratz Collection.
23. Kling, *Field of Divine Wonders*, 126–37.
24. The literature on Edwards's contribution to missions is extensive. See Piggin, "Expanding Knowledge of God," 266–96.
25. See chap. 6 in this volume.

evangelicals by even greater empirical proof.[26] By the early nineteenth century, Americans had become, in Ernest Sandeen's notable phrase, "drunk on the Millennium."[27] Griffin was convinced the church lived in that period which "is to extend to the morning of the millennium."[28] In sermons and other writings, he identified the year 1792 as the *annus mirabilis*, not only marking the beginning of four decades of continuous revival in America but also the year in which "the grand era of Missions" was launched in Kettering, England, by William Carey, John Ryland, Andrew Fuller, and others.[29]

Griffin was personally and directly connected to the beginnings of the American missionary movement. During his first pastorate, in New Hartford, Connecticut (1795–1800), he developed a close relationship with the nearby New Divinity pastor in Torringford, Samuel Mills, and got to know his son, Samuel Jr. Some years later, when Griffin was serving in New Jersey, Samuel Jr., who by then knew of Griffin's keen interest in missions, briefly studied theology with him in order to gain an influential ally for his missionary cause. Samuel's awareness of Griffin's support for missions was largely due to Griffin's 1805 sermon *The Kingdom of Christ*. Along with John H. Livingston's *The Everlasting Gospel* (1804), this sermon deeply influenced Mills and the Brethren at Williams College (a group dedicated to foreign missions), who reprinted the sermon in 1808. Its popularity reached other student missionary organizations such as the Society of Inquiry at Andover Theological Seminary, who also reprinted it. Clearly, Griffin's sermon inspired the first generation of American foreign missionaries and has a rightful place in the canon of prominent missionary sermons.

While serving as assistant pastor to the aging Alexander McWhorter at the First Presbyterian Church in Newark, New Jersey, Griffin was invited by the Presbyterian General Assembly to deliver the annual missionary sermon in 1805. Presbyterians had a long history of home missions to new settlements and Native Americans, but not until Griffin's sermon was an explicit call made for foreign missions. The sermon was

26. On Edwards and the millennium, see Wilson, "History, Redemption, and the Millennium," 132; McDermott, *One Holy and Happy Society*, 37–92.

27. Sandeen, *Roots of Fundamentalism*, 42.

28. Griffin, *Sermon, preached October 20, 1813*, 28. On millennial fervor among the New Divinity, see Kling, *Field of Divine Wonders*, 57–62; on millennialism in general, see Davidson, *Logic of Millennial Thought*; Bloch, *Visionary Republic*.

29. Griffin, *Sermon, preached October 20, 1813*, 31. See also Griffin, *Sermon preached September 14, 1826*, 24; Griffin, "Letter to the Rev. Dr. William Sprague," 359–60.

not only Griffin's first published sermon; it proved to be his best missionary sermon among those he delivered in the next three decades.³⁰ No other matched *Kingdom of Christ* for its clarity of expression, biblically rooted rationale for foreign missions, and indebtedness to Edwards's vision of world redemption. Griffin sensed its importance (or perhaps his own self-importance), for he sent a copy to John Ryland in England, who acknowledged receipt and queried whether Griffin was the same person at whose ordination "his excellent Tutor" Jonathan Edwards Jr. had delivered the sermon.³¹

Scholars have acknowledged that *Kingdom of Christ* was an important contribution to the rising interest in foreign missions but typically give it passing notice without a full examination of its contents.³² To be sure, it is not an original composition. In fact, *Kingdom of Christ* is essentially a distillation of Edwards's salient themes in the *History of Redemption* and *Concerning the End for Which God Created the World* (1765). It is, of course, impossible to confirm that Griffin had these works in hand when he composed the sermon; nevertheless, it reveals the extent to which Edwards's ideas and vocabulary permeated nineteenth-century Protestant culture. As an English reviewer noted, *History of Redemption* was "one of the most popular manuals of Calvinistic theology" in the nineteenth century.³³ To indicate Griffin's reliance on Edwards, I summarize Griffin's sermon (the numbers in parentheses are page numbers) and offer corresponding references to Edwards's works in the footnotes.³⁴

By introducing his sermon with a view to the "amazing purposes which God is carrying into execution" (3), Griffin mirrored Edwards's grand theme in the *History of Redemption*. Similarly, Griffin followed Edwards's reasoning for divine creation. God created out of God's very nature: "We must conceive an eternal propensity in the fountain of love to overflow, and fill with happiness numberless vessels fitted to receive it" (4).³⁵ The end of creation, as any orthodox Reformed theologian would

30. See Griffin, *Foreign Missions*; Griffin, *Sermon preached September 14, 1826*.

31. John Ryland to Edward D. Griffin, May 12, 1807, Gratz Collection. Edwards's sermon was *Duty of Ministers*.

32. Phillips, *Protestant America and the Pagan World*, 26; Chaney, *Birth of Missions in America*, 220.

33. Edwards W. Grinfield, *Nature and Extent of the Christian Dispensation* [. . .] (London, 1827), 427, quoted in Conforti, *Jonathan Edwards*, 48.

34. I cite from the reprint edition of Griffin, *Kingdom of Christ*, published by the Andover Society of Inquiry Respecting Missions.

35. For examples of Edwards's use of "propensity" (or "disposition," the word he uses more often), "fullness," and the "fountain" metaphor, see *WJE* 8:433–35, 438–42.

affirm and which Edwards uplifted, was "to enrich the universe with the knowledge of his glory, and to lay a foundation for a general confidence and delight in him.... The stupendous object which he contemplated was an immense and beautifully adjusted kingdom of holy and happy creatures, in which he should be acknowledged as the glorious head" (4).[36]

The fundamental significance Edwards attributed to God's redemption and his self-glorification was reiterated by Griffin, who, like Edwards, subordinated the doctrine of providence to that of redemption: "The whole plan of the world, including creation and providence, including every event from its beginning to the final judgment, was involved in the plan of redemption" (10).[37] The plan is one, yet its many parts "*are all designed to promote the glory of God*, though the *manner* cannot be explained" (11).[38] The means that God ordained to bring this about was through Jesus Christ, God's "viceregent," who acted as the "grand connecting bond between finite and infinite natures" (4–5). "All the works which God designed to produce throughout the universe, he delegated Christ to accomplish" (6).[39] God in Christ created and redeemed the earth; "*for* Christ the earth is also governed" (11). Under his government, "all things work together for good" (Rom 8:28); even "the revolution of empires, rebellions and wars, the councils of kings ... are all pressed into the service of Christ" (12). All that humans do—"secular employment, their social duties"—is subordinated to the kingdom and God's redemptive work (13).

Griffin then warms to the missionary challenge by turning to millennial themes that Edwards uplifted in *Humble Attempt*. A new age is approaching when "the everlasting gospel [Rev 14:6] shall be preached to every kindred, and tongue, and people.... Paradise will be restored"

---

36. On "end of creation," see Edwards, *Concerning the End for Which God Created the World*, in *WJE* 8, esp. 428–44; on "holy and happy," one of Edwards's favorite phrases, see *Humble Attempt*, *WJE* 5:338, 339, 365, 446.

37. According to Edwards, "All the decrees of God do some way or other belong to that eternal covenant of redemption that was between the Father and Son before the foundation of the world" (*WJE* 9:513; see also *WJE* 9:516 and Wilson, "Editor's Introduction," *WJE* 9:40–41).

38. In *Work of Redemption*, Edwards used two metaphors to describe the "many parts": rivers and streams that fed into the great providential ocean (*WJE* 9:517) and a building with its many constituent facets (ground preparation, materials, foundation, and superstructure), which, when completed with the top stone, demonstrates God's providential design of redemption (*WJE* 9:121–22).

39. Edwards, *WJE* 9: 130–32, 344–56.

(16).⁴⁰ But to reach this blessed state requires human effort, for human activity is the "established method of grace."⁴¹ Griffin exhorts his audience: "Awake, and generously expand your desire to encircle this benevolent and holy kingdom" (19). There is much to be done, for five-sixths of the world's population is dying in sin. Griffin moves Edwards's timetable forward: unlike previous generations that were content to pray, the present generation has been chosen to play "a conspicuous part in this blessed work" (20). "Great events appear to be struggling in their birth. . . . Men, warmed with apostolic zeal, have abandoned the comforts of civilized life, and are gone to the ends of the earth" to preach the gospel (20). To hasten the coming kingdom, more Christians should join their efforts and support the missionary cause (21).

Throughout *Kingdom of Christ*, Griffin's reliance on Edwards is unmistakable. In describing the unfolding of divine history in which human activity is crucial, he limns major themes in Edwards's works. Revivals and their extension into foreign missions are the glorious means by which God's work of redemption is accomplished.

EDWARDS IN NETTLETON: REVIVALS AT HOME

In 1812, Asahel Nettleton accepted a temporary appointment as an evangelist to the "waste places" (i.e., pastorless places) of eastern Connecticut. In the ensuing decade, he would become the New Divinity's greatest revivalist. Bennet Tyler, Nettleton's longtime associate and laudatory biographer, claimed (though it cannot be substantiated) that Nettleton was instrumental in the salvation of thirty thousand souls.⁴²

Nettleton was a product of the early New Divinity village revivals in New England. His conversion followed the paradigmatic New Divinity conversion narrative drawn largely from two of Edwards's works, *Faithful Narrative of the Surprising Work of God* (1737)—a work reprinted more than sixty times by the early nineteenth century—and his "Personal

40. On "paradise restored," see *Humble Attempt, WJE* 5:337.

41. According to Edwards, God's work of redemption "will be accomplished by means, by the preaching of the gospel, and the use of the ordinary means of grace" (*WJE* 9:459).

42. Tyler, *Memoir of Nettleton*, 17. According to Thornbury, *God Sent Revival*, twenty-five thousand is a more "conservative estimate" (233) but given the number of converts supplied in Tyler's *Nettleton and His Labours* and Smith's *Recollections of Nettleton*, even Thornbury's calculation seems high. A range of ten to fifteen thousand seems more reasonable.

Narrative," a brief account of his conversion written ca. 1740, first published in 1765, and frequently reissued in the late eighteenth and early nineteenth centuries. Although Edwards was indebted to his Puritan forebears' preparationist schemes or morphologies of conversion, he was not wholly reliant upon them. As he put it, "Some have gone too far towards directing the Spirit of the Lord, and marking out his footsteps for him, and limiting him to certain steps and methods."[43] Yet there were consistent themes to God's work of individual redemption, themes that reverberate throughout Nettleton's conversion narrative.

As a farm boy in rural Killingworth, Connecticut, Nettleton sat under the preaching of the New Divinity pastor Josiah Andrews.[44] At age seventeen, amid the outbreak of revival in Killingworth and surrounding areas in 1800—when, as Griffin observed, "I could stand at my doorstep in New Hartford . . . and number fifty or sixty congregations laid down in one field of divine wonders"—Nettleton was brought to saving faith.[45] Like any anxious sinner, he appropriated the standard means of grace. For ten tortuous months he "mourned in secret," imploring God out in the field and in the "closet," and yet "God seemed to pay no regard to his prayers." His problem: "He had not hated sin because it was committed against God, but had merely dreaded its consequences." He read the Bible. He pored over Edwards's *Faithful Narrative of the Surprising Work of God* and *Life of David Brainerd*, yet he experienced no breakthrough. He questioned the doctrines of divine sovereignty and election.

Eventually, in true New Divinity fashion, he came to realize the futility and sinfulness of his unregenerate doings: "He had been prompted by selfish motives. He saw that in all which he had done, he had not love to God, and no regard to his glory; but that he had been influenced solely by a desire to promote his own personal interest and happiness." Finally, after being seized by "an unusual tremor" during which the "horrors of mind were inexpressible" and thinking he was about to die, Nettleton "felt a calmness for which he knew not how to account." He thought he had lost all conviction, but then "a sweet peace pervaded his soul. The objects which had given him so much distress, he now contemplated with delight." Even so, for several days he did not consider himself to be saved. Not until he discovered that his views and feelings corresponded to those

---

43. Edwards, *WJE* 4:161.

44. For this paragraph and the paragraph that follows, see Tyler, *Memoir of Nettleton*, 17–30, 293 (Tyler quote).

45. Griffin, "Letter to the Rev. Dr. William Sprague," 360.

of others who had been converted to the Edwardsean way of salvation did he begin "to think it possible that he might have passed from death unto life." God had given Nettleton a new heart and a new taste for spiritual things. And so, first, "The character of God now appeared lovely." Then, "The Saviour was exceedingly precious; and the doctrines of grace, towards which he had felt such bitter opposition, he contemplated with delight." The months of Nettleton's spiritual travail, culminating in regeneration and conversion, confirmed in his mind the truth of New Divinity theology and gave him, according to Tyler, "a knowledge of the human heart which few possess."

Following the standard New Divinity educational route—college at Yale and pastoral preparation under a New Divinity pastor—Nettleton accepted an interim position as itinerant evangelist to eastern Connecticut. After outpourings of revival under his ministrations, Nettleton abandoned his earlier plan of becoming a foreign missionary. He had found the "field white unto harvest" in his own backyard. In the ensuing decade (1812–22), Nettleton experienced his greatest evangelistic success. Most of these years were spent in Connecticut, but he also visited New York (Saratoga County and Long Island), Rhode Island, and western Massachusetts—all regions with a significant orthodox Calvinist or New Divinity presence. In 1822, a severe bout with typhus forced Nettleton into semi-retirement. Though used as an instrument of scattered awakenings for the remainder of his life, his career as a full-time evangelist was finished.

Nettleton's extraordinary success as an awakener was largely indebted to selective application of Edwards's methods and message of revival. The New Divinity in general, and Nettleton in particular, followed Edwards's later more cautionary writings (e.g., *Religious Affections*) in conducting revivals and assessing their spiritual phenomena. Indeed, Nettleton was something of a control freak. At conference or inquiry meetings, which he perfected as a catalyst of revival, he insisted on complete quiet. As he put it, "God does not always speak *by words*."[46] He decried excessive conversation as indicative of spiritual pride and an impediment to the Spirit's work. To know God was to be still before God (Ps 46:10). "I love to talk to you," he told a group of inquirers, "you are so still. It looks as though the Spirit of God was here."[47] After counseling

---

46. Smith, *Recollections of Nettleton*, 135. Note: The emphasis in all subsequent quotes from Nettleton is his.

47. Tyler, *Memoir of Nettleton*, 145.

those under conviction, he advised them to leave the meeting quietly and deal with God alone. Crying out or bodily manifestations were met with removal from the meeting. On occasion, Nettleton preserved decorum by personally arranging placement of every chair in the conference room.

Behind this controlled environment were the hard lessons Edwards had learned from the Great Awakening and addressed subsequently in *Religious Affections*. These were lessons taken to heart by the New Divinity. By Griffin's reckoning, the "extravagances which took place in the days of Edwards and Whitefield put back revivals half a century."[48] No New Divinity minister would abide another James Davenport or other censorious itinerants whose rants and ravings during the Great Awakening both wreaked havoc with settled ministers and divided congregations. Davenport's and others' divide-and-conquer tactics, to which Edwards attributed the demise of the Great Awakening, were anathema to Nettleton, who, evangelizing in the very places Davenport had decimated, never conducted meetings without the express invitation and endorsement of the local pastor. Sane, sober, still, and orderly revivals—the Spirit worked within these New Divinity constraints.

Nettleton perceptively applied Edwards's insights to the dynamics of revival. He would typically visit established congregations where no extraordinary spiritual seriousness existed before his arrival and then urge weekly congregational concerts of prayer as a necessary prelude to the outpouring of divine showers, knowing that God "revives His work in the hearts of his own people" before "He awakens and converts sinners." Just as Edwards posited that the work of the Spirit ebbs and flows throughout history, so Nettleton claimed that "there is as really a season of harvest in the moral as in the natural world." At such propitious moments,

> The conversion of one sinner is often the means of awakening every member of the family, and the impulse is again felt through every kindred branch, and through the village and town, so one town may be the means of a revival in another, and that in another.... There is a crisis in the feelings of a people, which, if not improved [i.e., acted upon], the souls of that generation will not be gathered. In the season of a revival, more *may* be done—more *is* often done to secure the salvation of souls, in a few days, or weeks, than in years spent in preaching at other times.[49]

48. Griffin, *Sermon, preached September 2, 1827*, 15.
49. Tyler, *Memoir of Nettleton*, 296, 294–95; see also Nettleton, *Remains*, 309.

What happens on the large canvas of history also happens in the details of individual lives. The Spirit is poured out briefly for a sinner's eternal benefit and is then withdrawn: "The awakened sinner will not remain long in his present condition." Hence the need to repent immediately and respond to God's gracious offer of salvation. For some, however, "The sun has already passed the meridian." There are those who "have lost their day of grace." Once the Spirit has departed, they are lost for eternity.[50]

Nettleton was no match for the eloquence of Griffin, yet his simple, clear, and occasionally emotion-charged delivery had its desired effect. He preached the "hard sayings" of Calvinism (total depravity, human dependence, God's sovereignty, personal election, reprobation, divine grace, etc.), though modified by New Divinity "improvements"—doctrines that "did not *paralyze*, but greatly *promoted* the good work."[51] Nettleton emphasized "the duty of every sinner immediately to repent," yet he recognized that true repentance follows God's act of regeneration.[52] To assure sinners that they were still responsible for their condition, he distinguished between natural and moral ability ("The reason you will not come to Christ is not because you cannot, but because you will not").[53] To further cut out the props of excuses, Nettleton softened the "L" in the Calvinist "TULIP" (L = limited atonement).[54] He stressed the unlimited sufficiency of the atonement and portrayed God as the moral governor who "is disposed to do every thing in the best possible manner."[55] He did not dwell on this significant departure from traditional Calvinism but simply reiterated a view of the atonement that had become a New Divinity trademark.

50. Nettleton, *Remains*, 132, 21, 135.
51. Tyler, *Memoir of Nettleton*, 245.
52. Nettleton, *Remains*, 60; see also 352–58.
53. Nettleton, *Remains*, 122; see also 66–70, 116–27.
54. "TULIP" is an acronym for total depravity, unconditional election, limited atonement, irresistible grace, and perseverance of the saints.
55. Nettleton, *Remains*, 375, 295. For a summary of this view, see Kling, *Field of Divine Wonders*, 103–8. For selected primary sources, see Sweeney and Guelzo, *New England Theology*, 133–48.

CONCLUSION: EDWARDS IN A CONTESTED SECOND GREAT AWAKENING

Whether championing the cause of overseas missions, conducting a revival, or narrating the divine workings of God in the soul, proponents of the New Divinity movement stood tall in the long shadow of Edwards. From Edwards's corpus the New Divinity appropriated a vocabulary and theological framework to describe God's redemptive work in the grand scheme of history made evident by outpourings of revival at home and abroad. Griffin and Nettleton were emblematic of hundreds of New Divinity pastors and laypeople whose religious consciousness was shaped by Edwards, including the evangelist Charles Finney and the revivalist-theologian Nathaniel Taylor. To Nettleton and Griffin, however, Finney and Taylor betrayed Edwards's legacy. From the mid-1820s until his death, Nettleton spent much of his time and energy castigating the revival methods of Finney, the theological revisions of Taylor, and the New School Presbyterianism of his former revivalist colleague Lyman Beecher. Nettleton's correspondence reveals an indignant, defensive, and intransigent personality who likened his situation to that of Edwards and Brainerd. Just as they were "denounced in their day" for blowing "the trumpet of alarm," he too he had been denounced for defending "true" revivals of religion.[56] Reacting to what he considered Finney's out-of-control revivals, Nettleton sounded Edwards's alarm: "*False affections often rise far higher than those that are genuine.* . . . Feelings which are not founded on *correct* theology cannot be *right*; they must *necessarily* be spurious, or merely animal."[57] As for Taylor and Beecher, they had become "the guilty cause of all the present divisions in the New England & Presbyterian churches."[58]

For his part, Griffin joined in the publication fray by turning out works against Finney's new measures and Taylor's New Haven theology. He argued that Taylor mistakenly maintained "a liberty of will" and "everywhere denies divine efficiency" by telling sinners "they may and can succeed."[59] Finney besmirched "the honour of revivals and the salvation of men" by introducing the anxious seat and allowing "vulgar expressions"

---

56. Nettleton to Plumer, March 3, 1836, Plumer Papers.
57. Asahel Nettleton, quoted in Tyler, *Nettleton and His Labours*, 360, 362.
58. Nettleton to Plumer, September 5, 1838, Plumer Papers.
59. Griffin, *Causal Power*, 9; Griffin, *Doctrine of Divine Efficiency*, 43, 45.

of converts and public prayers by females in "promiscuous assemblies."[60] The new measures and new theology were bedfellows; they placed their adherents "within the pale of another denomination . . . between us and them as intervenes between Presbyterians and Methodists."[61]

"*If genuine religion is not found in revivals,*" wrote Nettleton, "*I have no evidence that it exists in the world.*"[62] All Edwardseans—be they Griffin and Nettleton or Taylor and Finney—would heartily agree. Contentions persisted over the correct means to and theological understanding of genuine religion. Edwards was *in* the Second Great Awakening of Griffin, Nettleton, and other like-minded New Divinity adherents. But Edwards was also *in* the revivals of their Edwardsean foes—proof enough that God's work of redemption in revivals of religion would remain at the core of Edwards's disputed legacy.

60. Griffin, *Letter to the Rev. Ansel D. Eddy*, 9, 6, 7.
61. Griffin, *Letter to a Friend*.
62. Nettleton, *Temperance and Revivals*, 2.

6

The New Divinity and the Origins of the American Board of Commissioners for Foreign Missions

THE THEOLOGICAL INFLUENCE OF the New Divinity in the formation and character of the American Board of Commissioners for Foreign Missions (ABCFM) is uncontested among scholars of American religious history and missions. Since the mid-nineteenth century, both partisans of missions and nearly all scholarly observers have attributed the origins of the modern American Protestant missionary spirit to the writings of Jonathan Edwards and his self-appointed heirs, those Congregational ministers who came to be called New Divinity men.[1] Edwards proposed a theology of cosmic redemption and supplied the exemplary missionary model in *Life of David Brainerd* (1749), his most popular and most frequently reprinted work.[2] Samuel Hopkins then furnished a theological rationale for missions by extending Edwards's aesthetic concept of a disinterested love to Being in general into a practical one of self-denial for the greater glory of God's kingdom and the betterment of humankind.

1. On the influence of the New Divinity generally and Samuel Hopkins in particular on the American foreign missionary movement, see Park, *Memoir of Nathanael Emmons*, 212; Foster, *Genetic History*, 129; Elsbree, *Rise of the Missionary Spirit*; Lowe, "First American Foreign Missionaries," chaps. 2–3; Sweet, *Religion in the Development of American Culture*, 231; Beaver, "Missionary Motivation," 121–26; Phillips, *Protestant America and the Pagan World*, chap. 1; Chaney, *Birth of Missions in America*, 74–84, 188–89, 192–95, 269–74; Conforti, *Samuel Hopkins*, 157–58; McCoy, "Women of the ABCFM," 62–82; McCoy, 'Reason for a Hope,' 175–92; Robert, *American Women in Mission*, 3–10.

2. Conforti, "David Brainerd," 309–29; Conforti, *Jonathan Edwards*, chap. 3.

In the early 1800s, the missionary spirit resonated among youthful converts in New Divinity–led revivals. One of those converts, Samuel J. Mills Jr., was convinced of his divine call to enter the foreign mission field. While enrolled at Williams College in Williamstown, Massachusetts, in the summer of 1806, he and four other students met in a grove of trees to pray for divine guidance and to discuss their religious faith and calling. During an afternoon rainstorm, Mills and the others sought refuge under a haystack. Undeterred, they continued their prayer meeting and consecrated their lives to overseas missions. This incident, later publicized as the Haystack Prayer Meeting and hailed as "the Antioch of our western hemisphere" by the ABCFM's corresponding secretary Rufus Anderson,[3] became the pivotal event in the launching of American Protestantism's foreign missionary movement. Mills and several comrades carried their vision from Williams to Andover Theological Seminary, where they created a more formal organization that eventually led to the establishment of the ABCFM in 1810. Two years later, five ABCFM missionaries—Adoniram Judson Jr., Samuel Nott, Samuel Newell, Luther Rice, and Gordon Hall—set sail for India, accompanied by three wives—Ann Hasseltine Judson, Rosanne Peck Nott, and Harriet Atwood Newell.

Such are the well-known developments surrounding the beginning of the American Protestant foreign missionary enterprise.[4] It was predominantly a New England Congregational effort, though as early as 1812 the Board elected Philadelphia and New York Presbyterian representatives to its corporation and in 1826 the United Foreign Missionary Society (representing Presbyterian and Reformed Dutch bodies) merged with the Board. And it was largely New Divinity in origins—in more ways than is commonly recognized.

While the creation of the ABCFM is largely attributed to the activism of Mills and his companions and to the ideas of Edwards and Hopkins, several critical developments are missing in this story. First, neither Edwards nor Hopkins provided an explicit theological rationale for overseas missions. To be sure, they provided the theological underpinnings for the possibility of foreign missions, but both must be understood as transitional figures. As Andrew Walls observes, Edwards "operated before the movement emerged in the English-speaking world as a distinct element

---

3. Quoted in Phillips, *Protestant America and the Pagan World*, 319.

4. Standard histories of the ABCFM include Tracy, *History of the American Board*; [Anderson], *Memorial Volume*; Strong, *Story of the American Board*; Goodsell, *You Shall Be My Witnesses*; Phillips, *Protestant America and the Pagan World*.

in Protestant consciousness."[5] And although Hopkins's correspondence attests that he was clearly aware of the missionary movement in England, he never lived to see the reality of the movement in America. A succeeding generation of Edwardseans—the subjects of this essay—extended and applied the implicit missionary theology of Edwards and Hopkins into an explicit theological justification for the creation of the ABCFM.

A second crucial development missing in accounts of the formation of the ABCFM is the impact of the New Divinity as a dominant cultural force among New England Calvinists. One cannot fully appreciate the contribution of Mills and other important players to the burgeoning missionary movement without recognizing that the ABCFM was but one instance of an expansive social and institutional network promulgating Edwardsean theology. Recent scholarship has demonstrated convincingly that the Edwardsean tradition flourished in the first three decades of the nineteenth century, to the point where, in the words of Douglas Sweeney, "It would not be inappropriate to speak of an Edwardsian enculturation of Calvinist New England."[6]

In this respect, we may view the New Divinity as a widespread movement insofar as it promoted an ideology (that is, a theology) and directed that ideology into organizations bent on influencing the nature of society. William Bentley, the Unitarian gadfly in Salem, Massachusetts, could not stomach Baptist exuberance, but he had an even greater antipathy to the New Divinity. When a Baptist minister observed that "Hopkinsianism [was] strongly associated with power," it was probably one of the few occasions that Bentley agreed with anything a Baptist said.[7]

I argue in this essay that the ABCFM—though officially devoid of creedal affirmations[8]—was a New Divinity creation, rooted in New Divinity theology, inspired by New Divinity revivals, and staffed by a well-established New Divinity social and institutional network. In making this claim, I hope to establish a working premise by which to comprehend some of the most compelling and complex issues raised by the ABCFM

5. Walls, "Missions and Historical Memory," 257.

6. Sweeney, *Nathaniel Taylor*, 40 (see also 10, 26, 142). Also see Sweeney, "Edwards and His Mantle," 114–15nn30, 31.

7. Bentley, *Diary of William Bentley*, 3:364.

8. In none of the fourteen articles of the Constitution is there any reference to doctrine or polity. According to Article 2, the object of the Board was "to devise, adopt, and prosecute, ways and means for propagating the gospel among those, who are destitute of the knowledge of Christianity." See American Board of Commissioners for Foreign Missions, *First Ten Annual Reports*, 11.

enterprise. Such issues include those of missionary motivation, the transmission of piety and theology on the mission field,[9] the impact of the Board's missionary enterprise on American culture,[10] and the creation of a systematic theology of missions,[11] to name but a few. My goal is to establish a context for examining the Board's activities, both at home and abroad, by charting the theological and social influences that brought the Board into being and shaped its early history. I begin with some general observations about the political, religious, and social climate favorable to the development of the foreign missionary enterprise. Second, I offer a cursory view of New Divinity theology, focusing on emphases that supported the universal spread of the gospel. Finally, I describe some of the principal ways in which the New Divinity manifested itself socially and institutionally by attending to the specific circumstances leading up to the formation of the ABCFM.

THE FOREIGN MISSIONARY CONTEXT

The creation of the American Board represents the convergence of three significant developments in American religious life. Two were of recent origins, while the other dated from the mid-eighteenth century. First, the Board's creation is evidence of a radical shift in religious authority occurring throughout the Western world between 1750 and 1850, signaled by the breaking apart of the *corpus christianum*. In the United States the dissolution of the unity of church, state, and society accelerated in the years following the American Revolution. As state-sponsored religion crumbled under the weight of First Amendment sentiments, Americans fashioned an alternative vision of religion's place in the social order that enabled denominational institutions and voluntary societies to flourish. Although Congregationalists in Massachusetts and Connecticut had long resisted severing official church-state ties, even amid bitter disputes over disestablishment,[12] they were busy developing new strategies and creat-

---

9. A fine case study is McCoy, "Women of the ABCFM Oregon Mission"; McCoy, "Edwardsean Spirituality and the Nez Perce."

10. See Andrew, *Rebuilding the Christian Commonwealth*.

11. See Chaney, *Birth of Missions in America*; Corr, "'The Field is the World.'"

12. The term "disestablishment" comes from the "establishment clause" in the U.S. Constitution, First Amendment—"Congress shall make no law respecting an establishment of religion"—meaning that the federal government cannot establish an official religion or unduly favor one religion over another.

ing voluntary institutional bodies to address specific religious concerns. In 1812, the year the ABCFM was legally incorporated, Boston alone had more than thirty benevolent, charitable, and religious societies.[13]

Second, although the American Board owed its structure to this shift in religious authority, it owed its outlook—one of unabashed millennial optimism—to a dramatic change in evangelical self-understanding. In 1790 no one could have predicted that evangelicals would become a cultural shaping force in America. In the aftermath of the American Revolution, the infant nation was beset by a host of political, social, economic, and religious ills that threatened its fragile health. Because Americans faced clear-cut choices over fundamental issues, competing political and religious groups engaged in a frenzy of activity for the hearts and minds of the people. To paraphrase Carl Becker, the Revolution settled the issue of home rule, but it remained for future generations to determine who would rule at home. A sense of urgency, born of the conviction that they lived in an era of national and religious crisis, stirred the New Divinity men (and other evangelicals as well) to fill the social vacuum and shape the course of history according to what they believed was God's design. That vacuum was soon filled by revivals whose spiritual energies were channeled into numerous voluntary societies (such as the ABCFM) to provide what Donald Mathews in his now classic essay called "an organizing process."[14] By 1810, after nearly two decades of revivals, evangelicals faced the future with considerably more confidence than they had in 1790. "The long expected day is approaching," declared the Board in its first address to the public, "a new scene, with us, is now opening.... The Lord is shaking the nations ... and unprecedented exertions are making for the spread of divine knowledge, and the conversion of nations."[15]

Third, the New Divinity and the ABCFM are appropriately understood as part of a larger transatlantic evangelical movement encompassing the English-speaking world since the eighteenth century.[16] Calvinist evangelicals had exchanged thousands of personal letters, pamphlets, sermons, tracts, and magazines to create the mid-eighteenth-century

13. Andrew, *Rebuilding the Christian Commonwealth*, 18. See also Field, *Crisis of the Standing Order*, chaps. 4–5. On the emergence of voluntary religious institutions, see Sassi, *Republic of Righteousness*, 136–44, 163–84.

14. Mathews, "Second Great Awakening," 23–43.

15. American Board of Commissioners for Foreign Missions, *First Ten Annual Reports*, 13, 14.

16. For a discussion and application of wide-ranging expressions of evangelicalism, see Noll et al., *Evangelicalism*.

transatlantic revival.[17] Although that exchange slowed from 1775 to 1825, the continuing transatlantic transfer of ideas and information fueled Anglo-American missions. For example, the English Baptist Calvinist and missionary advocate John Ryland corresponded with the American Edwardsean Edward Dorr Griffin. In an 1807 letter to Griffin, Ryland acknowledges receipt of a packet from Griffin that included a letter with queries to Andrew Fuller, the Baptist theologian and first secretary of the Baptist Missionary Society, adding that he has enclosed Fuller's reply. Ryland also observes that he carried on a two-decade correspondence with Jonathan Edwards Jr. (the younger) and expresses his "peculiarly high regard" for Edwards and "his venerable Father." He then thanks Griffin for his 1805 *Missionary Sermon on the Kingdom of Christ* and closes by giving his respects to Samuel Miller, the American Presbyterian minister and educator. This one letter alone gives the impression of a lively transatlantic correspondence among Calvinist evangelicals.[18]

Moreover, it is well known that Edwards's thinking was deeply influenced by British thinkers and, in turn, that his *Life of David Brainerd* and other theological treatises initially had a more receptive audience abroad than in America. Indeed, his *Life of David Brainerd* and his *Humble Attempt*, with its call for a "united concert of prayer," directly inspired England's foray into overseas missions.[19] As Samuel Hopkins wrote in a letter to Andrew Fuller, he was "pleased to hear that Edwardean principles are gaining ground" and that William Carey, England's leading missionary light, had "imbibed these principles."[20]

For their part, American evangelicals adopted British organizational models, borrowed freely and extensively from their missionary publications, incorporated British eschatological speculations into their writings, and circulated sermons from their British counterparts, including those that may bear directly on the origins of the ABCFM.[21] For example, the Reverend Kiah Bayley, writing to the secretaries of the American Board in 1854, recalled,

---

17. O'Brien, "Transatlantic Community of Saints," 811–32; O'Brien, "Eighteenth-Century Publishing Networks," 38–57.
18. John Ryland to Edward Dorr Griffin, 12 May 1807, Gratz Collection.
19. van den Berg, *Constrained by Jesus' Love*, 92–93, 123; Rooy, *Theology of Missions*, 292–93; O'Brien, "Transatlantic Community of Saints," 831; Conforti, *Jonathan Edwards*, 68–69; Davies, "Jonathan Edwards," 60.
20. Samuel Hopkins, quoted in Lowe, "First American Foreign Missionaries," 2.
21. See Foster, *Errand of Mercy*, chaps. 5–6.

A short time before my ordination at Newcastle, Maine, in 1797, the Rev. Alexander McLean, of Bristol, had received from his friends in Scotland the sermons delivered in London by Dr. Haweis and others at the formation of the London Missionary Society. He was charmed with them, and lent them to me. I took the pamphlet to my wife, who was then in Newburyport, and she lent it to her friends, who read it with great avidity. A subscription paper was immediately issued, and a printer engaged. The work was soon in circulation. Dr. Samuel Spring and others in Newburyport caught the sacred flame. I know not that there was any other reprint of those sermons in America. Thus I have pointed out one little rill from which your Society rose. There were others, no doubt, but I believe this was the leader. *The sermons preached in London were sent to Scotland to Maine, and from Maine to Newburyport.*[22]

Bayley's account is but one instance of the sort of communication that, from the beginning of the eighteenth century, helped to link English and American evangelicalism—nationalistic interests of the early nineteenth century notwithstanding. During its initial organizational stage, at a time when diplomatic relations between the United States and England had degenerated to the breaking point, the ABCFM sent Adoniram Judson to England in 1810 to inquire about the willingness of the London Missionary Society to co-sponsor an American mission party to India.

With the actual outbreak of the War of 1812—the very year that the ABCFM sent out its first missionaries—Congregational clergy such as the Reverend Elijah Parish, a New Divinity minister in Byfield, Massachusetts, pled for peace between the "two Englands." Americans and the British transcended political animosities on the basis of a shared cultural background that included evangelical beliefs and attitudes. As Parish noted, "Like a parent and a child, they have united together to promote the glorious gospel. Shall they not, like the two luminaries of heaven, continue to aid each other in giving light and glory to the world?"[23] Not all evangelicals shared Parish's antiwar, Anglophile sentiments. Methodists and Baptists branded him a "young Judas,"[24] but even they reaffirmed

---

22. Rev. Kiah Bayley, quoted in [Anderson], *Memorial Volume*, 44–45, emphasis added.

23. Elijah Parish, *A Sermon [. . .] before the Society for the Propagation of the Gospel Among the Indians and Others in North-America*, 25, quoted in Phillips, *Protestant America and the Pagan World*, 12.

24. Quoted in Gribbin, *Churches Militant*, 25.

their evangelical ties after the war by engaging in cooperative missionary endeavors with their English brethren.[25] According to the British scholar David Bebbington, these nineteenth-century American and British evangelicals shared four primary beliefs and attitudes. Bebbington describes them as conversionism—a belief in the necessity of the new birth; activism—an individual or corporate emphasis on religious duties and social involvement; biblicism—a stress on the Bible alone as the source of religious authority; and crucicentrism—an emphasis on the redeeming work of Christ.[26] By their application of these characteristics in a particular scheme, the New Divinity men initiated America's first foreign missionary venture.

A MISSIONARY THEOLOGY

In the aftermath of the Great Awakening, the most visible party to emerge within New England Congregationalism was the Edwardseans or the "New Divinity." Criticized as theological innovators, the New Divinity men identified themselves as Calvinists and the rightful heirs of the Puritan tradition who were seeking to revive or "improve" traditional Calvinist doctrines, to make them "consistent" in meeting the intellectual challenges of their day. By the 1790s, critics had had a field day with the provocative theological positions of Samuel Hopkins (that one must be willing to be damned for the greater glory of God) and Nathanael Emmons (that the saved in heaven should rejoice in God's just condemnation of the unrepentant in hell).

Yet there was another side to the New Divinity, a moderate side, which defined the basic contours of their theology. Despite a relative diversity of thought that occasioned family feuds, the New Divinity men agreed upon what Leonard Woods called "the grand principles" of Edwardseanism.[27] Although detractors accused them of fruitless metaphysical speculation, the Edwardseans put these principles to work in reviving the spiritually "stupid" and evangelizing the "benighted heathen." To a large extent, their overall effort represented a Reformed response to the Enlightenment critique that God's sovereignty and human freedom are

---

25. American Baptists created their own foreign missionary society in 1814, the Methodists in 1819.

26. See Bebbington, *Evangelicalism in Modern Britain*, 2–17; Bebbington, "Introduction," 6.

27. Woods, *History of the Andover Theological Seminary*, 39.

incompatible and that truly virtuous behavior required little more than the inculcation of moral teaching.

Two basic doctrines formulated for evangelistic purposes defined the Edwardseans' theological agenda. First, they embraced Edwards's teaching on the will. In *Freedom of the Will* (1754), Edwards responded to critics (Arminians and enlightened rationalists) who questioned why God holds naturally depraved sinners responsible for a condition that they have no power to change. He argued that humans were both free and determined, reconciling this apparent contradiction by distinguishing between the natural ability and the moral ability to obey God. Many aspects of life, reasoned Edwards, are governed by natural necessity. Such necessity refers to actual physical hindrances or conditions, which, no matter what we may wish, are out of our control and for which we cannot be held responsible. For example, someone ordered to move a mountain cannot be held responsible for not carrying out the impossible. Neither can a crippled girl be accountable for her inability to walk. In the world of nature, physical limitations preclude a person's will from affecting the outcome.

In another area of human experience, however, one's moral ability does affect the outcome and, indeed, inclines people to act in certain ways for which they were held accountable. According to Edwards, the crippled girl could not be held accountable for her inability to walk, but a healthy girl was entirely accountable for her refusal to walk. Nothing but, say, stubbornness prevented her from walking. Such an inclination (or disinclination) was entirely voluntary and prompted by the will. The girl could choose, but she was not free to choose *what* she chose. Humans thus had freedom, but because sin had so blighted moral agency, their freedom always led to wrong choices and sinful behavior. As the New Divinity pastor Charles Backus put it, "The unregenerate are not under the same kind of inability of loving and serving God, as a deaf man is of hearing sounds, or as a blind man is of discerning colors; but their inability arises from a heart which is opposed both to the law and the gospel."[28] In making these distinctions, the goal was to hold the unsaved responsible for their condition—and so arouse them out of their spiritual lethargy. Original sin had not eradicated the human capacity to obey divine commands but had only disoriented the human will and affections so that the

---

28. Backus, *Scripture Doctrine of Regeneration*, 20.

sinner no longer desired what was right. Humans had freedom, but that freedom inevitably led to wrong choices and sinful behavior.

A second New Divinity theological view derived from Edwards was the insistence on immediate repentance. God demanded "the immediate duty of sinners, to hear the voice of Christ, and comply with his gracious proposals," stated one Edwardsean minister.[29] God never asked the impossible, for God gave to sinners the natural ability to obey. Only their obdurate, incorrigible, but voluntary will kept them from carrying out their duties. To passively wait and do nothing about one's condition was tantamount to committing spiritual suicide.

To advance the missionary cause, the New Divinity also adopted Edwards's view of providential history. In *An Humble Attempt to Promote [. . .] Union Among God's People* (1747) and in *A History of the Work of Redemption* (published posthumously in 1774), Edwards proposed that the spiritual awakenings in Europe, Great Britain, America, and elsewhere portended the dawn of the millennium. This new age would arrive not through cataclysmic events (as earlier interpreters proposed) but through natural means by the work of God's Spirit poured out in Christian teaching, preaching, and religious activity. According to this optimistic post-millennial view, the world was gradually improving, setting the stage for Christ's return. Christian activity hastened the coming of the Lord, for Christians who participated in missionary activity played a divinely ordained role in ushering in the coming kingdom of Christ. Edwards's millennial views thus linked revivalism and missions in a providential scheme.

Working within Edwards's general theological framework, the New Divinity restated and reiterated his views, and at other times they revised and extended them. Whatever the case, by the 1790s, as the English launched their first missionary venture and as "great and remarkable" New Divinity revivals spread throughout New England, the New Divinity had at its disposal a well-stocked arsenal of effective evangelical weapons. Wielded initially in the battle for souls on the home front,[30] they were soon aimed at the distant shores of foreign lands. In particular, the New Divinity advanced the missionary cause under the banner of five theological convictions. To be sure, these convictions reflected an emerging theological consensus among Anglo-American evangelicals,

---

29. Washburn, *Sermons on Practical Subjects*, 299.
30. See Guelzo, *Edwards on the Will*, chap. 4; Kling, *Field of Divine Wonders*, chap. 3.

yet at the same time the New Divinity affirmed these convictions while working within the somewhat provincial constraints of New England theological discourse.

First, the New Divinity insisted on the absolute necessity of the new birth. This biblically rooted idea became the dominant motif of the eighteenth-century Anglo-American evangelical revival and, subsequently, the trademark of all evangelicals, including the New Divinity. An outward profession of faith or baptism was not deemed sufficient proof of one's Christian status; rather, the inner, palpable work of the Holy Spirit had to be confirmed. Christianity became a matter of the heart, validated by a visible, perceivable experience. In addition, like other eighteenth-century evangelicals, the New Divinity men severed the experience of the new birth from belonging to a particular community. Their conception of the new birth modified (if not repudiated) traditional Puritan notions of a civil or corporate sense of covenant theology. Consequently, this re-envisioning of the Christian community—from a nation that itself was elect to a nation of elect individuals—enabled the Edwardseans to think less parochially, less in terms of America's divine election, and more in terms of God's providential designs for the whole world.[31] No longer was a gathered people buffered from the Almighty through corporate covenants with God. "External covenant relations" of a nation or church, insisted a New Divinity minister, "will prepare no one for heaven."[32] There was no refuge in solidarity—except for the church as the collective expression of the visible saints—for what ultimately mattered was the solitary soul's direct encounter with God.

Although the New Divinity deconstructed the national covenant, by the early nineteenth century they asserted that America (read: New England) was providentially favored to carry the gospel overseas. Theirs was a spiritual noblesse oblige linked inextricably to a developing American nationalism wherein God raised up the United States as a beacon of gospel light to the world. In its 1811 "Address to the Christian Public," the Board noted that missionary opportunities were open to all nations, "but to no nation is it more inviting, than to the people of New England" since

31. See Perry, "American Board of Commissioners," 378–79; Noll, *One Nation under God?*, 49–51; Valeri, "New Divinity," 741–69; Grasso, *Speaking Aristocracy*, 66–85, 128–42; Sassi, *Republic of Righteousness*, 34–46.

32. Strong, *Sermon, delivered at the Consecration*, 11. To be sure, the New Divinity expressed a certain ambivalence regarding the body politic, for while Edwardseans labored to save individual souls, they expected that the sum of regenerate individuals would save the collective soul of the nation.

"no nation ever experienced the blessings of the Christian religion more evidently and uniformly."[33]

The admixture of this enlarged sense of obligation and the necessity of the new birth became a potent prescription for global missions. With a vision of the whole world and an individual conception of the Christian faith, evangelicals divided the world into heathen and Christian without regard to social status or geographic residence. To describe this circumstance, the New Divinity relied upon the vocabulary of Enlightenment science. Just as universal, scientific "laws" control the universe, so universal Christian laws control the human race. "The laws of Christianity are suited to govern mankind of every nation and climate," asserted Leonard Woods in his 1812 ordination sermon for the ABCFM's first missionaries. "These laws rest on general principles, and extend equally to the whole human race. The corruptions which they require us to subdue are found in every child of Adam."[34] In a similar vein, in his 1816 sermon before the ABCFM, Henry Davis, the New Divinity president of Middlebury College, noted that all peoples are "members of the same family; as candidates for the same immortality; and to be saved, if saved at all, with the same everlasting salvation."[35] From this perspective, a privileged New Englander who had been baptized, attended worship, and lived an upright life was no better off eternally than the "millions groveling in ignorance, in sottishness and pollution."[36] As historians of missions have observed, the spiritual equality of all unregenerate peoples—at home and abroad—had profound missionary consequences.[37]

If then all were unregenerate and in need of salvation, how would they hear? A second feature of New Divinity theology wedded to the universal spread of the gospel was an emphasis on the "means of grace" or "means of salvation." The quintessential defense of the use of means was, of course, William Carey's famous plea for foreign missions, *An Enquiry into the Obligations of Christians to Use Means for the Conversion*

---

33. American Board of Commissioners for Foreign Missions, *First Ten Annual Reports*, 28, 29. See also Chaney, *Birth of Missions in America*, 187; Hutchison, *Errand to the World*, 44–45.

34. Woods, *Sermon, delivered at the Tabernacle*, 262.

35. Davis, *Sermon, delivered before the American Board*, 24.

36. Davis, *Sermon, delivered before the American Board*, 24.

37. Walls, "Evangelical Revival," 310; van den Berg, *Constrained by Jesus' Love*, 84–86. Rooy traces this idea back to seventeenth-century Puritanism, noting that "all men, whether the lawyers at Grey's Inn or the Indians in America, were alike." Rooy, *Theology of Missions*, 314.

of Heathens (1792). In this broadside aimed at answering antimission hyper-Calvinists, Carey urged Christians to abandon fatalistic notions of God's sovereignty and argued that the Great Commission (Matt 28:19–20) applied as much to Christians in his day as it did to first-century disciples. Carey himself had been influenced (at least indirectly) by the efforts of Edwards to reconcile the doctrine of divine sovereignty with human responsibility.[38]

The New Divinity engagement with this issue—initially in the context of revivalism at home rather than mission activity abroad—represented a response to Old Calvinist emphases on preparation. The New Divinity typically referred to the means of grace as "unregenerate doings," for in a depraved condition no one could truly please God. Moreover, renouncing evil habits, attending divine worship, and reading Scripture—making apparent progress in the faith—only worsened, not bettered, one's sinful state by making the impenitent all the more culpable. That was precisely the point. An attention to means demonstrated how far one fell short of the glory of God. The transition from an unregenerate to a regenerate state was neither a growth experience nor "a gradual change of reason which triumphs over passions and appetites," for there was "an essential" difference between the two.[39] Thus sinners were instructed to exhaust all human effort, repent immediately, and leave it to God to regenerate instantaneously.

It was out of this intramural debate with fellow Calvinists that the New Divinity appealed to the use of means in missionary outreach. Always quick to assert that "the day of miracles is past," the Edwardseans looked to secondary, natural means to win the heathen to Christ. In his 1818 sermon delivered at the annual meeting of the ABCFM, Samuel Spring affirmed that "God has given us the means of instruction" through ministers of the gospel, and that "means and ends are closely connected in the course of divine administration."[40] Although there was no necessary connection between the use of means and conversion, the use of means was God's "ordinary" way of giving renewing grace. Make no mistake, "God is the author of salvation . . . the efficient cause of regeneration." And yet, Spring continued, God "prepares the way for the salvation of sinners, by his ministers, his missionaries, or agents. God does not

---

38. van den Berg, *Constrained by Jesus' Love*, 126–27; Orr, *Eager Feet*, 89.
39. Griffin, *Series of Lectures*, 114; Backus, *Scripture Doctrine of Regeneration*, 65.
40. Spring, *Sermon, preached at New Haven*, 6.

operate alone."[41] The missionary armed with Scripture—the "grand instrument of converting the world"—co-labored with God.[42]

A third buttress to a missionary theology emerged from the New Divinity's most striking theological innovation, the advocacy of Christ's unlimited atonement. According to Dortian "five-point Calvinism," the merits of Christ's death did not extend to all of humanity but only to those whom God pleased to predestine to eternal life. However, in an effort to uphold moral accountability and to assure sinners that "whosoever will may come," New Divinity theologians rejected what Nathanael Emmons mocked as Calvinism's "darling doctrine of a limited atonement."[43] They reversed the emphases in the traditional Reformed understanding of the sufficiency, design, and effectiveness of the atonement. The New Divinity stressed the unlimited sufficiency of the atonement (Christ's death was sufficient to save each and every sinner; salvation was freely offered to all) and de-emphasized the limited design of the atonement (Christ's death was designed to save only God's elect or chosen people). "This great atonement," assured Leonard Woods, "is as sufficient for Asiatics and Africans, as for us.... The mercy of God is an ocean absolutely exhaustless." Christians "are not straightened in God," but they "have a warrant from God to strive for the salvation of the whole world."[44] In sermons and systematic treatises, the New Divinity emphasized repeatedly that the atonement was, in the words of Samuel J. Mills Sr., "sufficient for the whole world—offered indiscriminately to all."[45]

The fourth and most memorable New Divinity theological contribution to missionary motivation was derived from the phrase that made Samuel Hopkins famous—"disinterested benevolence." The term itself was not unique to Hopkins or to Edwards but was in currency among British moral philosophers and employed in a wider discussion of the

---

41. Spring, *Sermon, preached at New Haven*, 6–7.

42. Griffin, *Series of Lectures*, 173.

43. Emmons, "Two Sermons," 132. In other parts of the English-speaking world, missions-minded moderate Calvinists, such as the Independent Edward Williams, made similar efforts to reconcile divine sovereignty with human responsibility, though they retained the doctrine of a limited atonement. According to Stuart Piggin, Williams "relegated to *adiaphora* particular election and limited atonement and claimed that while, in effect, Christ's death was a surety only for the elect, it justified, even demanded, the universal invitation to sinners to come to God, because it paid the Eternal Judge a price sufficient for all men." Piggin, *Making Evangelical Missionaries*, 83.

44. Woods, *Sermon, delivered at the Tabernacle*, 260.

45. Mills, "Religious Sentiments of Christ," 8.

nature of "true virtue."[46] Edwards equated true virtue with the condition of the regenerate and defined it as a love or "benevolence to Being in general."[47] True Christians are given a new disposition (or "taste" or "relish") for God and all things that God has brought into existence, and, consequently, they have a love of "being in general." There is no private or selfish interest involved; rather, God is loved, adored, and worshiped for who and what God is. What Edwards proposed was an aesthetic, beatific vision that Hopkins found incomplete and in need of "improvement."

In a very real way, Hopkins brought Edwards back to earth by locating true virtue in social behavior, in an ethic, not an aesthetic, of disinterested benevolence. Whereas Edwards saw true virtue culminating in a holy consciousness, Hopkins viewed it as culminating in holy action. In the words of Mark Noll, "What was for Edwards an aesthetic principle with ethical implications became for Hopkins a practical principle with aesthetic connotations."[48] True Christians, then, expressed themselves in unselfish acts of love and mercy (even in a willingness to die and be damned) in order to bring glory to God and further God's kingdom. And what could be more unselfish than leaving the comforts of civilization for the hardships of foreign missionary service? Whether expressed as duty, benevolence, or a "pure and holy love," the concept of disinterested benevolence moved those who embraced it to action. When joined to spiritual revival, it set off an explosion of vast human energy, both at home and abroad.

Almost without fail, every sermon, discourse, or tract that addressed the subject of missions dealt with the theme of disinterested benevolence, either explicitly or implicitly. I will cite two examples. Addressing the ABCFM in 1814, the Reverend James Richards, an Edwardsean pastor of Newark's First Presbyterian Church, cited the apostle Paul as an exemplary missionary, "who did not seek his own glory in this work . . . but the glory of God."[49] Richards then moved from this traditional Westminster-sounding confessional language to Hopkinsian phraseology, noting that some missions have been undertaken with the selfish motive of adding numbers to a church or "a wreath to the crown of individual talent." But God took no delight in such sacrifices:

46. For a helpful discussion of the wider context, see Conforti, *Samuel Hopkins*, chap. 7.
47. Edwards, *WJE*, 8:540.
48. Noll, *America's God*, 274.
49. Richards, *Spirit of Paul*, 16, 17.

Will he delight in us, unless we delight in his cause, abstracted from our own private views and interests? He is a God of love, and has made a spirit of disinterested affection the spring of all acceptable duty. It is this alone which can elevate us to the purity and dignity of the ancient churches, and give us a zeal for the spread of the gospel, sincere and permanent as theirs.[50]

For Levi Parsons, the expression of disinterested benevolence approached martyrdom. Following his graduation from Andover Theological Seminary and prior to his departure as the ABCFM's first missionary to Palestine, he addressed the seminary's Society of Inquiry on the Subject of Missions. "True religion," he declared,

implies a disposition to forsake Father and Mother, Friends and Country for Christ. Every devoted Christian will enquire, not where he can enjoy the most ease, create the most trouble, obtain the most wealth, or honor, but where he can most successfully labor in the cause of Christ & promote the salvation of men Better, my brethren, wear out and die in three years, than live forty years in slothfulness.[51]

Finally, the origins of the ABCFM are inconceivable without the Edwardseans' embrace of millennial fervor. Drawing from an Anglo-American tradition of millennial speculation, evangelicals of the late eighteenth and early nineteenth centuries were, to borrow Ernest Sandeen's felicitous phrase, "drunk on the Millennium."[52] Throughout Christian history, millennialism waxed during dramatic times and waned during ordinary times. America's Revolutionary and post-Revolutionary period (1776–1800)—a dramatic time indeed—unleashed a torrent of millennialist predictions, some premillennial, others postmillennial, but, as Ruth Bloch has observed, no one vision carried the day.[53] However, as revivals of the late eighteenth and early nineteenth centuries advanced in both intensity and duration, a confidence grew that the millennium was an approaching reality. The apocalyptic element of millennial thought, which was associated with the destruction of the world prior to Christ's return, gave way to more hopeful millennial expectations.

50. Richards, *Spirit of Paul*, 17–18.
51. Parsons, "Address to the Society," vol. 9 (Sept. 23, 1817), Records of the Society of Inquiry, Series 7: Dissertations, Andover Theological Records, Yale Divinity School Library .
52. Sandeen, *Roots of Fundamentalism*, 42.
53. Bloch, *Visionary Republic*, 105–10.

An evolution in prophetic understanding can be seen in statements made over a period of two decades. Readings of the signs of the times ranged from Samuel Hopkins's gloomy forecast in 1793 that "that time of greatest suffering is yet to come,"[54] to the cautious optimism of a writer in the New Divinity–sponsored *Connecticut Evangelical Magazine* in 1803 who stated "that the events of the time are favorable to the hypothesis of an increasing of the church of Christ both in numbers and graces,"[55] to the blushing confidence expressed in the ABCFM annual report a decade later:

> If the Messiah was then the Desire of all nations, his millennial reign is no less now.... Prophecy, history, and the present state of the world, seem to unite in declaring, that the great pillars of the Papal and Mahommedan impostures are now tottering to their fall.... In the great conflict between truth and error, what Christian will refuse to take an active part?... Ultimate victory is secure, as is promised by Him.[56]

James Davidson has noted that "postmillennialism ... came into its own only when divines consciously argued that Christ's figurative millennial reign demanded human action"—the kind of action called for in the ABCFM's report. Only then, Davidson continues, could postmillennialism be "used as a lynchpin to hang a rationalized psychology of motivation."[57] The importance of eschatology as a major motivator to missions cannot be overstated, notwithstanding R. Pierce Beaver's assessment that end-times speculation "showed a tendency to degenerate into imminent apocalyptic expectations of the millennium."[58] Such degeneration was, in fact, the fuel that propelled the missionary engine in the early republic as well as in subsequent periods of fervid missionary activity.[59]

---

54. Hopkins, "Serious Address," 215.
55. "Analysis of the Book of Daniel," 51.
56. American Board of Commissioners for Foreign Missions, *First Ten Annual Reports*, 27–28.
57. Davidson, *Logic of Millennial Thought*, 262.
58. Beaver, "Missionary Motivation," 124.
59. For example, early-twentieth-century Pentecostal and evangelical missionary outreach was motivated by the conviction that "Jesus is coming"—a premillennial expression to be sure, with an even more pronounced apocalyptic element than postmillennial views. But whether one is convinced that "Jesus is coming soon" or that "the kingdom of Christ is fast approaching," the psychological motivation is functionally the same. Both expressions are premised on the notion that a new era of the Spirit has come and that God is using Christians as God's agents of world redemption. On Pentecostal

A MISSIONARY MOVEMENT

The Edwardseans not only constructed a theological rationale for missions, but they harnessed that rationale to an organization that became the first and the largest in the United States. By 1850, the Board was sponsoring 157 ordained missionaries—40 percent of all missionary personnel in the United States—and had an annual budget exceeding $300,000.[60] The stature of the Board is all the more impressive in light of a radical shift occurring in American denominational allegiances. From 1776 to 1850, Congregationalists fell precipitously from 20 percent of all religious adherents in the United States to 4 percent, whereas Methodists grew at an astronomical rate from a mere 2.5 percent to over 34 percent of all religious adherents. "For Congregationalists," surmise Roger Finke and Rodney Stark, "the shift approached total collapse."[61] Thus, while aggressive Methodists (and Baptists) saturated the frontier and even displaced Congregationalists in their own New England backyard, the ABCFM expanded its reach around the world—thanks to the vitality of an emboldened New Divinity movement.[62]

A partial explanation for the ABCFM's numerical strength over other missionary agencies lies in the disparity of formal education between elite and popular denominations. Obviously, an advanced level of education (or the genius of a "simple cobbler" like William Carey) was necessary in order to learn and translate a foreign language.[63] But because the

---

apocalyptic thought and missions, see Land, *Pentecostal Spirituality*. On evangelicals, see Robert, "'Crisis of Missions,'" 29–46.

60. Strong, *Story of the American Board*, 157; Hutchison, *Errand to the World*, 45; [Anderson], *Memorial Volume*, 160. The total number of persons serving under the Board in 1850, including wives, teachers, physicians, and missionaries, was 395. Strong, *Story of the American Board*, 160.

61. Finke and Stark, *Churching of America*, 55.

62. One could take the "market share" approach of Finke and Stark in *Churching of America* and argue that once Congregationalists were shut out of the domestic market, they turned their sights overseas. As intriguing as this reasoning may be (and Finke and Stark do not suggest this conclusion, for they omit any discussion of foreign missions), it distorts the real successes of Congregational evangelism on the frontier. For a critique of Finke and Stark's approach to the Congregationalist loss of the domestic share, see Rohrer, *Keepers of the Covenant*, chap. 8. A related argument—one that I do not find entirely convincing—is advanced by Andrew (*Rebuilding the Christian Commonwealth*), who locates the impetus for overseas missions in social and religious turbulence at home.

63. Actually, Carey studied for two years under the direction of John Sutcliffe and was keenly aware of the importance of education. The Serampore Trio (William Carey, Joshua

absence of formal education was something of a badge of honor among American Baptists and Methodists, they were less prepared and, hence, less inclined than well-educated Congregationalists and Presbyterians to enter foreign missionary service. Clearly, educational background did matter as a criterion for missionary service. With their traditional emphasis on a "learned ministry," perhaps it was only natural that Congregationalists and Presbyterians predominated in the early stages of the American foreign missionary movement. Yet educational preparation was only one reason, and certainly not the most compelling reason, for the ABCFM's dominance in the first half of the nineteenth century. To understand that dominance we must view the ABCFM within the wider context of the New Divinity as a dynamic cultural movement.

Like other broad-based movements, the New Divinity identity was not confined to a shared belief system but evolved into a well-defined social group that resorted to collective action and, over time, promoted new processes of socialization and community formation. Drawing upon social theories of movement organization, we may understand the growth and development of the New Divinity in terms of how social movements organize themselves toward achieving their goals; how they recruit, consolidate, and deploy members; and how they sustain their organization and maintain leadership. Beginning in 1750, the New Divinity men evolved from a handful of devotees of Jonathan Edwards to the point that, by the early 1800s, they dominated the religious, educational, and cultural life of New England (except for Unitarian-controlled Boston and Harvard). Modest social backgrounds, shared educational bonds (first at Yale, then at New Divinity theological finishing "schools of the prophets"), conservative political views (nearly all were Federalists), kinship networks, and fraternal connections through correspondence, pulpit exchanges, and team preaching and revivalism—these designated the collective Edwardsean identity.[64]

Between 1750 and 1825, from the First through the Second Great Awakenings, the New Divinity men established firm roots in New England. These heirs of Edwards followed in his steps by promoting ecclesiastical

---

Marshman, and William Ward) complained to the Baptist Missionary Society that the educational level of missionaries sent out to them was deficient. Piggin, *Making Evangelical Missionaries*, 160; also see chaps. 6–8 for a discussion of British missionary training.

64. Birdsall, *Berkshire County*, 33–74; Conforti, *Samuel Hopkins*, chap. 2; Kling, *Field of Divine Wonders*, chap. 1. For a broader discussion of group identity formation, see Hall, *Organization of American Culture*. On the transmission of knowledge, see Brown, *Knowledge Is Power*.

reform, education, publication projects, and revivals. In ecclesiastical affairs, they succeeded where Edwards had failed (at Northampton) in overturning the Half-Way Covenant (1662) and establishing Congregational churches on pure church principles. Joseph Bellamy, derisively called "our Sovereign Lord Bellamy" by the moderate Calvinist Ezra Stiles, president of Yale College, seized control of the ecclesiastical machinery and turned the Litchfield Association of Congregational ministers into a New Divinity credentialing operation.[65] In Berkshire County, western Massachusetts, Stephen West, Edwards's successor in Stockbridge, and Samuel Hopkins of Great Barrington maintained New Divinity orthodoxy by creating the Berkshire Association of Congregational Ministers in 1763. To the east, Nathanael Emmons controlled the Mendon Association, and later he had a hand in the creation of the General Association of Congregational Ministers in 1802—the very group approached in 1810 by four Andover Theological Seminary students who came seeking advice for their missionary vision.

The most important intergenerational structure for communicating Edwardsean theology was the New Divinity "parlor seminaries" or "log colleges." Just as Edwards had tutored several disciples (for example, Hopkins and Bellamy), so his namesakes followed suit. In postbaccalaureate informal "schools of the prophets," the Edwardseans educated clerical aspirants in the piety and theology of the New Divinity at the home or on the farm of a leading minister. In so doing, they provided the infrastructure for the growth and longevity of the New Divinity movement. Between 1750 and 1825, over five hundred young men studied under the tutelage of a New Divinity mentor.[66] Eight New Divinity pastors trained at least thirty clerical aspirants, with Nathanael Emmons of Franklin, Massachusetts, leading the way in educating ninety students, followed by Joseph Bellamy of Bethlehem, Connecticut, and Asa Burton of Thetford, Vermont (sixty each), and Charles Backus of Somers, Connecticut (fifty-eight). The educational paternity of these finishing schools has a direct lineage to foreign missions. For example, John Smalley, a student of Bellamy's, tutored Ebenezer Porter, a leading pastor-revivalist in Washington, Connecticut, and later professor of homiletics and president of Andover Theological Seminary. During his pastorate at Washington, Porter trained both Gordon Hall and Harvey Loomis, Williams

---

65. Stiles, *Literary Diary of Ezra Stiles*, 3:374.
66. For a more comprehensive view of these practices, see chap. 7 in this volume.

College graduates (1807) who, at the 1806 Haystack Prayer Meeting, were among those who dedicated their lives to overseas missionary service. Not surprisingly, from the critical mass of New Divinity pastors and theologians emerged leaders in higher education. Yale College is often cited for supplying the many provincial college presidents of northern antebellum New England, when in fact the schools of the prophets played an important mediating role by stamping these sons of Yale with the peculiar New Divinity imprimatur. In the late eighteenth and early nineteenth centuries, Edwardseans permeated New England and New York's provincial colleges. New Divinity presidents and faculty guided colleges such as Williams, Yale, Dartmouth, Middlebury, Amherst, Union, and Hamilton—those very institutions that contributed nearly 75 percent of all missionaries (124 out of 170) to the ABCFM before 1840.[67]

In addition, as Andover Theological Seminary, America's first postgraduate theological school (founded in 1808) replaced schools of the prophets as centers of ministerial training, it too counted Edwardseans among its supporters, founders, professors, and, of course, students, who were introduced to Edwards's *Religious Affections* and *Life of David Brainerd*.[68] Though Andover was established upon an Old Calvinist-New Divinity compromise, William Bentley was rightly convinced that "the Calvinists have been made to play into the hands of the Hopkinsians."[69] The seminary was stacked with Edwardsean faculty, including Edward D. Griffin, Moses Stuart, Ebenezer Porter, and Edwards A. Park, and it ensured that future faculty remained so with its "Hopkinsian" Associate Creed.[70] From the beginning, Andover was the training center of the ABCFM's missionaries. During the first decade of the Board, all but one of its missionaries was educated at Andover, and within thirty-eight years, one hundred students had carried the New Divinity message to the ends of the earth.[71]

The New Divinity also kept the Edwardsean legacy alive by engaging in an extensive campaign to republish Edwards's works and to publish many of his unpublished manuscripts. In the last half of the eighteenth

---

67. Figures are extrapolated from the table in Phillips, *Protestant America and the Pagan World*, 29.

68. Woods, *History of the Andover Theological Seminary*, 169.

69. Bentley, *Diary*, 3:403.

70. On New Divinity influence at Andover, see Conforti, *Jonathan Edwards*, 20, 112; Sweeney, "Nathaniel William Taylor," 144; Field, *Crisis of the Standing Order*, 161–71.

71. Woods, *History of the Andover Theological Seminary*, 199–200.

century and well into the nineteenth, Edwards's reputation as a spokesman for true Christianity grew to heroic proportions. Between 1780 and 1800, his works were republished more extensively in America than in the twenty years following his death in 1758.[72] And in the nineteenth century, his works were so popular that runs of reprints totaled in the hundreds of thousands.[73] On both sides of the Atlantic, his name was invoked with reverence as the popularity of his writings spread through and beyond the Calvinist community, among clergy and laity alike, including ABCFM missionary wives.[74] Edwards's hagiographic *Life of David Brainerd*, reprinted and republished more than any of his works, had its greatest impact on American missionaries. Prospective missionaries consumed its contents, carried it to the field, and emulated Brainerd's life of disinterested benevolence.[75] What Athanasius's *Life of Anthony* was to the early monastic movement, Edwards's *Life of David Brainerd* was to the modern missionary movement. For ABCFM missionaries, *Life of David Brainerd* became the spiritual yardstick by which to measure the fidelity of their own willingness to endure physical, emotional, and spiritual hardship and, yes, even a Hopkinsian willingness to die for the greater glory of God. Gordon Hall, one of the original five missionaries to be sent out by the ABCFM, penned these words to his parents before sailing to Bombay: "It will be trying to your parental tenderness to see your son leaving you to live and die in a foreign land. But have you not given me away in covenant to God?" He then assured his parents that "death will separate us whether we consent or not."[76]

In transmitting the piety, theology, and writings of Edwards through several generations, the New Divinity laid the basis for the Calvinist revivals of the Second Great Awakening in New England.[77] In turn, these

72. For a list of reprints, see Kling, *Field of Divine Wonders*, 80n7.

73. Sweeney, "Nathaniel William Taylor," 142. Bentley noted the printing of Edwards's works was "employed as a vehicle of disseminating the Doctrine of Special Election, which he has associated with this doctrine of the will." Bentley, *Diary*, 3:462 (October 1, 1809). The whole print impression was sold, totaling $20,000.

74. Robert, *American Women in Mission*, 7–8; McCoy, "Women of the ABCFM," 63, 73. On the influence of Edwards abroad, see Kling and Sweeney, *Jonathan Edwards at Home and Abroad*, pt. 3, "Edwards around the World."

75. Conforti, *Jonathan Edwards*, 74–78.

76. Horatio Bardwell, *Memoir of Rev. Gordon Hall, A.M., One of the First Missionaries of the American Board of Commissioners for Foreign Missions, at Bombay* (Andover, MA, 1841), 21–22, quoted in Conforti, *Jonathan Edwards*, 76.

77. On the Second Great Awakening in Connecticut, see Keller, *Second Great Awakening in Connecticut*; Shiels, "Connecticut Clergy"; Kling, *Field of Divine Wonders*.

spiritual outpourings did more than anything else to augment an already expanding Edwardsean movement and to supply the young male converts who comprised the nucleus of the Board's missionaries.[78] Following Edwards's prescription for revival, New Divinity ministers sparked spiritual interest by sponsoring circular fasts and concerts of prayer and then inflamed it through impassioned preaching, small group evangelistic conference meetings, and team revivalism. Hundreds of members were added to the church rolls. A renewed spiritual fervor heightened millennial expectations and anticipations of the global spread of Christianity.

One of the earliest institutional expressions of this spiritual awakening was the Connecticut Missionary Society, formed in 1798. Organized and controlled by Edwardseans, the Society expressed the millennial conviction reiterated incessantly in antebellum America that "the time is near in which God will spread his truth through the earth."[79] For the CMS, that truth was spread to New Englanders living in the "waste places" of recently settled frontier areas and to the "heathen" Native Americans. From 1798 to 1818, 148 itinerant missionaries—nearly all Edwardseans—served new settlements in Vermont, New York, Pennsylvania, and the Ohio Territory.[80] Over a decade before the creation of the ABCFM, the New Divinity was actively engaged in frontier evangelism.

America's first foray into overseas missions thus may be seen as a continuation and extension of home revivals and frontier missions. Clearly, conditions were conducive for the contemplation of overseas missions. Edwardseans had gained experience in home missions. From revivals flowed the willpower and energy to begin and sustain foreign missions. And in their periodicals, such as the *Massachusetts Missionary Magazine*, the *Connecticut Evangelical Magazine*, and the *Panoplist*, Edwardseans shared their missionary vision through articles authored by their own contributors or reprinted from English missionary magazines. It was only a matter of time before New Divinity leaders, inspired by a student missionary movement, inquired into the possibility of sponsoring their own overseas missionary venture.

If we retrace the developments leading up to the creation of the ABCFM as sketched at the outset of this essay and fill in the details, the presence of a vibrant New Divinity movement becomes all the more

---

78. On future missionaries converted during revivals, see Woods, *Memoirs of American Missionaries*, 39–189; Perry, "American Board of Commissioners," 573.

79. Connecticut Missionary Society, quoted in Rohrer, *Keepers of the Covenant*, 62.

80. Rohrer, *Keepers of the Covenant*, 13, 52–101.

apparent. Consider the specific circumstances beginning with Samuel J. Mills Jr., the "father of American foreign missions," and culminating with the election of the first Board officers in September 1810. Mills's life offers a New Divinity biographical model.[81] He was born into a New Divinity parsonage that was frequented by a train of visiting New Divinity ministers, including his father's longtime friend Samuel Hopkins. At an early age, Mills's mother dedicated her son to missionary service and read to him of the missionary heroics of John Eliot and David Brainerd. First stirred during a New Divinity revival in 1798–99 at his father's church in Torringford, Connecticut, the fifteen-year-old Mills found no spiritual peace until 1801. He then prepared for collegiate studies under James Morris, an Edwardsean and proprietor of a respected academy at South Farms in Litchfield who would later serve as a trustee of the Board's Cornwall Indian School in Cornwall, Connecticut. Morris himself had studied theology under Joseph Bellamy at the same time as his Yale College classmate, Adoniram Judson Sr., the future father of the famous ABCFM-turned-Baptist missionary who was his namesake.[82]

In 1806 Mills entered Williams College, then a fledgling provincial school with New Divinity sympathies in northwestern Massachusetts.[83] Mills's choice of Williams is noteworthy for it illustrates the modest social backgrounds of the hundreds of New Divinity men who attended newly established, low-cost provincial colleges such as Union in New York (founded in 1795), Middlebury in Vermont (founded in 1800), and Amherst in Massachusetts (founded 1821) and who later served as missionaries under the ABCFM.[84] Mills's choice of Williams also illustrates New Divinity intergenerational connections operating at personal and institutional levels. The Reverend Ammi Robbins, a trustee of Williams

81. Biographical details are found in Spring, *Memoir of Samuel John Mills*; Richards, *Samuel J. Mills*.

82. Morris, *Memoirs of James Morris*, 13.

83. For a continued discussion of Mills and Williams College, see chap. 8 in this volume.

84. On the dynamic shift in student social backgrounds from the colonial to the early national periods, see Allmendinger, *Paupers and Scholars*, chap. 1. For Williams' tuition, see "Minutes of the Meetings of Trustees of Williams College," April 24, 1785–March 27, 1868, 2 vols. (microfilm), Williamsiana Collection. For Yale's tuition, see Story, *Forging of an Aristocracy*, 98–100. On the social backgrounds of missionaries, see Woods, *Memoirs of American Missionaries*, 39–189; Lowe, "First American Foreign Missionaries," 195–98; Phillips, *Protestant America and the Pagan World*, 30–31.

and a colleague and relative of Samuel's father, encouraged Samuel to attend the college.[85]

Under similar circumstances, other students made their way to the remote college in the Berkshires. For example, Moses Hallock, an Edwardsean pastor in Plainfield, Massachusetts, supplemented his modest salary by preparing boys for college. Through his personal tutelage, many young men entered Williams, including future ABCFM missionaries James Richards, William Richards, Levi Parsons, Jonas King, and Homan Hallock.[86] By continuing their studies at Andover Theological Seminary, they ensured that their entire formal education—from the academy to the college to the seminary—was obtained under the aegis of New Divinity teachers.

Following the spontaneous commitments made at the Haystack Prayer Meeting, Mills created the secret missionary society of "the Brethren," comprised of students who pledged to commit themselves to missions to the "heathen." The group republished missionary sermons, sought to enlist prominent ministers in their cause, and through correspondence spread their missionary zeal to other colleges. One of the missionary sermons republished by the Brethren was Edward D. Griffin's *The Kingdom of Christ*.[87] Delivered initially before the Presbyterian General Assembly in 1805, Griffin challenged Presbyterians to take the lead in foreign missions. An erstwhile colleague of Samuel J. Mills Sr. in Connecticut, one of the greatest revivalists of his day, and the future president of Williams (1821–36), Griffin argued that "the whole plan of this world . . . was involved in the plan of redemption," which is "designed to promote the glory of God."[88] A new age was approaching, Griffin assured his audience, when "the everlasting gospel shall be preached to every kindred, and tongue, and people . . . . Paradise will be restored."[89] But that restoration required human initiative, the "established method of divine grace." We must, he insisted, fulfill the Great Commission, for "the

---

85. Richards, *Samuel J. Mills*, 24.

86. Yale, *Godly Pastor*, 326.

87. Charles Chaney considers Griffin's sermon "one of the superior sermons of the Nineteenth Century." Chaney, *Birth of Missions in America*, 220. Another influential sermon republished by the Brethren was by the Reformed Dutch theologian and educator John Henry Livingston: *The Everlasting Gospel*. On Livingston's contribution to the modern missionary movement, see Kennedy, "From Providence to Civil Religion," 11–23; Beardslee, "John Henry Livingston," 1–21.

88. Griffin, *Kingdom of Christ*, 10, 11.

89. Griffin, *Kingdom of Christ*, 16.

conversion of the single pagan [was] of more value than all the wealth that omnipotence ever produced."[90] Inspired by this and other missionary sermons, Williams led all other colleges by 1840 in the number of missionaries serving under the Board.[91]

In addition to his leadership of the Brethren, Mills also became a moving force in the recently formed Theological Society, which met fortnightly for prayer and theological discussion. During the first decade of its existence, the society evidenced an unmistakable allegiance to New Divinity theology. The recorded minutes of the society reveal a gathering of pious young men engaged in discussing vital topics of missionary theology. At a meeting in December 1809, for example, members debated, "Is the atonement sufficient for all?" They decided—in keeping with New Divinity revisionist theology—in the affirmative. In March 1810, the majority of the society members distanced themselves from Hopkinsian idiosyncrasies by deciding "negative" to the infamous query, "If a person ought to be willing to be damned in order to be saved?" In November, the novice theologians also debated questions like, "Is regeneration preceded by the proper efficacy of means or by the immutable power of God?" And the following October 1811: "What sort of inability is it which prevents unholy men from performing their duty; and is their inability so great as to render it certain that they will not truly repent and believe without the special divine influence?"[92]

Following graduation in 1809, Mills and other missionary-minded colleagues continued their studies at the newly formed Andover Theological Seminary. Sometime in 1810, they transferred the records of the Brethren to Andover, and, shortly thereafter, they created the Society of Inquiry on the Subject of Mission, an organization open to all Andover students and committed to the cause of missions in general. Among the society's records are "dissertations"—papers delivered by students that dealt with a range of missionary topics: objections to foreign missions, missionary motivation, histories of missions, and the benefits of foreign missions upon churches at home, to name a few. An Edwardsean piety permeates these papers, whether expressed in references to Brainerd, a sense of duty, or selflessness.[93]

90. Griffin, *Kingdom of Christ*, 24.

91. Hewitt, *Williams College and Foreign Missions*, 29.

92. "Theological Society Proceedings, 1809–1822," box 1, folder 1, Williamsiana Collection.

93. For example, see Richards, "Arguments in Favor," vol. 4 (April 23, 1811); Chancey

As Mills would do throughout his career as the man behind the scenes in creating evangelical societies, he relied upon personal relationships with New Divinity men to advance the foreign missionary cause. In June of 1810, after consultation with several Andover faculty members, Mills and three other missionary-minded Andover students approached the General Association of Ministers at their annual meeting in Bradford, Massachusetts. The association was not a legal body per se but an organization of evangelical ministers (primarily New Divinity men) formed in 1802 to support Calvinist orthodoxy against the menace of expanding Unitarianism in eastern Massachusetts. The students presented their ideas in writing, "noting that their minds have been long impressed with the duty and importance of personally attempting a mission to the heathen." They then sought the advice of their elders:

> Whether, with their present views and feelings, they ought to renounce the object of missions as visionary or impracticable; if not, whether they ought to direct their attention to the eastern or western world; whether they may expect patronage and support from a Missionary Society in this country, or must commit themselves to the direction of a European society; and what preparatory measures they ought to take, previous to actual engagement.[94]

In response, the association appointed a committee to form a board, consisting of nine members—five chosen by the General Association of Massachusetts and four by the General Association of Connecticut. The ABCFM, which was created and first met at Farmington, Connecticut, in September of 1810, had a distinct New Divinity profile. Its highest-ranking officers were inveterate New Divinity men. John Treadwell—lawyer, judge, governor of Connecticut (1809–11), deacon, and original trustee and president of the Connecticut Missionary Society from 1798 to 1822—presided over the ABCFM until his death in 1823. A theologian in his own right, Treadwell remarked that his "scheme of faith was forever settled by reading Edwards on the Will."[95] He contributed articles

---

Booth, "What are the peculiar encouragements for missionaries?," vol. 4 (February 11, 1812); Amzi Benedict, "Missionary biography," vol. 8 (August 27, 1817); Levi Parsons, "Address to the society," vol. 9 (September 23, 1817), all in Records of the Society of Inquiry, Series 7: Dissertations, Andover Theological Records, Yale Divinity School Library.

94. American Board of Commissioners for Foreign Missions, *First Ten Annual Reports*, 10.

95. Olmsted, *Memoir of John Treadwell*, 16.

on New Divinity theology to religious periodicals, debated the fine points of theology with New Divinity ministers, and conveyed his Edwardsean convictions in his *Summary of Christian Doctrine for Pioneers in Western Settlements* (1804).[96] Samuel Spring, an influential New Divinity pastor in Newburyport, served as the Board's vice president from 1810 to 1819. He was among the New Divinity founders of Andover Theological Seminary, and, under his preachments, wealthy merchant parishioners bequeathed substantial sums to the seminary and to the ABCFM.[97] Finally, the Reverend Samuel Worcester of Salem was elected the Board's corresponding secretary, a position to which he dedicated long hours until his untimely death in 1821. Worcester was such a stiff-necked New Divinity man that, during a five-year controversy in an earlier pastorate, the term "Hopkinsian" became such a derogatory term that schoolboys used it as an epithet.[98] Such was the leadership of the ABCFM during its first decade of existence. Except for Jedidiah Morse, a moderate Calvinist co-opted by the Edwardseans, the Board's most influential leaders were New Divinity men to the core.[99]

CONCLUSION

"If the two major sources behind nineteenth century Anglo-American missions could be isolated," observed James De Jong, "a convincing case could be constructed for their being the theology of Jonathan Edwards and the example of David Brainerd."[100] This essay has confirmed De Jong's observation: Edwards's theological ideas had missionary consequences, and Brainerd's exemplary life attracted a cadre of dedicated missionaries. Nevertheless, De Jong and other historians of American missions have too often played historical leapfrog, jumping a half-century from Edwards to the creation of the ABCFM. To be sure, these historians point to the significant missionary contributions of the English, Samuel Hopkins, Samuel Mills, and home missionary societies. Still, in exploring the

---

96. Olmsted, *Memoir of Treadwell*, 16–21; Porter, *Sermon*, 11–16.

97. Sprague, *Annals of the American Pulpit*, 2:85–89; Andrew, *Rebuilding the Christian Commonwealth*, 16.

98. Sprague, *Annals of the American Pulpit*, 2:398–407; Worcester, *Life and Labors*, 1:282.

99. On Morse's relationship to the New Divinity, see Sweeney, "Nathaniel William Taylor," 143.

100. De Jong, *As the Waters Cover the Sea*, 137.

antecedents of American missions, they have underestimated not only the New Divinity theological revisions undertaken to make explicit a missionary theology but also the social and cultural forces that enabled a missionary theology to take root, gain an audience, and locate itself in the institutional life of New England. In this essay I have attempted to redress these inadequacies.

At the same time, what I have offered is a prolegomenon to America's first overseas missionary enterprise. Establishing the New Divinity origins of the ABCFM raises as many questions as answers, some of which have been addressed by historians but only in an episodic way.[101] Larger questions remain. For example, what were the extent, duration, and outcome of New Divinity influences on the mission field? What were its strengths and shortcomings? How long was Edwardsean theology a moving force among the Board's leadership? Did the concept of disinterested benevolence lose its specific theological content in the mission field and become, as it did at home, a diffuse concept employed in the many contexts of humanitarian reform? I have suggested a point of departure. While recent research has uncovered a profound Edwardsean legacy in Great Britain's foreign missionary enterprise, the American Edwardsean missionary legacy begs for further inquiry.[102]

---

101. See McCoy, "Women of the ABCFM Oregon Mission"; Conforti, *Jonathan Edwards*, chap. 3.

102. Efforts to explore this British legacy are found in Walls, "Missions and Historical Memory"; Piggin, "Expanding Knowledge of God."

7

New Divinity Schools of the Prophets, 1750–1825

A Case Study in Ministerial Education

SCHOLARS HAVE LONG RECOGNIZED the Great Awakening (ca. 1735–45) as an important moment in the history of American higher education. As increasing numbers of young men experienced conversion and entered the ministry, leaders seized the opportunity to establish educational institutions that furthered the aims of the revival. Within a generation after the Awakening, pro-revivalist groups founded four new colleges: the College of New Jersey at Princeton by Presbyterians in 1746, Rhode Island College (renamed Brown University) by Baptists in 1764, Queen's College (renamed Rutgers) by Dutch Reformed in 1766, and Dartmouth College by the Congregationalist Eleazar Wheelock in 1769.

Less well known yet crucial to our understanding of ministerial education from 1750 to 1825 was the emergence of a distinct group within New England Congregationalism associated with Jonathan Edwards and his disciples, the New Divinity men.[1] Identifying themselves as Calvinists and heirs of the Puritan tradition, they sought to revise or "improve" traditional Calvinist doctrines. Critics tarred them with the brush of innovation, claiming that they had devised a "new divinity," but the Edwardseans responded that they were recontextualizing their Puritan heritage to meet the intellectual challenges of the day. Despite the

---

1. Recent book treatments of the New Divinity include Conforti, *Samuel Hopkins*; Conforti, *Jonathan Edwards*; Ferm, *Jonathan Edwards the Younger*; Guelzo, *Edwards on the Will*; Kling, *Field of Divine Wonders*; Valeri, *Law and Providence*.

relative diversity of New Divinity thought, the Edwardseans shared a great deal of theological unity and collegiality. In brief, their distinctive views turned upon two fundamental convictions. First, to undercut spiritual indifference and spark revival, they reiterated Edwards's distinction between one's natural and moral ability to obey God. In *Freedom of the Will* (1754), Edwards argued that Adam's original sin had not eradicated the natural ability of humans to obey divine commands. No natural or physical impediment stood in the way of sinners obeying God's law. Unrepentant sinners could no longer blame God for their condition; rather, as moral agents, they voluntarily willed not to love God, and in so doing were culpable. The New Divinity acknowledged that they could never fully comprehend what was essentially the mystery of God's sovereign intentions. "The disposing hand of God over moral agents while they remain free and accountable," declared a New Divinity supporter, "is a process in the divine government attended with obscurity and incapable of explanation by the limited powers of men."[2] Second, to emphasize the eternal consequences of remaining unconverted, the New Divinity followed Edwards in pressing the unsaved to repent immediately. To be sure, salvation was by God's grace alone, but as the apostle Paul urged the Corinthians, "Now is the day of salvation" (2 Cor 6:2; see also Isa 45:22). Working from these dual theological principles, Edwards and his disciples championed revivals and heartfelt, "affectionate" religion as a genuine expression of the Spirit.

This essay considers the primary mechanism by which the New Divinity transmitted theological knowledge. Displeased with but reluctant to abandon Yale as an initial training ground for ministry, the Edwardseans provided postbaccalaureate theological education through informal academies typically referred to as "schools of the prophets." While the term had long been used in New England to designate an institution whose primary function was to train clergy, it became synonymous with New Divinity clerical education during the last half of the eighteenth century. These schools of the prophets educated clerical aspirants in the piety and theology of the New Divinity at the home or on the farm of a leading New Divinity minister. In so doing, they provided the infrastructure for the growth and longevity of the New Divinity movement. The profound and widespread influence of the schools of the prophets not only enabled the New Divinity movement to prosper but also distinguished them as America's single most important source of ministerial training from the

2. Newton, "View of God," 83.

mid-eighteenth century to the establishment of seminaries in the early nineteenth century.

Despite monopolizing theological training for well over half a century, the schools of the prophets have either been overlooked or, more often, underappreciated. In 1963, Clarence C. Goen recognized the schools as "a phenomenon of major magnitude in ministerial training," and yet a decade later, in his introduction to *The Great Awakening and American Education*, Douglas Sloan made no mention of New Divinity mentoring practices. In 1990, Glenn Miller corrected this omission, noting that the New Divinity theologians "made 'reading divinity' an art." Other historians have devoted significant space to these schools, but the influence of New Divinity schools of the prophets on the religious and social life of New England—even the world, if one considers their impact on the modern missionary movement—has been vastly understated.[3]

The numbers alone are impressive: between 1750 and 1825, over five hundred clerical aspirants studied in New Divinity schools of the prophets. Long-term influences are even more impressive. These schools transmitted the piety, theology, and legacy of the Great Awakening through several generations and thus profoundly contributed to a "second" Great Awakening (ca. 1790–1835). Moreover, Yale College is often credited for producing many provincial college presidents of northern antebellum New England, when in fact the schools of the prophets played an important mediating role by stamping these sons of Yale with the peculiar New Divinity imprimatur. A similar claim can be made for New Divinity influence in the training of clergy for home and foreign missionary service. Some of the earliest missionary organizations in America (for example, the Connecticut Missionary Society, the Massachusetts Missionary Society, and the American Board of Commissioners for Foreign Missions) owe their origins largely to the inspiration of the New Divinity men and their schools.[4] Not until the rise of the professional seminary,

---

3. Goen, "Changing Conceptions," 297; Sloan, *Great Awakening and American Education*; Miller, *Piety and Intellect*, 55. See also Gambrell, *Ministerial Training*, chaps. 6, 7; Bainton, *Yale and the Ministry*, chap. 5; Conforti, *Samuel Hopkins*, chap. 2.

4. Conforti, *Samuel Hopkins*, chap. 11; and esp. Kling, *Field of Divine Wonders*; Hall, *Organization of American Culture*, 162. The following Yale alumni who became college presidents received theological instruction in the schools of the prophets: Azel Backus (Hamilton), Henry Davis (Middlebury, Hamilton), Edward Dorr Griffin (Williams), and Heman Humphrey (Amherst). Other New Divinity-trained ministers who became college presidents included Jonathan Edwards Jr. (Union), Zephaniah Swift Moore (Williams, Amherst), and Stephen Chapin (Columbia). Conforti, *Samuel Hopkins*, 157–58; Rohrer, *Keepers of the Covenant*.

beginning with Andover Theological Seminary in 1808, did the hegemony of schools of the prophets among New England Calvinists weaken, although in some quarters New Divinity mentoring practices persisted well into the 1820s. For nearly three-quarters of a century, schools of the prophets proliferated, reproducing the teaching, preaching, and mentoring practices of the New Divinity in a remarkably consistent fashion. New Divinity theology—the first and perhaps the most enduring of indigenous theologies in America—owed its sustaining power to these schools. Moreover, the medium was an indispensable part of the message, for in the environment of personal interaction students imbibed not only a theology but a way of life. In these household seminaries, the light of the gospel and the heat of heartfelt religion passed through three and sometimes four generations of ministers.

ORIGINS OF THE SCHOOLS OF THE PROPHETS

The origins of the New Divinity informal seminaries may be illustrated by the ministerial preparation of three generations in the Robbins family of eighteenth-century Connecticut. Philemon Robbins graduated from Harvard in 1729, briefly taught school, studied theology under the Reverend Nathaniel Appleton in Cambridge, and then accepted a call from the Congregational Church in Branford, Connecticut. Ordained in 1732, Philemon is remembered as a New Light sympathizer of the Great Awakening, a popular preacher, and an ardent patriot of the American Revolution. His son, Ammi Ruhamah, followed a similar path into the ministry. After a short stint at Nassau Hall (Princeton), he transferred to Yale and graduated in 1760. Convinced of his ministerial calling, Ammi pursued theological studies with Joseph Bellamy in Bethlehem, Connecticut, and was subsequently licensed and ordained at Norfolk, Connecticut. Like his father, Ammi embraced New Light sentiments, although his were of the Edwardsean or New Divinity variety, thanks to Bellamy's influence. For over fifty years, Ammi preached the verities of the New Divinity in his rural parish, and he witnessed the ingathering of several hundred souls during periodic revivals, including the conversion of his son Thomas. For several years after graduating from both Williams and Yale Colleges in 1796, Thomas alternated between teaching in village schools during the winter months and apprenticing under local ministers during the balance of the year. Like his father, Thomas studied with New Divinity pastors, initially under Ephraim Judson of Sheffield, Massachusetts, then in the summer and fall of 1797 with Stephen West, a pillar of the New Divinity and successor to Jonathan Edwards at Stockbridge, Massachusetts, and finally under Samuel Mills Sr. of Torringford, Connecticut.[5]

The path the Robbinses followed into the ministry is a familiar one to students of eighteenth-century New England. Throughout the colonial period and well into the nineteenth century, preparation for the Congregational ministry followed a pattern indebted to sixteenth- and seventeenth-century English Puritanism. Puritans viewed the university as representing an essential element in the preparation of a preacher but not the sole element. Beyond formal instruction at Oxford or Cambridge, the influence of a mentor—be he a tutor, a preacher, or a pastor—was often decisive in "equipping the ministry." Training at the university was often followed by an apprenticeship under a respected minister. This pattern of supervision, developed early within the Puritan movement, became widespread in England, was transported to America in the seventeenth century, and, as we have seen, continued throughout the eighteenth century. Thus, training for the ministry followed a two-step process of formal education and brief apprenticeship. In her study of ministerial training in eighteenth-century New England, Mary Gambrell calculated that of the more than eight hundred ministers ordained between 1740 and 1810, fewer than twenty were not definitely known to have been awarded a college degree.[6] At both Harvard and Yale, a classical liberal arts education, permeated with the study of Protestant theology ("theoretical divinity"), informed the college curriculum.

A college education may have provided training *for* the ministry, but a settled clergyman provided training *in* the ministry. Under the tutelage of an experienced practitioner, clerical candidates received the rudiments of professional preparation. Despite the high value placed upon a learned ministry within the Calvinist tradition, Congregationalists in New England and Presbyterians in the Middle Colonies—the two largest religious

---

5. On Philemon Robbins, see Sprague, *Annals of the American Pulpit*, 1:367; Weber, *Rhetoric and History*, chap. 1. On Ammi Robbins, see Dexter, *Biographical Sketches*, 2:670–73; Sprague, *Annals of the American Pulpit*, 1:369–70. On Thomas Robbins, see Robbins, *Diary of Thomas Robbins*, 1:iii–vii.

6. Cragg, "Training in the Ministry," 226–29. For examples of the continuity of these tutorial practices in America, see Shewmaker, "Training of the Protestant Ministry," 150–52; Gambrell, *Ministerial Training*, 52. The realization of the educational ideal for ministers represented a continuation of past practices. Gambrell calculated that between 1640 and 1740, of 250 ministers known to have been ordained, only twenty-five were not definitely known to have held a college degree. Gambrell, *Ministerial Training*, 21–22.

bodies in colonial America—imposed no formal, uniform training upon their ministers beyond a college education. Typically, a ministerial candidate "read divinity" or "studied theology" with another pastor—whether a relative, a local pastor, or a well-known teacher such as Bellamy—or with the president or a professor of divinity at Harvard or Yale.[7]

Apprenticeship practices were not confined to the Congregationalists or Presbyterians, nor were such practices limited to ministerial education, for aspiring lawyers and physicians prepared for their careers in much the same way. The antecedents for apprenticeship training are found, of course, in the distant past of the medieval guild system and more directly in English nonconformist practices. In addition, the peculiar demands and conditions of the new world, created first by distance and then exacerbated by the sundering of European ties following the Revolution, encouraged apprenticeship practices. Lacking their own universities or official credentialing agencies in America and often faced with critical shortages, such groups as Lutherans, Episcopalians, and a number of Reformed bodies (Presbyterian, Dutch Reformed, and Associate, Associate Reformed, and Reformed Presbyterian) supplied an educated ministry through "household seminaries."[8] In some cases, private teachers or academies were denominationally appointed, created, and regulated; in others, they emerged spontaneously as a means of addressing the need for an educated ministry. Depending upon a student's prior preparation as well as the educational demands of a particular religious group, the length and nature of study ranged from several months of informal reading to a prescribed four-year curriculum. Following this "seminary" training, such as it was, a student became eligible for ordination into the work of the ministry.

As long as stability and general unity characterized New England Puritanism, decisions regarding study with a settled minister followed the path of expediency. That is, the personal knowledge of a minister or the proximity of a minister to where the candidate resided largely determined the pairing of candidate and teacher. The Great Awakening, however, fractured Puritanism and, in so doing, challenged long-standing practices of ministerial education.

---

7. Mead, "Rise of the Evangelical Conception," 242. Harvard established the Hollis chair in divinity in 1721, Yale its chair in 1756.

8. On general educational efforts prior to the advent of formal seminaries, see Simpson, "Early Ministerial Training in America," 117–29; Shewmaker, "Training of the Protestant Ministry," 71–197; McCloy, "History of Theological Education," 449–53.

The stinging criticisms of Gilbert Tennent, George Whitefield, Jonathan Edwards, and others, who contended that colonial colleges offered "light but no heat," knowledge but no piety, resulted in a profound reordering of ministerial education throughout the colonies. The fragmentation of Puritanism in New England and Presbyterianism in the Middle Colonies into pro- and anti-revivalist parties (New Lights and Old Lights among Congregationalists, New Sides and Old Sides among Presbyterians) bred competition and a struggle for power over whose churches, schools, colleges, and form of religiosity would ultimately prevail. The result was aggressive attempts by "new" evangelical parties to advance their convictions on the relationship between religion and learning, between experiential knowledge of Christ and education.

While pro-revivalists made efforts to institutionalize the Great Awakening with the founding of new colleges, other more immediate forces were at work to sustain the evangelical Calvinists' goal of coupling piety with learning. For Scots-Irish Presbyterians, this goal was advanced first by William Tennent's Log College (founded 1727) and then, following the Old Side–New Side split in 1741, by New Side academies established by Tennent's students.[9] To the north, New Light Edwardseans sought to maintain evangelical piety and learning by working within the well-established structures of ministerial education yet bending those structures to their own purposes.

Although New Side Presbyterians largely succeeded in creating their own alternative educational institutions, New Lights were stymied by the heavy hand of Old Light rule at Yale. (Actually, New Sides themselves had experienced Old Light policies, for Yale had been a viable educational alternative for Presbyterians prior to the Awakening.) Under the imperious President Thomas Clap, Yale instituted measures to snuff out any threat of New Light enthusiasm or censoriousness. And so David Brainerd was expelled in 1741 for his refusal to make public confession for an offhanded private comment that his tutor "had no more grace than the chair" he was leaning on. Three years later the brothers John and Ebenezer Cleaveland were expelled for attending a Separatist meeting while at home with their parents. Such Old Light actions created martyrs to the New Light cause (as Edwards cast Brainerd in his biography) and consequently heightened the controversy over Yale's fitness to train evangelical ministers of the gospel.[10]

9. Sloan, *Scottish Enlightenment*, chap. 2.

10. For a general treatment of Yale's response to the Great Awakening, see Hofstadter and Metzger, *Development of Academic Freedom*, 163–77; Kelley, *Yale*, 49–55.

Shortly after Brainerd's dismissal, in *Some Thoughts Concerning the Present Revival of Religion in New England* (1742), Edwards attacked the New England colleges for abandoning their "original and main design of which is to train up persons, and fit them for the work of the ministry." These colleges, he wrote, should be "nurseries of piety" and "fountains of ... holiness," where men are trained "to be ambassadors of Jesus Christ and to lead souls to heaven," but instead "one can't send a child thither without great danger of his being infected as to his morals." If the colleges expected to live up to their mission as "schools of the prophets," concluded Edwards, then "certainly there ought to be extraordinary care taken to train 'em up to be Christians."[11]

Edwards and other friends of the Awakening, realizing that their interests were not shared by officials at either Yale or Harvard, sought alternative means to perpetuate vital piety in ministerial training. For the more radical Separatists, this meant complete repudiation of the spiritually corrupt colleges and the erection of the short-lived "Shepherd's Tent" (1742-43) in New London, Connecticut. The brainchild of Timothy Allen and James Davenport, the tent—no more than the second floor of a house—functioned as a school to aid and abet the most radical of religious enthusiasts. It was at New London, by the instigation of Davenport and with the hearty support of students, that citizens burned heretical books and worldly clothing in March 1743. To Old Lights, such actions were bad enough, but when these radicals claimed the direct inspiration of the Holy Ghost for their actions, even New Lights such as Edwards and Joseph Bellamy repudiated them, and the Shepherd's Tent folded. Criticizing existing colleges was one thing; creating an institution based on divine revelation was quite another.[12]

In the wake of the Shepherd's Tent debacle, moderate New Lights continued to bemoan spiritual decay in the colleges, but their dismay did not result in a wholesale rejection of existing institutions. Yale was valued and respected for it provided the rudiments of ministerial education, especially instruction in languages and literature. But Yale was not enough, nor was just *any* pastor an appropriate theological guide. There emerged, then, a self-conscious desire among New Light clerical aspirants to complete their ministerial preparation under sympathetic ministers. Indeed, the ousted John Cleaveland so admired Philemon Robbins's evangelical

---

11. Edwards, *WJE* 4:510-12.
12. On this episode, see Warch, "Shepherd's Tent," 177-98.

preaching that he chose Robbins as his ministerial mentor.[13] As the moderate New Light party evolved into the New Divinity in the 1760s, the schools of the prophets were born both out of protest and by default. Because Yale failed as a nursery of piety, the burden now fell upon New Divinity men to ensure that the theology and vital piety of the Awakening were transmitted to the rising generation of ministers. Consequently, while Yale was led by Old (or Moderate) Calvinist presidents for the remainder of the century (Thomas Clap until 1766, Naphtali Daggett from 1766 to 1777, and Ezra Stiles from 1777 to 1795), increasing numbers of graduates completed their ministerial preparation in New Divinity schools of the prophets. Rather than studying with the familiar neighborhood pastor or a reverend uncle, ministerial candidates consciously sought out those with proven New Divinity theological credentials and evangelical piety. Within the broad pattern of Congregational ministerial training, an intentionally directed form of apprenticeship arose in the years following the Awakening.

AN EMERGING CULTURAL MOVEMENT

With the emergence of New Divinity schools of the prophets, a movement was born. Growing slowly in the years after Edwards's death in 1758 and increasing rapidly by the end of the eighteenth century, a uniquely Edwardsean theological culture emerged. Sustained primarily through the schools of the prophets, this culture maintained its identity through educational ties to Yale, an intricate kinship network, extensive correspondence, steady personal contact, and team preaching / revival tours. As more New Divinity pastor-teachers opened their homes to prospective ministers, the movement increased in number and expanded its local and translocal ties. In the interval between 1765 and 1783, New Divinity men occupied fully one-half of New England's pulpit appointments. By 1800, the Edwardseans had secured footholds along the Eastern seaboard and in Vermont and New Hampshire and could claim northwestern Connecticut and western Massachusetts as their own territory. Samuel Hopkins, one of the patriarchs of the New Divinity movement, calculated that the number of New Divinity clergy grew from a handful in 1756 to nearly fifty in 1773 and by 1797 topped the one hundred mark. By Yale president Ezra Stiles's reckoning in 1792, over one-third of the Connecticut Congregational pulpits ("58 or 60 out of 168") were filled with New

13. Jedrey, *World of John Cleaveland*, 40.

Divinity men, and their numbers were increasing. In 1813, the Reverend William Bentley, the proto-Unitarian from Salem, Massachusetts, proffered grudging tribute to the New Divinity, recording that it was "the basis of the popular theology in New England."[14] From 1750 to 1825, over five hundred men passed through the schools of the prophets, imbibed Edwardsean theology, and thus collectively established the most powerful theological movement in New England.[15]

Several dozen New Divinity pastors trained clerical candidates, but a few eminent divines tutored significant numbers over the course of their ministerial careers. Jonathan Edwards took in students such as Samuel Hopkins and Joseph Bellamy, who in turn trained a generation of New Divinity men. Bellamy was the first to establish a school for the training of New Divinity pastors, and over the course of his career he trained some sixty ministers at his parsonage in Bethlehem, Connecticut. His fame as a revivalist preacher, coupled with the publication of *True Religion Delineated* (1750), established him as a leading proponent of the New Divinity. Consequently, students began showing up at Bellamy's "log college" to study with "the pope of Litchfield County." Near the end of Bellamy's career, Nathanael Emmons of Franklin, Massachusetts, emerged as *Herr Doktor Professor* of the New Divinity. Initially, Emmons had no intention of beginning a school, yet over a period of fifty years he put over ninety students through the rigors of his brand of New Divinity theology. Charles Backus of Somers, Connecticut, and Asa Burton of Thetford, Vermont, trained about sixty ministers each.[16] When the infirmities of age and then death removed Backus from the scene, Asahel Hooker maintained the tradition in Connecticut by taking in over thirty students during the first decade of the nineteenth century. Other Connecticut New Divinity men such as Benjamin Trumbull of North Haven, John Smalley of Berlin, Levi Hart of Preston, Jonathan Edwards Jr.

14. Valeri, *Law and Providence*, 4; Hopkins, *Sketches*, 102-3; Stiles, *Literary Diary of Ezra Stiles* 3:463-64; Bentley, *Diary of William Bentley*, 4:302.

15. This figure was calculated by first identifying New Divinity pastor-teachers and then identifying their students. Sources: Sprague, *Annals of the American Pulpit*, vols. 1-4; Dexter, *Biographical Sketches*, vols. 1-5; Godell, "John Smalley," 362; Vaill, "Theological Education in Connecticut," 137-42; Durfee, *Williams Biographical Annals*. See also listings of New Divinity men in Wright, *Beginnings of Unitarianism*, 288-91; Conforti, *Samuel Hopkins*, 227-32; Kling, *Field of Divine Wonders*, 245-50.

16. Park, *Memoir of Nathanael Emmons*; Dahlquist, "Nathanael Emmons," 1:203-4. On Backus, see Sprague, *Annals of the American Pulpit*, 2:61-68; Vaill, "Theological Education in Connecticut," 139. On Burton, see Burton, *Life of Asa Burton*; Sprague, *Annals of the American Pulpit*, 2:140-47.

of New Haven, Nathan Perkins of West Hartford, and Ebenezer Porter of Washington educated about ninety students, ranging between eight and thirty each. In western Massachusetts, a hotbed of New Divinity sentiment from 1775 to 1825, Stephen West, Ephraim Judson, Jacob Catlin, Theophilus Packard, Alvan Hyde, and Edward Dorr Griffin trained over seventy-five students (see figure 2).

FIGURE 2

New Divinity Schools of the Prophets, 1750–1825

Pastor-Teacher (of eight or more students)	Number of Students
Jonathan Edwards (1703–58) Northampton, Mass.	(8)
Joseph Bellamy (1719–90) Bethlehem, Conn.	(60)
John Smalley (1734–1820) New Britain, Conn.	(30)
Benjamin Trumbull (1735–1820) North Haven, Conn.	(8)
Stephen West (1735–1818) Northampton, Mass.	(11)
Levi Hart (1736–1808) Preston, Conn.	(8)
Ephraim Judson (1737–1813) Sheffield, Mass.	(8)
Jonathan Edwards, Jr. (1745–1801) New Haven, Conn.	(14)
Nathanael Emmons (1745–1840) Franklin, Mass.	(90)
Nathan Perkins (1748–1838) West Hartford, Conn.	(30)
Charles Backus (1749–1803) Somers, Conn.	(58)
Asa Burton (1752–1836) Thetford, Vt.	(60)
Asahel Hooker (1762–1813) Goshen, Conn.	(33)
Alvan Hyde (1768–1833) Lee, Mass.	(15)
Theophilus Packard (1769–1855) Shelburne, Mass.	(31)
Edward Dorr Griffin (1770–1837) Williamstown, Mass.	(8)
Ebenezer Porter (1772–1834) Washington, Conn.	(8)

Source: See note 15.

SCHOOLS OF THE PROPHETS BY THE NUMBERS

A detailed pedagogical genealogy of New Divinity men can be reconstructed by tracing three and sometimes four generations of education in schools of the prophets. Jonathan Edwards mentored Bellamy and Hopkins, who established their own schools; John Smalley, a student of Bellamy's, continued the tradition by training twenty students, including Nathanael Emmons. And so it went. By 1800 hundreds of New Divinity men could trace their pedigree back through several teachers to Edwards himself. Unraveling this complex web of New Divinity relations reveals that Congregationalists who played major roles in the outpouring of the early-nineteenth-century revivals as well as in the formation of and participation in the modern missionary movement received their instruction, direction, and inspiration in New Divinity schools of the prophets.[17] For example, Hopkins trained Edwards's son, Jonathan Jr., who in turn trained Edward Dorr Griffin, a leading revivalist, seminary professor, and college president. In the early 1820s, during the first years of his presidency at Williams College, Griffin continued the tradition of New Divinity mentoring by instructing recent graduates.

From Bellamy's rustic school there issued a number of influential New Divinity leaders, including Levi Hart who trained Charles Backus and Asa Burton—two men whose prodigious teaching efforts have already been cited. Backus, in turn, mentored three college presidents—his nephew Azel Backus of Hamilton; Zephaniah Swift Moore of Williams and later Amherst; and Henry Davis of Middlebury and later Hamilton. Included among Backus's students who initiated their own parlor seminaries were Alvan Hyde and Jacob Catlin, colleagues in Berkshire County, Massachusetts. To cite a final example: John Smalley, a student of Bellamy's, tutored Ebenezer Porter, a leading pastor-revivalist in Washington, Connecticut, and later professor of homiletics and president of Andover. During his pastorate at Washington, Porter trained both Gordon Hall and Harvey Loomis, Williams College graduates (1807) who, at the famous 1806 Haystack Prayer Meeting at Williams, were among those who dedicated their lives to overseas missionary service.

17. For example, see the pedigree chart in Kling, *Field of Divine Wonders*, 31. This informal web of connections characterizes purposive movements in general. The New Divinity movement closely followed bonding patterns of the English Puritan movement. As David D. Hall notes in *Faithful Shepherd*, "Family intermarriage, familial patterns of recruitment, and a complex set of spiritual relationships were other bonds among the members of the [Puritan] brotherhood" (50).

In addition to creating linkages between the awakenings, New Divinity schools of the prophets generated discrete group identities. Indeed, the schools of the prophets not only functioned as parlor seminaries and ministerial placement centers but also furnished the social matrix for marriage and associational bonds. In some cases, students married the daughter or relative of their mentor; in others, a spouse was discovered within the larger New Divinity social network. Levi Hart not only listened to the words of Bellamy but found a wife in his daughter. Jeremiah Hallock joined the New Divinity extended family by marrying the sister to the wife of his mentor, Abraham Fowler.

The schools of the prophets also created a sense of social cohesiveness that enabled the movement to flourish. With college acquaintances renewed, friendships made, values shared, and piety enhanced, teacher and students set about their common task. Moreover, prospective pastors were initiated into the private as well as the public side of ministerial life. Their mentor not only imparted theology in the study and preached the Word in the meetinghouse, but he also proffered pastoral advice and provided a model of godly living. Nathanael Emmons "often discoursed upon the duties, difficulties, advantages and trials of ministers" and exhorted his students "to give themselves wholly to their work, and never encumber themselves with the concerns of the world, or dissipate their minds by mixing with vain and unprofitable company." Beyond mere words, pastor-teachers lived lives their impressionable students emulated. In his deportment at home with his wife and children and in his pastoral relations, the teacher transmitted attitudes and values that his students carried with them into their own ministerial careers. Heman Humphrey, a 1805 graduate of Yale and later president of Amherst College, recalled his tenure of instruction with Asahel Hooker: "Living in his family, observing how he went out and came in, how he walked before his flock, ... enjoying his daily conversations, sitting under his ministry, and getting insensibly as it were, initiated into the duties of the pastoral office, by the light of his example, were among the most important benefits enjoyed in his school."[18]

Not all of the students' waking hours were dedicated to theological preparation. Some "seminarians" offset their expenses by regular farm work or by tutoring their instructor's children and so relieved their mentor of secular distractions. On occasion, students took to the fields to

18. Emmons, "Memoir of Nathanael Emmons," 1:xxv; Sprague, *Annals of the American Pulpit*, 2:321; see also Vaill, "Theological Education in Connecticut," 141–42.

assist their teacher in the harvest of his crops. At other times, they were pressed into a different and more consequential harvest—that of souls. Asahel Hooker, whose congregation experienced repeated revivals from 1799 to 1807, regularly enlisted the aid of his students to instruct and counsel potential converts.[19] In much the same way, Charles Backus's school included a practicum component. As students neared the end of their instruction and after they obtained a preaching license, Backus allowed them to preach from his pulpit and in neighboring churches. Students also refined their communication skills in the more intimate setting of the "conference" meeting, a weekly gathering for the instruction and edification of parishioners. Here, Backus would call upon several students to speak briefly on a selected passage of Scripture, after which he summarized their comments and made application.[20]

The course of study as well as the demands placed upon students in schools of the prophets varied from instructor to instructor. Clerical apprentices spent most of their time in independent study, which, as one student claimed, "was admirably fitted to put a young man upon his own resources." Payson Williston, who studied for a year with Benjamin Trumbull, considered him an "abundantly competent" instructor but not particularly demanding. "Nearly all that he did," recalled Payson, "was to hear our recitations in Vincent's Catechism, to direct us in regard to our reading, and occasionally to criticise our arguments and compositions." Trumbull's relaxed standards and general attitude toward his own North Haven parish, however, do not fit the normal profile of New Divinity theological instructors and pastors. Students of Bellamy and Emmons recalled the exactitude and "the ordeal . . . of criticism" to which these two New Divinity giants subjected them.[21]

THE CURRICULUM

However rigorous or relaxed the requirements, New Divinity instruction followed scholastic patterns of theological education: directed reading,

19. Clark, *New England Ministry*, 34.

20. Vaill, "Theological Education in Connecticut," 141; Sprague, *Annals of the American Pulpit*, 2:63–64. Bellamy permitted and encouraged his students to preach in the outlying areas of Bethlehem. See Bellamy, *Works of Joseph Bellamy*, 1:lvii.

21. Student quoted in Emmons, *Works of Nathanael Emmons*, 1:220; Williston quoted in Sprague, *Annals of the American Pulpit*, 1:590; Bellamy, *Works of Bellamy*, 1:lvii; Emmons, *Works of Nathanael Emmons* (1861), 1:220 (quotation).

personal instruction, and answering questions in "polemical" (systematic) or didactic theology. Theological study was foremost, as is attested by the long hours (thirteen to eighteen hours a day) some New Divinity instructors spent wrestling with post-Great Awakening theological issues. The other three areas of the traditional fourfold pattern of theological education (church history, practical theology, Bible) were subordinated to the study of theology. As one might expect, instructors ignored the early church fathers, paid scant attention to scriptural exegesis or linguistics, and slighted the notion of doctrinal development other than to relate the usual tale of medieval corruptions and Reformation correctives.[22] In the charged atmosphere of theological debate and emerging Protestant pluralism during the last half of the eighteenth century, polemical theology was de rigueur for the New Divinity.

Accounts of actual instruction are fragmentary, but piecing them together yields a remarkably consistent picture of New Divinity training practices for three-quarters of a century. Students were presented with a series of theological questions in a fashion reminiscent of catechetical instruction. With the questions before them, Joseph Bellamy's students wrote "dissertations"

> on such subjects as the existence, attributes, and moral government of God; our moral agency, and the law under which we are placed; the sinful state and character of mankind; the need of a divine revelation, and the fact that one has been given; the great doctrines of revelation, especially of the gospel; the character, offices, and work of Christ; the atonement, and regeneration through the truth, and by the Holy Spirit; justification by faith; the distinguishing nature and fruits of repentance, love, and other Christian graces; growth in grace; the perseverance of the saints; death, the resurrection, and final judgment; heaven and hell, the nature of the church; particular churches, their officers and ordinances; the nature, uses, and ends of church discipline, etc.[23]

Bellamy thus covered the standard topics in Protestant scholastic theology in a kind of "short course" that, in a modern divinity school setting, might constitute a year-long survey of dogmatic theology.

The informal nature of the schools of the prophets dictated against standardized educational procedures. A degree of coherence was

22. Gambrell, *Ministerial Training*, 135.
23. Bellamy, *Works of Bellamy*, 1:lvii.

maintained, however, through constant interaction among New Divinity men or by teachers simply duplicating the methods and questions of their New Divinity predecessors. Bellamy and Hopkins exchanged correspondence over a common core of theological questions, and in 1756 Bellamy went so far as to suggest that they coauthor a text of questions to be used in the schools. Because Bellamy's school was one of the earliest and the most popular of the day, his system of teaching became the New Divinity modus operandi. John Smalley followed Bellamy's pedagogical lead, as did his student Nathanael Emmons. Other instructors such as Charles Backus, Jonathan Edwards Jr., Stephen West, and Asahel Hooker supplied questions and required students to write dissertations on standard theological topics.[24]

To answer theological questions, students consulted Scripture and read a variety of theological treatises—both orthodox and heterodox. They then discussed their dissertations and assigned readings with their teacher for an hour or two in the afternoon or evenings. A rather revealing indicator of the growing theological contentiousness during the last half of the eighteenth century (or perhaps a testimony to a more comprehensive approach to theology) is the increasing number of questions added to the instructor's list. Jonathan Edwards, for example, compiled a list of ninety questions for his students; Bellamy suggested a list of between two and three hundred questions; a generation later, Edwards's son's list ran to over three hundred. Jonathan the Younger's questions ranged from the standard catechetical queries ("For what purposes was revelation necessary?" "Was Christ a son from eternity?") to specific New Divinity concerns ("What is the difference between natural and moral necessity?" "What do you mean by disinterested love?" "Do the unregenerate grow better in the use of means?"). Maltby Gelston, a student of the younger Edwards, kept a notebook in which he recorded the answers to some five hundred questions covering the basics of didactic theology. Presumably, all of his answers were committed to memory.[25]

The small libraries of rural New Divinity parsons and the narrow focus of theological study dictated that priority be given to depth of

---

24. Conforti, *Samuel Hopkins*, 37; Emmons, *Works of Nathanael Emmons*, 1:xxiv. On West, see Sprague, *Annals of the American Pulpit*, 1:553. On Hooker, see Sprague, *Annals of the American Pulpit*, 2:320-21. On Backus, see Vaill, "Theological Education in Connecticut," 141.

25. See *Theological Questions*; Joseph Bellamy to Samuel Hopkins, 30 Jan. 1756, Gratz Collection; Gambrell, *Ministerial Training*, 134.

understanding, not breadth of knowledge. This approach accorded with the practices of other theological instructors such as David Tappan, Hollis Professor at Harvard, whose reading requirements were comparable to those of New Divinity instructors. The difference, of course, was that Tappan's students had access to the substantial holdings of Harvard's library, whereas students of New Divinity men were limited to their teacher's personal holdings. A singular exception among the New Divinity was the library of Nathanael Emmons. His holdings included not only his own but the parish's and the town's—the latter representing the personal bequest of Benjamin Franklin. More typical was the collection of Asa Burton, whose works filled a six-foot shelf. The meager libraries of New Divinity instructors often included a few works by rationalists and deists (such as those of Lord Herbert of Cherbury, Daniel Whitby, and David Hume) so that students could engage the argument of the "enemy," with the balance of these libraries filled with works by agreeable authors. A student of Stephen West recalled that "the books to be read were few, among them were Hopkins's *System of Divinity* [1793; i.e., *System of Doctrines*] and a few other important works such as might be expected in the library of a country minister." For three-quarters of a century, the New Divinity canon built upon the writings of Edwards and Bellamy and then, as they came available, expanded to include the works of other New Divinity authors—Hopkins's *System of Doctrines* and selected theological treatises by Stephen West and John Smalley.[26]

THE IDEAL PASTOR

After studying with a New Divinity teacher for as little as three months or with several teachers intermittently for three years, after reading and learning New Divinity dogmatics, and after living with a pastor, his family, and a few other students, what expectations did an aspiring pastor take with him into the ministry? What goals did New Divinity teachers have for their students? Indeed, what was the ideal New Divinity minister? Despite the far-reaching changes to New England's ministry from 1750 to 1850—variously characterized by scholars as "from office to profession"

---

26. See Sprague, *Annals of the American Pulpit*, 1:553 (quotation); "List of Books," 326. For an extended discussion of New Divinity library holdings, see Gambrell, *Ministerial Training*, 108–24. On Emmons's holdings, see Dahlquist, "Nathanael Emmons," 102–10. For other references to New Divinity "reading lists," see Robbins, *Diary of Thomas Robbins*, 1:36–50; Park, *Memoir of Nathanael Emmons*, 218–19.

or "from job-oriented to congregation-oriented"—the New Divinity pastoral model remained remarkably consistent. To be sure, New Divinity men were at once affected by and contributed to this altered perception of ministry.[27] In some cases, the New Divinity–trained "parson" of the mid-eighteenth century became, by the early decades of the nineteenth century, a professional, whether as a college president, seminary professor, religious newspaper editor, or benevolent society employee. At the same time, the New Divinity pastor-teachers remained indebted to the classical Protestant conception of the evangelical minister as one who preached the Word of God for the salvation and edification of his hearers. Richard Baxter's *The Reformed Pastor* (1655) remained a popular handbook for Congregational ministers throughout the colonial era and well into the nineteenth century. This classic of pastoral theology emphasized the primacy of theological study but subordinated its study to practical ends. Perhaps for this reason—for its utilitarian bent—the New Divinity never found the pastoral Baxter as compelling as the more speculative Edwards.

New Divinity ordination sermons, published during the last half of the eighteenth century, reiterated the evangelical view of the ideal pastor. At the same time, the New Divinity highlighted prominent themes in Edwards that emphasized the role of the minister as a theologian. Edwards's 1744 ordination sermon, "The True Excellency of a Gospel Minister," served as a paradigm for the New Divinity conception of the ministry. Taking his text from John 5:35 (where Christ observed that John "was a bright and shining light"), Edwards averred that "light and heat must be united in a minister of the gospel." By "light" he meant that ministers must possess correct doctrinal knowledge, or "great speculative knowledge." In order to reveal the mind and will of God, the gospel minister knew the things of God. Light, however, was not sufficient. As Edwards had noted some years before, the people of his congregation in Northampton, Massachusetts, did not so much need their "heads stored" with knowledge as their "hearts touched" by God. To be able to touch the heart, the gospel minister needed "heat," consisting of a "holy zeal," an

---

27. Scott, *From Office to Profession*; Andrew, *Rebuilding the Christian Commonwealth*, 39. Kling, *Field of Divine Wonders*, 35–42, discusses this changing conception of ministry in the context of clerical mobility, salary disputes, personal ambition, and increasing factiousness between pastor and parishioners.

"ardour in his heart," or a "heart warmed and inflamed with a great love to Christ."²⁸

Ordination sermons elaborated upon the Edwardsean twofold model. The overarching qualifications for the ministry remained consistent: to advance the kingdom of Christ through the promotion of salvation and piety. To that end, a faithful New Divinity minister of the gospel met three qualifications. First, he himself was spiritually regenerate, having an "experimental acquaintance with Christianity." The contentions raised during the Great Awakening over "an unconverted ministry" remained foremost in the New Divinity mind. A minister could not preach "Ye must be born again" without being reborn himself. The Reverend Nathan Perkins of West Hartford posed a simple question: "How can one whose eyes were never opened lead the blind?"²⁹ Typically, New Divinity ministerial aspirants experienced conversion in their late teens or early twenties, during that critical period when a previous "calling" to the ministry now approached the actual assumption of the ministerial task.

A second qualification for ministry was knowledge. Thoroughly grounded in the ancient languages, Scripture, and doctrine, the New Divinity pastor was a "workman" engaged in "deep thought" and "hard study," "mighty in Scriptures, and expert in reasoning upon divine subjects."³⁰ During the last decades of the eighteenth century, a period that increasingly emphasized the ability of humans to take control of their personal and political destinies, the New Divinity considered the defense of the Calvinist faith as a primary qualification to the ministry. "You will be unworthy of your station," noted Charles Backus to his nephew Azel Backus, "if you are not able to contend earnestly for its divine original, and heavenly doctrines." A godly minister, then, was a "watchman," ever vigilant in defense of the faith against corrupting influences, whether in the form of spiritual apathy among parishioners or of outright challenges posed by "deists" and "infidels."³¹

Piety, the final qualification for the ministry, outwardly expressed an inwardly changed heart. True virtue or self-giving love was a fruit of

---

28. Edwards, *WPE* 10:506. For a sensitive treatment of Edwards's conception of the ministry, see Westra, "'Above All Others,'" 209–19.

29. On the qualifications for ministry, see Perkins, *Sermon*, 8 (quotation), 23; Backus, *Faithful Ministers*, 7; Burton, *Sermon*, 16; Hart, *Christian Minister*, 8–9.

30. Trumbull, *Sermon*, 7; Backus, *Qualifications and Duties*, 10–12; Edwards Jr., *Duty of Ministers*, 13; Perkins, *Sermon*, 16; Emmons, *Sermon*, 22.

31. Backus, *Faithful Ministers*, 22, 24 (quotation); Trumbull, *Sermon*, 8; Backus, *Ministers Serving God*, 11; Hooker, *Immoral and Pernicious Tendency*, 23.

salvation, the result of the work of Christ in one's heart. A man of piety, or "a real good man" as the New Divinity called him, exhibited a love of Christ and relished "the moral beauty of scripture doctrines."[32] A godly minister thus gave evidence of the work of grace in his life.

Having met these prerequisites, the New Divinity pastor fulfilled his ministerial duty by preaching the gospel. Speaking the Word of God—primarily in Sabbath sermons but also in mid-week lectures, in conferences, and in house visitations—was the God-ordained means of bringing sinners to salvation and saints to edification. The title of Levi Hart's ordination sermon "The Christian Minister, or *Faithful Preacher of the Gospel Described*" (emphasis added) aptly depicted the New Divinity's virtual identification of ministry with preaching. Administering the ordinances and visiting the sick were incumbent upon all pastors but clearly of secondary importance.

Finally, the medium was inseparable from the message. How the sermon was preached was as important as its content. In the span of three-quarters of a century, alterations in composition and style occurred, and yet the New Divinity men remained constant champions of evangelical preaching. Such sermonizing was "plain," "bold," "tender," "convincing," and directed to the "hearts and consciences of hearers." New Divinity men had mixed success as preachers: some, like Hopkins, stupefied their congregations; others, like Griffin, stunned. However, they all enjoined a manner of preaching congruent with Edwards's teaching on the head and the heart.[33] For the Edwardseans, knowing religion and being religious constituted inseparable aspects of a single reality, and the preached sermon was the most appropriate God-ordained vehicle for apprehending this reality.

In addition to this primary preaching task, New Divinity ministers counseled the display of "distinguishing marks of conversion." These marks included self-sacrifice in placing the cause of Christ before personal pleasure, zealousness in the work of God, and devotion to the spiritual life. Edwards's advice became the constant refrain through the years: "As to the things of the world, you are not to expect outward ease,

---

32. Perkins, *Sermon*, 8; Edwards Jr., *All Divine Truth Profitable*, 37; Emmons, *Discourse, preached*, 14; Backus, *High Importance of Love*, 9.

33. Perkins, *Discourse delivered at the Ordination*, 12–18; Trumbull, *Sermon*, 8; Backus, *Qualifications and Duties*, 18; Edwards Jr., *Duty of Ministers*, 16; Emmons, *Discourse, delivered*, 21–22. For the varying approaches, attitudes, and successes of New Divinity preaching, see Kling, *Field of Divine Wonders*, chap. 4.

pleasure, and plenty; nor are you to depend on the friendship and respect of men, but [you] should prepare to endure hardness, as one that is going forth as a soldier to war." New Divinity teachers urged their students to practice constant self-examination in order to know the true condition of their corrupt hearts and thus to affirm their dependence upon a sovereign yet merciful God. Moreover, what mentors demanded of themselves they enjoined upon their students: rigorous study, disciplined habits, and single-minded devotion to the ministry. Criticizing "indolence" as "inexcusable" and a form of "worldliness," they fulfilled the divine calling with a self-denying holy zeal. Wary of unprofitable conversation (even with parishioners!), ever mindful of the need for vigilance against the powers of darkness (whether real or imagined infidelity), and captured (at times enraptured) by a vision of God's glory, the New Divinity viewed the calling to the ministry as an either/or proposition. "There can be no neuters in the cause of Christ," warned Nathanael Emmons. "He that is not for him, must be against him. You must be conformed either to Christ or to the world."[34]

CONCLUSION

Standard histories of theological education in New England typically conclude the story of the New Divinity schools of the prophets with the opening of Andover Theological Seminary in 1808. This first seminary, after all, had New Divinity men among its founders and first professors and thus siphoned off potential students from schools of the prophets. The professional seminary filled the obvious need to train the growing number of male converts from the Second Great Awakening who felt called into full-time Christian service. And so the overworked New Divinity pastor-teacher, with his meager collection of books and desultory educational requirements, happily yielded to seminary professors, well-stocked theological libraries, and formal curricula. Coincident with the professions of law and medicine, the study of divinity went the way of general professionalization.[35] Together, these developments betokened the final chapter in the history of the schools of the prophets.

34. Emmons, *Sermon, Delivered*, 8, 29 (quotation); Edwards, *WPE* 10:509; Perkins, *Sermon*, 16; Edwards Jr., *Duty of Ministers*, 15. Regarding unprofitable conversations, see Backus, *Qualifications and Duties*, 9.

35. See Gambrell, *Ministerial Training*, chap. 8; Bainton, *Yale and the Ministry*, chap. 7; Woods, *History of the Andover Theological Seminary*. On the rise of these professions, see Haber, *Quest for Authority*.

There is, however, an epilogue to the story, for just as the professional study of law and medicine did not immediately displace traditional apprenticeship practices, so the opening of Andover did not lead to an abrupt closing of the schools of the prophets. Even with the founding of additional seminaries (Princeton in 1812, Harvard in 1815, Bangor in 1816, Auburn in 1818, General in 1819, and Yale in 1822), the schools of the prophets, albeit in considerably reduced numbers, persisted. We may view the years from 1808 until the mid-1820s as a transitional phase during which a number of options lay before clerical aspirants. Some continued to receive all of their post-graduate theological training with a New Divinity "prophet"; others studied with a pastor *and* at a seminary; still others made the transition complete by preparing exclusively at one of the newly established divinity schools.

A vital component in the continued influence of the schools of the prophets was the New England provincial college. Whereas Yale had served as the primary feeder to schools of the prophets throughout the eighteenth century, rural New England colleges emerged as the primary feeders during the first quarter of the nineteenth century. Just as many church-related colleges today function as feeder schools to denominational seminaries, so in the early republic a number of newly formed colleges funneled aspiring ministers to New Divinity finishing schools. The reason for this development is obvious: New Divinity men filled leadership posts in these colleges and thus strongly influenced the choice of a graduate's theological training. Presidents and professors at Dartmouth, Williams, and, to a lesser extent, Hamilton and Union channeled graduates to established New Divinity teachers such as Charles Backus, Nathanael Emmons, Ephraim Judson, Alvan Hyde, and Asa Burton.

The early history of Williams College, from 1793 to 1836, provides an instructive example of how New Divinity influence at an undergraduate institution was parlayed into continued New Divinity mentoring practices. Williams's first institutional leaders were all men of the New Divinity stripe, with connections to the schools of the prophets. They served as the college's first three presidents (1793–1836), as its first five vice presidents, and as members of the board of trustees.[36] Though not

36. For an extended treatment of the New Divinity at Williams, see chap. 8 in this volume. The college's presidents were Ebenezer Fitch, 1793–1815; Zephaniah Swift Moore, 1815–21; and Edward Dorr Griffin, 1821–36; the first five vice presidents were Stephen West, Alan Hyde, Samuel Shepard, Timothy Mather Cooley, and Emerson Davis; New Divinity members of the board included Reverends Daniel Collins, Seth Swift, Job Swift, Ammi Robbins, and Jacob Catlin.

always successful in imposing New Divinity views upon Williams, these men influenced the institution theologically and nurtured men of piety and evangelical zeal who ministered at home and abroad.

With this potent New Divinity presence, professors, presidents, and board members influenced the choice of theological education of graduates who intended to serve as pastors or missionaries. Prior to Andover's establishment, 70 percent (thirty-eight of fifty-five) of Williams's alumni who entered the ministry apprenticed with a New Divinity pastor-teacher.[37] Beginning with the graduating class of 1807, ministerial and missionary candidates sought opportunities for professional theological education at Andover and then at Princeton after 1812. Nevertheless, the schools of the prophets continued to draw their fair share. Between 1807 and 1822, of the 120 alumni seeking theological education, thirty-five studied with a New Divinity pastor, forty-two studied at Andover, and eleven studied at Princeton.

After 1822 only a handful of students preferred the schools of the prophets, but New Divinity connections persisted and remained crucial during Edward D. Griffin's presidency from 1821 to 1836. These alliances are illustrated in personal relationships that translated into institutional ties between Williams, a nondenominational but informally Congregational college, and Auburn Theological Seminary, a Presbyterian institution with close ties to the New Divinity. Griffin and James Richards, professor of theology at Auburn (1823–42), had known each other since the early 1800s, when both held pastorates in New Jersey—Griffin in Newark and Richards in Morristown. They maintained close ties through the years and shared upwardly mobile career paths by moving from prestigious pastorates to seminary professorships. More importantly, they shared Edwardsean theological views. When Richards accepted a position as professor of Christian theology at Auburn, Griffin deliberately sent Williams graduates in his direction. Between 1824 and 1837, forty-five Williams graduates attended Auburn, the second highest number among feeder institutions to the seminary.[38]

---

37. These and subsequent calculations on Williams graduates (unless otherwise noted) are based upon Durfee, *Williams Biographical Annals*.

38. For the Edwardsean views of Griffin, see Kling, *Field of Divine Wonders*. For Richards, see Sprague, *Annals of the American Pulpit*, 4:99–112; Adams, *History of Auburn Theological Seminary*, 73; Gridley, "Biographical Sketch," 86–87; Richards, *Lectures on Mental Philosophy*, 97–153, 476–501. For Williams graduates, see Adams, *History of Auburn Theological Seminary*, 94.

During this same interval, however, no graduates studied in schools of the prophets. Clearly, by this time the transition was complete; ministerial education had become the exclusive domain of the seminary.[39] Although the demise of the schools of the prophets did not necessarily portend the demise of New Divinity theology, it undoubtedly hastened it. The medium was indispensable to the message, for the staying power of the New Divinity was linked to a specific educational environment. Indeed, for three-quarters of a century, the New Divinity flourished—quite literally—in homes of its own.

---

39. For a helpful discussion of the rise of the theological seminary, see Naylor, "Theological Seminary," 17–30.

8

The New Divinity and Williams College, 1793–1836

THE STORY IS A familiar one, found in nearly every narrative text of American religious history. In the summer of 1806, five Williams College students met in a grove of trees to pray for divine guidance and to discuss their religious faith and calling. While seeking refuge from a summer rainstorm under a haystack, Samuel J. Mills Jr., and the other four students consecrated their lives to overseas missions. This incident, later publicized as the Haystack Prayer Meeting, became the pivotal event in the launching of American Protestantism's foreign missionary movement. Mills and several comrades carried their vision from Williams to Andover Theological Seminary, where they created a more formal organization that eventually led to the establishment of the American Board of Commissioners for Foreign Missions (ABCFM) in 1810. In the hagiography of missions, Mills is revered as the "father" of American foreign missions and Williams as the birthplace. Subsequently, Mills's "sons"—alumni of Williams—followed his precedent: from 1810 to 1840, Williams provided more missionaries to the ABCFM than any other American college.[1]

Since the mid-nineteenth century, partisans of missions and nearly all scholarly observers have attributed the origins of this missionary spirit at Williams to the writings of Jonathan Edwards and his self-appointed heirs, those Congregational ministers who came to be called New Divinity men.[2] Edwards supplied the exemplary missionary model in *Life of*

---

1. Phillips, *Protestant America and the Pagan World*, chap. 1.
2. On the influence of the New Divinity generally and Samuel Hopkins in particular

David Brainerd (1749), his most popular and most frequently reprinted work.³ Samuel Hopkins then furnished an explicit theological rationale for missions by revising Edwards's aesthetic concept of "disinterested benevolence" to God (i.e., a love for God because of who God is) into a practical one of self-denial for the greater glory of God's kingdom. Edwards A. Park, the man most responsible for the resuscitation of Edwardseanism in the nineteenth century, observed that "Williams College was intimately associated with the cause of Hopkinsianism, as well as the cause of Missions, the one cause being a precursor of the other."⁴

But why this intimate association between Williams College and the New Divinity? This essay addresses this question with three observations. First, scholarship of the last two decades has convincingly refuted older estimations that the New Divinity was little more than Calvinist scholasticism run wild, that it was an obscurantist movement guaranteed to quench the fires of revivalism, and that grim, moralistic Edwardseans betrayed the living piety of their namesake.⁵ To be sure, the New Divinity engaged in metaphysical speculation, and its adherents tended to be stiff-necked moralists. In such matters, however, they were certainly no different than Edwards himself. Far from aloof pedagogues whose preaching stupefied their congregations, these "great men of their day," as Henry May once called them,⁶ promoted revivals of the Second Great Awakening and provided clerical leadership to a host of emergent voluntary societies in the early republic. Among their organizing efforts that, until

---

on the American foreign missionary movement, see Elsbree, *Rise of the Missionary Spirit*; Sweet, *Religion in the Development of American Culture*, 231; Beaver, "Missionary Motivation," 121–26; Phillips, *Protestant America and the Pagan World*, chap. 1; Chaney, "God's Glorious Work"; Conforti, *Samuel Hopkins*, 157–58; McCoy, "Women of the ABCFM Oregon Mission," 62–82.

3. Conforti, "David Brainerd," 310–11.

4. Park, *Memoir of Nathanael Emmons*, 212. Arthur Latham Perry stridently dissented with the view that linked the New Divinity with missions at Williams College. In his intriguing but at times bombastic *Williamstown and Williams College*, he called Park's quote "untrue" (222). Perry's animosity toward the perceived intolerance and fruitless metaphysical speculations of the New Divinity prevented a fair evaluation of its impact upon Williams.

5. This older view was given classic formulation in Haroutunian, *Piety versus Moralism*, and advanced by Morgan, "American Revolution as an Intellectual Movement," 11–33; Berk, *Calvinism versus Democracy*. For representative samples of revisionist scholarship, see Breitenbach, "Piety and Moralism," 177–204; Conforti, *Samuel Hopkins*; Guelzo, *Edwards on the Will*; Kling, *Field of Divine Wonders*; Valeri, *Law and Providence*.

6. May, *Enlightenment in America*, 59.

recently, has gone largely unnoticed was their guiding influence in the formation of New England regional colleges such as Williams.

Second, the origins of Williams College had nothing to do with New Divinity Edwardseanism, yet the early history of the college exemplified nothing less than its institutionalization. Unlike Dartmouth, Amherst, and Mount Holyoke, colleges whose origins clearly reflected Edwardsean influences,[7] Williams College claimed no such paternity. Williams, however, perhaps more than any of these institutions, reflected the ongoing penetration of the New Divinity into the frontier regions of New England. The Haystack Prayer Meeting represented neither the culmination nor an exceptional instance of New Divinity influence; rather, it epitomized a trend in the New Divinity enculturation of Williams. For over forty years, beginning in 1793 with its first president, Ebenezer Fitch, and extending throughout the presidencies of Zephaniah Swift Moore (1815–21) and particularly of Edward Dorr Griffin (1821–36), a distinct New Divinity theological culture shaped the character of Williams College.

Finally, viewed in a wider context, the intimate association between Williams College and the New Divinity illustrates the vitality of the New Divinity movement throughout New England, whether in cities such as Boston and Hartford or, more typically, in rural villages.[8] The realignment and internal upheaval within Congregationalism (e.g., disestablishment, the rise of Unitarianism) and the external challenges from upstart Methodists and other popular religious groups should not be seen as detracting from a revitalized Edwardseanism whose devotees championed revival and home and foreign missionary work and who created and staffed educational institutions to promote their cause.

The New Divinity hegemony at Williams College, then, reflects the consequences of an emboldened, not a quiescent, Calvinism. More specifically, the opening of the college coincided with the apogee of New Divinity clerical strength in Berkshire County as well as with the outbreak of New Divinity revivals in western Massachusetts and northwestern Connecticut.[9] Accordingly, the religious character of Williams

7. See Richardson, *History of Dartmouth College*, 1:239–40; Fuess, *Amherst*, 30; Conforti, "Mary Lyon," 69–89.

8. For contemporary references to the New Divinity in the greater Boston area, see Bentley, *Diary of William Bentley*, 3:334, 364–65, 402–3, 445, 447, 462, 496, 527, 549; 4:159; Lee, *Memoirs of Rev. Joseph Buckminster*, 330. For other major New Divinity outposts, including Hartford, see Guelzo, *Edwards on the Will*, 92–93 (including maps); and n9 below.

9. On New Divinity strength in Berkshire County, see Birdsall, *Berkshire County*,

was profoundly influenced by New Divinity clergy chosen to sit on the board of trustees as well as by the influx of pious students such as Samuel Mills, who numbered among the hundreds of converts in New Divinity revivals at the turn of the century. Far from being a desiccated scholarly movement, the New Divinity captured the hearts and minds of hundreds of ordinary young men such as Mills who appropriated the essential features of New Divinity theology. In doing so, they espoused a moderate Edwardseanism that fit comfortably into the early republic's evangelical ethos.

That Mills attended Williams College and made it the epicenter of missions was not happenstance. New Divinity connections influenced his decision to choose this fledgling institution over Yale, his father's alma mater, which was located considerably closer to his home in Torringford, Connecticut. Apart from its New Divinity hegemony, Williams's low cost and convenient location for the rural youth of Massachusetts, Vermont, and New York made the college a natural choice. Whether these students arrived informed or ignorant of the New Divinity, or whether they embraced or rejected New Divinity teaching at Williams, one thing was certain: they could not escape the shaping of this institution by New Divinity interests.

THE ORIGINS OF WILLIAMS COLLEGE

Several ironies attend the making of Williams College as a hotbed of New Divinity sentiment. First, the college was never, in a legal or formal sense, a religious institution.[10] Unlike Yale, after which Williams patterned its curriculum, the college's articles of incorporation articulated no mission of training "an educated ministry." In fact, religious purposes of any kind were not mentioned. The reason for this omission lies with Williams's benefactor, Colonel Ephraim Williams (1715–55), whose will stipulated the creation of a "Free School," not a college. Williams, a bookish bachelor, intended the school to serve the educational needs of the sons of men who had served in the militia.[11] Consequently, the charters for the short-lived free school (1791–93) and the college that evolved from it expressed

---

33–74; Conforti, "Rise of the New Divinity," 37–47; and chap. 7 in this volume. On New Divinity revivals, see Kling, *Field of Divine Wonders*.

10. Rudolph, *Mark Hopkins and the Log*, 91.
11. Fitch, "Historical Sketch," 47–53.

no religious goals. Despite spiritually nurturing and then graduating hundreds of students who entered the ministry in some capacity, Williams never officially identified with a denomination (though it was unofficially associated with Congregationalism) or a religious mission.

A second and greater irony is that the Williams name ever came to be associated with an institution bearing an Edwardsean stamp. Ephraim Williams was a Calvinist, but an Edwardsean he was not. A member of the Williams clan, the most prominent family among the so-called "river gods" of the Connecticut valley and "mountain gods" of the Berkshire region, Ephraim thoroughly identified with the family's Old Calvinist ties.[12] In the aftermath of the Great Awakening, several distinct but related disputes erupted between Jonathan Edwards and his cousins of the Williams clan. While the quarrel among kinsmen involved issues of personality and politics, fundamental to their disagreement were religious convictions. Edwards and the Williamses clashed often and bitterly over Edwards's New Light Calvinism, particularly his "pure church" ecclesiology. Against the Puritan and then Old Calvinist ideal of a seamless church and society, Edwards rent the two apart, arguing that the church must be reserved for the regenerate alone. Edwards and his New Divinity disciples rejected the Half-Way Covenant and any other temporizing criteria for church membership. In opposition, the Williams family defended the Puritan idea of a commonwealth, the integration of church and society.

On three separate occasions and at three different venues, the powerful Williams clan challenged Edwards's convictions. Beginning at Northampton, the Reverend Solomon Williams responded to Edwards's *Humble Inquiry* (1749)—a definition and defense of visible sainthood as a criterion for church membership—with *The True State of the Question concerning the Qualifications Necessary to Lawful Communion in the Christian Sacraments* (1751).[13] Ephraim Sr., the college founder's father, also publicly entered the controversy by supporting Edwards's dismissal from his Northampton congregation. When Edwards moved on to candidate at Stockbridge in 1751, father and son lobbied unsuccessfully to prevent his settlement. Ephraim Jr. conveyed his displeasure with Edwards, finding him "unsociable . . . unable to teach" and a "very great

---

12. My discussion of the Williams family and their conflict with Edwards is indebted to Sweeney, "River Gods and Related Minor Deities," 2:413–95. See also Tracy, *Jonathan Edwards, Pastor*, 171–94.

13. For a discussion of this dispute, see Hall, "Editor's Introduction," 68–77.

bigot."[14] A final conflict—and a portent of the Edwardsean domination of western Massachusetts—had less to do with Edwards himself than with the attractiveness of his pure church teachings. In 1754, Williams family members tried in vain to prevent the inclusion of strict ecclesiastical principles in the covenant of the Reverend Edward Billings's church in Greenfield. One of the few dissenting members of the council that dismissed Edwards from Northampton, Billings became, according to Kevin Sweeney, the "mid-Connecticut valley's first avowed follower of Edwards."[15]

A year later, Ephraim Williams Jr. initiated what became a long and convoluted chain of events that led to the creation of Williams College. In July 1755, shortly before he was killed in an ambush by French soldiers and Indians at the battle of Bloody Morning Scout during Britain's Great War for Empire, Williams executed his last will and testament, setting aside the residuum of his estate to establish a free school in the "West Township" of Massachusetts. The executors of the estate, Deacon Israel Williams of Hatfield and John Worthington of Springfield, followed Ephraim's wishes, but the turmoil of the War for Independence, a boundary dispute with New York, and site selection snafus delayed the creation of the free school for over thirty-five years. Finally, in 1791, the school opened, consisting of two departments, a tuition-charging academy and an English-instruction free school.[16] Shortly thereafter, the trustees petitioned the state legislature for a new charter as a college. Thirteen months after the free school opened, the general court incorporated Williams College. In October 1793, Williams was organized and three classes were admitted.[17] This progression from academy to college, albeit rapid, typified the evolution of newly established colleges in the early republic.[18]

By 1793, Israel Williams was dead, but another family member assumed direction of the fledgling school. William Williams of Dalton, Israel's son, presided over the board of trustees during the period of transition from free school to college. A devoted churchman who helped

14. Ephraim Williams Jr., quoted in Sweeney, "River Gods and Related Minor Deities," 2:469–70.

15. Sweeney, "River Gods and Related Minor Deities," 2:488.

16. The academy functioned as a college, offering college-level courses, whereas the English free school offered reading and writing in the English language to boys from the upper classes in the town schools. See Durfee, *History of Williams College*, 61.

17. On the origins of Williams College, see Perry, *Williamstown and Williams College*, 151–226.

18. See Robson, *Educating Republicans*, 188.

to establish the Congregational church in Dalton, Williams retained the family's Old Calvinist sympathies. In a letter penned to his wife in 1802, he summarized those convictions:

> Religion, genuine religion, is not a flash of devotion which dies with the feelings of the moment or occasion but a rational consecration of the whole man or woman to God in Christ. . . . Fiery, flaming zeal in religion, and a Christian as cold as a corpse are extremes to be avoided—Happy He or she who has found and can keep the proper medium.[19]

A balanced, rational Calvinism that embraced the Westminster Confession and promulgated the inclusivity of church and society characterized Williams's brand of Christianity. Had he had his way, Old Calvinism would have prevailed at Williams College. The early history of Williams, however, was far different. The ghost of Edwards returned to haunt the Williams clan, appearing in New Divinity apparitions. From the highest reaches of the presidency and board of trustees to the student body, Edwards's second-, third-, and fourth-generation disciples shaped the religious character of Williams College. For forty years, they read New Divinity works, taught New Divinity theology, discoursed in New Divinity language, behaved in New Divinity ways, and promoted New Divinity revivals.

THE NEW DIVINITY MOVEMENT

The New Divinity enculturation at Williams College represents a microcosm of a larger movement. During the early nineteenth century, New Divinity Edwardseanism permeated other areas and other institutions throughout New England. Andover Theological Seminary, for example, had a distinctive Edwardsean theological cast.[20] Joseph Conforti has taken note of Mary Lyon, founder of Mount Holyoke College, as an exemplar of what he calls "the cultural revival of Jonathan Edwards."[21] Williams College, however, founded a generation earlier than Mount Holyoke, is less an instance of the revitalization of Edwards than the continued

---

19. William Williams, quoted in Sweeney, "River Gods and Related Minor Deities," 2:663.

20. See Woods, *History of the Andover Theological Seminary*; Conforti, *Jonathan Edwards*, chap. 5.

21. Conforti, "Mary Lyon."

expansion and penetration of the New Divinity into the farthest reaches of the Massachusetts frontier. By the 1790s, New Divinity pastors in Berkshire County and other counties of western Massachusetts dominated the Congregational establishment.[22] In their ministerial roles as traditional shapers of culture, they exerted a collective influence, whether in the organization of ecclesiastical associations, the formation of libraries and academies, or the advancement of colleges such as Williams.

Like other broad-based movements, the New Divinity identity was not confined to ideology (i.e., doctrine) but evolved into a well-defined social group. This socioreligious milieu promoted new processes of socialization and community formation. Modest social backgrounds, shared educational bonds (first at Yale, then at New Divinity theological finishing "schools of the prophets"), conservative political views (nearly all were Federalists), kinship networks, and fraternal connections through correspondence, pulpit exchanges, and team preaching—all these characterized the New Divinity theological culture.[23]

During the forty-year interlude between the First and Second Great Awakenings, between Edwards's humiliating defeat at Northampton and the founding of Williams College, New Divinity men set down firm roots in northwestern Connecticut and western Massachusetts. Edwards may have lost the initial battle, but his heirs eventually won the cultural war. Joseph Bellamy, derisively called "our Sovereign Lord Bellamy" by Ezra Stiles, seized control of the ecclesiastical machinery and turned the Litchfield Association of Congregational ministers into a New Divinity credentialing operation.[24] In Berkshire County, Stephen West of Stockbridge and Samuel Hopkins of Great Barrington maintained New Divinity orthodoxy by creating the Berkshire Association of Congregational Ministers in 1763. With these organizational mechanisms in place, and with the attraction of these frontier regions to abstemious, missionary-minded New Divinity men, Litchfield and Berkshire counties acquired reputations as dens of New Divinity. Critics referred to the "Litchfield Divinity" or the "Berkshire Divinity," pejoratives for the New Divinity theological hold in these counties.

In the midst of this New Divinity institutional ascendancy, Williams College was established. Its founding reflected a growing national

22. Birdsall, *Berkshire County*, 50.

23. See Birdsall, *Berkshire County*, 41–49; Conforti, *Samuel Hopkins*, chap. 2; Kling, *Field of Divine Wonders*, chap. 1.

24. Stiles, *Literary Diary of Ezra Stiles*, 3:374.

awareness that higher education benefitted the expanding frontier regions as well as produced virtuous citizens and leaders of the republic. Williams was thus one of over fifteen newly founded colleges to address the needs of the new nation.[25] Although the laws of the college did not specify that its board members be clerics, the early leaders of Williams College followed the tradition of Harvard, Yale, and other colleges by selecting clergy to sit on the board of trustees as well as to preside over the college. Unlike at Harvard, though, where a Unitarian-controlled board of overseers was in the process of dispensing with the last vestiges of Calvinism, Williams's clerical board members affirmed its New Divinity variant. These trustees, though always a minority within the seventeen-member board, profoundly influenced college affairs.[26] From their choice of a president to their active recruitment of students, they shaped the religious character of the college.

During the presidencies of Fitch, Moore, and Griffin, the clerical board reads like a "who's who" of New Divinity men.[27] Stephen West of Stockbridge and Alvan Hyde of Lee served as the college's first two vice presidents. West was a natural choice. A pillar of the New Divinity in Stockbridge (he was Edwards's successor) and a respected community leader, West was married to Colonel Williams's half sister Elizabeth. Thus, by dint of kin and character, he was chosen the college's first vice president, a position he held until 1812. West was succeeded by Hyde, a trustee since 1802 and vice president from 1812 to 1833. The Edwardsean ancestry of these two divines could not have been more direct: West was a student of Hopkins and editor of his mentor's autobiography (and Hopkins was a student and biographer of Edwards); Hyde was a student and biographer of West.

The guidance of vice presidents West and Hyde, the self-perpetuating character of the board, and the predominance of New Divinity pastors in Berkshire County ensured New Divinity allegiances among the college's ministerial board members. By default—that is, by a critical mass of numbers—as well as by design, Williams assumed a New Divinity identity. The first ten clerical board members were Daniel Collins (1793–1809)

25. See Robson, *Educating Republicans*, chap. 6.

26. The 1793 board had six clergy and eleven civilians; subsequently, during President Griffin's tenure, the board reached a more balanced composition of eight clergy and nine civilians.

27. Biographical data on vice presidents and the board of trustees are found in Durfee, *Williams Biographical Annals*, 36–97.

of Lanesboro, Massachusetts; Seth Swift (1793–1807) of Williamstown, Massachusetts, and his brother Job Swift (1794–1802) of Bennington, Vermont; Ammi Robbins (1794–1810) of Norfolk, Connecticut; and five others from western Massachusetts—Jacob Catlin (1807–22) of New Marlborough; Theophilus Packard (1810–25) of Shelburne; Thomas Snell (1817–25) of Brookfield; Heman Humphrey (1820–25) of Pittsfield; Isaac Knapp (1822–26) of Westfield—and Ezra Fisk (1823–33) of Goshen, New York. All ten pastors had prepared for the ministry under a New Divinity pastor-teacher; all distinguished themselves as inveterate New Divinity men; and nearly all led or witnessed New Divinity revivals in their parishes. The Reverends Robbins and Catlin, for example, directed young male converts from New Divinity revivals to attend Williams;[28] Packard, Hyde, and Catlin trained aspiring pastors (many of them Williams graduates) in their parlor seminaries;[29] and Humphrey went on to further the cause of Edwardseanism as the president of Amherst College (1823–45).[30]

THE NEW DIVINITY ESTABLISHED: PRESIDENT FITCH (1791–1815)

In 1791, when the trustees of the free school hired Ebenezer Fitch as preceptor, there was no reason to suspect his New Divinity sympathies. After all, he had been the right-hand man of Ezra Stiles, Yale's Old Calvinist president and a consistent critic of the New Divinity. What the board wanted was a good teacher of moral character, a person of intellectual attainment, and a Yale man.[31] With a heavy representation of Yale alumni (eight of thirteen) on the college's original board of trustees, corporation members naturally looked to their alma mater for an appropriate candidate.[32] Fitch, a senior tutor and librarian at Yale, accepted the challenge of leading the infant school. Following Fitch's short stint as preceptor of the grammar school, the board unanimously elected him president of the college.

28. See Griffin, *Sermon preached September 2, 1828*, 20.
29. See chap. 7 in this volume.
30. See Fuess, *Amherst*, 82–97; [Humphrey], *Memorial Sketches*.
31. Perry, *Williamstown and Williams College*, 199.
32. Perry, *Williamstown and Williams College*, 287. Stephen West did not join the board until the college was established.

Like other college presidents of his day, Fitch cared as much for the spiritual development of his students as for their intellectual achievement. To confirm his religious desires for the institution, as well as to conform to the tradition of college presidents as ministers, Fitch was ordained by New Divinity brethren prior to the commencement of the first graduating class in 1795. In the ordination sermon, the Reverend Ephraim Judson of Sheffield urged students to give heed not only to the classical instruction of their new president but also to his religious counsel. "You are informing characters for eternity," he declared. "Religion is of infinite importance."[33] To Judson, to President Fitch, to presidents Moore and Griffin, to any New Divinity man, character formation meant spiritual formation, which meant the touchstone of evangelical Christianity—spiritual regeneration. A truly virtuous citizen and leader was a Christian, for only through God's act of regeneration upon the sinner's heart could a person truly love God and behave in virtuous ways. Edwardseans referred to this behavior as "disinterested benevolence"—the willingness to sacrifice self-interest for the greater glory of God and God's kingdom. In his 1799 baccalaureate address, Fitch uplifted this theme by exhorting the graduates to pursue their best talents, adding that "there is still a more excellent way," a more "glorious way"—the way of holiness. "Talents without piety, gifts without grace, will not profit you at last.... But true virtue alone can procure the divine favor, and ensure the rewards of a better life."[34]

Regeneration, true virtue, disinterested benevolence—Fitch reiterated New Divinity fundamentals that had been in place for nearly half a century. During his first year as president, in an effort to ensure that Williams students imbibed New Divinity theology, he assigned Samuel Hopkins's just-published *System of Doctrines* (1793) as a required text. This work, the first true compendium of New Divinity doctrine, was viewed by Fitch and clerical board members as the best work on systematic theology to date. The civilian trustees, operating on the assumption that Fitch would simply replicate Yale's curriculum, knew nothing about this change. Upon their discovery, however, they mounted opposition. No doubt Old Calvinist William Williams could not abide the Edwardseanism that his family had long opposed;[35] other civilian board members, not wanting the fledgling institution to become a center of New Divinity

33. Judson, *On Preaching the Word*, 25.
34. Fitch, *Useful knowledge and religion*, 31.
35. See Perry, *Williamstown and Williams College*, 221–22.

sectarianism and thus threaten the school's survival, outvoted the clerical board in rejecting *System of Doctrines* as required reading. "It was introduced as a classical study without the order of the corporation," Stephen West explained to Hopkins.

> The President introduced it because, as he told me, he thought it much exceeded anything of the kind he had seen. But the civilian part of the board, it seems, were of another opinion. They judged that its being recited would be injurious to the reputation of our new institution. The matter was considerably discussed. The clerical part of the board were all of one mind; and were greatly opposed to its being rejected. But when the vote for its rejection was taken, every hand was up excepting those of the ministers.[36]

In March 1797, Fitch surrendered to the demands of the civilian members of the board by replacing Hopkins's work with Philip Doddridge's popular college text *A Course of Lectures* (1763).

Although the president and clerical board could not get away with foisting a New Divinity text upon students, they found another, less conspicuous way of exposing students to the New Divinity perspective. Hopkins's *System of Doctrines*, quashed as a text, appeared on the shelves in the college library—along with other New Divinity works. Between 1794 and 1828, the college acquired the primary corpus of New Divinity publications. In addition to Hopkins's writings and the many theological treatises and sermons by Edwards, the library added the works of noted New Divinity apologists Charles Backus, Nathanael Emmons, Nathan Strong, Benjamin Trumbull, Stephen West, John Smalley, Job Swift, Joseph Bellamy, Jacob Catlin, and Edward Dorr Griffin.[37]

How often students opened the covers of these weighty theological treatises is unknown, but a clue to the popularity of these works may be found in the library of the Adelphic Union, an all-inclusive student society at Williams. That its library contained Edwards's *A History of the Work of Redemption*, Emmons's *Sermons on Various Subjects*, Hopkins's *Two Discourses*, and Strong's *Sermons on Various Subjects* attests to the attraction of New Divinity works among students.[38] But, even granting that students read these works with avidity, New Divinity men would be

36. Stephen West, quoted in Durfee, *Sketch of the Late Rev. Ebenezer Fitch*, 45–46.
37. See *Catalogue of Books, in the Library of Williams College* (1794, 1802, 1812, 1821, 1828).
38. *Catalogue of Books, in the Library of Williams College* (1821).

the first to admit that head knowledge without heart knowledge figured for naught in God's plan of redemption. What the New Divinity called "speculative knowledge" was merely a precondition of, never sufficient for, salvation. Heads full of divinity meant little without a heartfelt love of God. Whether students' heads were full or empty, one thing was certain: their hearts were cold. During the first seven years of the college's existence, Edward Griffin identified a mere five "professors" of Christianity among the ninety-three graduates. In 1801, however, "The religious character of the college received an important change from the accession of the Freshman class of four young men from the revivals in Litchfield county." It was from this revival-soaked county that "the influence of a new era" of continuing revivals and missionary outreach "crept upon the college."[39] Not until 1806, however, when a revival at Seth Swift's Williamstown church spread to the college, did Williams College experience its first revival. Thereafter, "town and gown" revivals broke out periodically. Converts won in revivals at the Williamstown Congregational Church augmented the steady influx into the college of recent converts from the revivals in Litchfield and Berkshire counties. The resulting spiritual heat ignited three college revivals during Fitch's tenure, bringing about the conversion of nearly seventy students.[40]

The most celebrated student to energize Williams with the revival and missionary spirit was, of course, Samuel Mills. Stirred during a 1798 revival at his father's church in Torringford, Connecticut, the fifteen-year-old found no peace until 1801. While engaged in farming, he prepared for collegiate studies under the tutelage of James Morris, an Edwardsean and proprietor of a respected academy at South Farms in Litchfield. In 1806, Mills entered Williams. His choice of Williams over Yale is noteworthy, for it is emblematic of the New Divinity social identity. First, his selection of Williams illustrates the primary attraction of the New Divinity in less established, rural areas, away from centers of urban growth. The unsophisticated, isolated setting of Williams relative to Yale offered few distractions. Second, as it did for the flood of rural "paupers" who inundated New England provincial colleges, cost figured into Mills's decision to attend Williams over Yale.[41] Affordability was a primary reason for the attraction of such country colleges as Williams,

39. Griffin, *Sermon preached September 2, 1828*, 18, 20.
40. See Griffin, *Sermon preached September 2, 1828*, 25, 26.
41. On the dynamic shift in student social backgrounds from the colonial to early national periods, see Allmendinger, *Paupers and Scholars*, chap. 1.

and it was indicative of the modest social backgrounds of New Divinity men. In 1807, Williams's yearly tuition of twelve dollars was exactly one-half of Yale's; moreover, living expenses were far less.[42] Finally, Mills's preference for Williams College demonstrates the pervasive influence of the New Divinity social network. Through the encouragement of Ammi Robbins, a trustee of the college and a colleague and relative of Samuel's father, Mills chose Williams.[43]

The organizational genius that served Mills so well in his later endeavors soon surfaced at Williams. Following the Haystack Prayer Meeting, he created the secret missionary society of the Brethren, and he also became a moving force in the Theological Society. Formed a year before Mills entered Williams, the society numbered three hundred members (including clergy) by 1828.[44] The group met every other Sunday evening for prayer and theological discussion. During its first decade of existence, the society evidenced an unmistakable allegiance to New Divinity theology. The recorded minutes of the society reveal a gathering of pious young men engaged in discussions of the most pressing New Divinity theological issues. At a meeting in December 1809, for example, members debated, "Is the atonement sufficient for all?" In March 1810, the majority of society members distanced themselves from Hopkinsian idiosyncrasies by deciding "negative" to the infamous query, "If a person ought to be willing to be damned in order to be saved?" The novice theologians also debated questions like "Is regeneration preceded by the proper efficacy of means or by the immutable power of God?" (November 18, 1810), and a year later they tackled "What sort of inability is it which prevents

---

42. For Williams's tuition, see "Minutes of the Meetings of Trustees of Williams College," April 24, 1785–March 27, 1868, 2 vols., Williamsiana Collection. For Yale's tuition, see Story, *Forging of an Aristocracy*, 98–100.

43. See Richards, *Samuel J. Mills*, 24. The New Divinity feeder network operated simultaneously on personal and institutional levels. For example, Moses Hallock was an Edwardsean pastor in Plainfield who supplemented his salary by preparing boys for college. Through his personal influence, many young men entered Williams, including missionaries James Richards, William Richards, Levi Parsons, Jonas King, and Homan Hallock. See Yale, *Godly Pastor*, 326.

44. See Membership List, "Theological Society Proceedings, 1809–1829," box 1, folder 1, Williamsiana Collection. By way of comparison, the questions discussed and books read by the members of the Theological Society at Princeton Theological Seminary reflected more traditional (Old School) Calvinist concerns. At the same time, the group occasionally wrestled with the same issues that preoccupied their counterparts at Williams and, as late as 1831, debated Edwards's theory of the will. See "Princeton Theological Seminary, Theological Society," box 1, nos. 1, 5, Speer Library, Archives and Special Collections, Princeton Theological Seminary, Princeton, New Jersey.

unholy men from performing their duty; and is their inability so great as to render it certain that they will not truly repent and believe without the special divine influence?" (October 20, 1811). During the next five years, such questions as these recurred.[45]

Particularly striking in the students' discussions is the focus on conversion. Clearly, their concerns were more practical than speculative or metaphysical. To opponents of Hopkinsian New Divinity, a practical New Divinity theology was well-nigh oxymoronic, for their very repulsion with this "new divinity" as it emerged initially in the 1760s and 1770s had been with its tendency to speculate fruitlessly about the ways of God with humankind that neither the Bible nor the Westminster Confession addressed. Foes had pronounced devotees of the New Divinity as "metaphysic mad," claiming their teaching was a "chaos of divinity."[46] By the 1790s, critics had had a heyday with the provocative theological positions of Hopkins (that one must be willing to be damned for the greater glory of God, that unregenerate doings were not only useless but condemnatory) and Nathanael Emmons (that the saved in heaven should rejoice in God's just condemnation of the unrepentant in hell). But there was another side to the New Divinity, a moderate Edwardsean side, that defined the contours of this essentially Calvinist theology. In the main, the New Divinity upheld Edwards's insistence on a church of the regenerate, his defense of revivals, his explication of affectional religion, his view of the will, his definition of true virtue, and his millennialism that linked revivalism and missions in a providential pattern. Such was the New Divinity that prevailed at Williams College among students (hence, their negative response to Hopkins's "damned for the glory of God" assertion), faculty, and presidents. The lively speculative debate among Edwardseans in the nineteenth century over the "taste" and "exercise" schemes (concerning the disposition of the will in reconciling divine sovereignty and human moral accountability) and the wider contest over the meaning of Edwardseanism apparently found no audience within the Williams community.[47]

45. "Theological Society Proceedings, 1809–1829," box 1, folder 1, Williamsiana Collection.

46. Andrew Fuller and William Hart, quoted in Kling, *Field of Divine Wonders*, 75.

47. I am not suggesting that New Divinity men associated with Williams stood aloof from these controversies. Alvan Hyde and Edward Dorr Griffin, for example, vehemently opposed Nathaniel W. Taylor's "improvements" of Edwards, and Griffin wrote a treatise defending the exercise scheme. However, there is no evidence to suggest that such controversies raged at Williams. For extended discussions of New Divinity

One of the earliest members of the Theological Society to grapple with New Divinity concerns was Justin Edwards (graduated 1810), later a well-known temperance crusader, Sabbatarian reformer, and president of Andover Theological Seminary (1836–42). Edwards's conversion prior to entering Williams and his subsequent efforts to grow in the faith illustrate the New Divinity clutch on some of the young men entering the college. The circumstances surrounding his conversion also illustrate the New Divinity's penchant for linking their own present revivals to Jonathan Edwards and the Great Awakening. It was Phebe Bartlett, the very same four-year-old girl extolled in Jonathan Edwards's *Narrative of Surprising Conversions* (1736), who became instrumental in Justin's conversion. In 1804, the doddering saint visited her son, a neighbor of Justin's family in Westhampton. There, Phebe took sick and died, but not before she had so impressed Justin with her faith and serenity that he was "hopefully" converted. "Thus," writes Justin's biographer, "he was one of the fruits, through the power and grace of Him . . . of 'The Great Awakening of 1740.'"[48] Justin Edwards's spiritual biography translated into a spiritual genealogy. His conversion represented a prime example of the New Divinity penchant for historical revisionism—their repristination of Jonathan Edwards and the Great Awakening in order to assert their own legitimacy as the true heirs of God's work of redemption.[49]

Following his conversion, Justin Edwards established a rigorous reading schedule of devotional works and theological treatises. In particular, he pored over Edwards's *Religious Affections* (1746) and *Life of David Brainerd* (1749) and Charles Backus's *The Scripture Doctrine of Regeneration* (1800). Entering Williams College in 1807, Edwards maintained a reading schedule in which he devoured some two hundred volumes, including Edwards's *Freedom of the Will* (1754).[50]

Despite the religious intensity exhibited by the likes of Mills and Edwards, Williams College was hardly a nursery of piety. Not unlike other colleges in the early republic, Williams had its share of rebellious and

---

theology, see Breitenbach, "Unregenerate Doings," 479–502; Breitenbach, "Consistent Calvinism," 241–64; Conforti, *Samuel Hopkins*; Kuklick, *Churchmen and Philosophers*, chap. 4; Guelzo, *Edwards on the Will*, chaps. 3, 4; Kling, *Field of Divine Wonders*, chap. 3.

48. Hallock, "Light and Love," 11–12.

49. For an extensive analysis of this phenomenon, see Conforti, "Invention of the Great Awakening," 99–118.

50. See Hallock, *"Light and Love,"* 16, 18–19.

disorderly youth.[51] Some students were enamored of French infidelity in the 1790s; others defied the college's strict laws through a variety of unseemly behaviors, including absences from prayer and chapel, drunkenness, fire setting, vandalism, unauthorized leaves, and "rioting."[52] The college faculty—the enforcers of discipline—dealt with infractions through traditional but largely ineffective disciplinary measures: fines, suspensions, "rustications" (where an incorrigible student was quite literally "farmed out" to live with a minister for a stipulated period of time), and expulsions.[53]

Where fear of temporal punishment often failed to produce orderly students, fear of eternal punishment increasingly succeeded. Throughout antebellum America, nearly all college authorities came to embrace revivals as a means not only to eternal salvation but also to internal self-discipline and social harmony.[54] Piety served conservative interests, engendering order and regulating desires. As more pious students entered Williams and as more impious Williams students converted, the tone of the college became increasingly religious and decidedly Edwardsean. Before the revival of 1812, wrote Professor Albert Hopkins, "It became a trial to live in college, especially in the building occupied by the two lower classes."[55] Then, in April and May, revival at the church spread to the college, primarily to the three lower classes.[56] "The results," Hopkins noted, "were permanent. Those various petty mischiefs and tricks which had been so common before, entirely disappeared, and during the three years followed, the students pursued their appropriate pursuits, in an atmosphere quiet and tranquil, congenial to mental improvement as well as growth in divine things."[57]

Student-initiated prayer meetings, conducted since the college's beginnings, grew in frequency and number. Edwardsean faculty,

51. See Novak, *Rights of Youth*; Allmendinger, *Paupers and Scholars*, 108–10.

52. On French infidelity, see Jedidiah Bushnell (graduated 1797) to Albert Hopkins, November 15, 1840, Williams College Autographs, vol. 2, no. 5, Williamsiana Collection. On disorderly students, see "Records of the Faculty of Williams College, 1821–1871," Williamsiana Collection; and "Minutes of the Meetings of Trustees of Williams College," Williamsiana Collection.

53. "Records of the Faculty of Williams College, 1821–1829," Williamsiana Collection.

54. See Allmendinger, *Paupers and Scholars*, 119.

55. Hopkins, "Revivals of Religion," 348.

56. Griffin, *Sermon preached September 2, 1828*, 25.

57. Hopkins, "Revivals of Religion," 351.

particularly Chester Dewey, became the prime movers of revival. Their efforts resulted not only in the salvation of souls but also eased their role as student disciplinarians. A Williams alumnus and theological student of Stephen West, Dewey returned to the college as tutor before becoming professor of mathematics and natural philosophy (1810–27). He drew from his own religious experience at Williams, for, in his senior year during Fitch's presidency, Dewey found the Savior in a student revival.[58] After leaving Williams, he was succeeded by Albert Hopkins (Williams graduate, 1826), one of the many students moved in the revivals under President Griffin. Like Dewey, Hopkins encouraged student revivals and initiated noonday prayer meetings as a means of maintaining spiritual fervor.[59]

THE NEW DIVINITY REITERATED: PRESIDENT MOORE (1815–21)

Following Fitch's resignation in 1815, the board looked for a replacement within the New Divinity social matrix. Leonard Woods, professor of theology at Andover, was both Fitch's and the trustees' first choice. After Woods declined their offer, they found their New Divinity man in Zephaniah Swift Moore, a professor of languages at Dartmouth.[60] A 1793 graduate of Dartmouth, Moore studied theology with Charles Backus and then pastored at Leicester, Massachusetts, from 1798 to 1811. Under Moore, the church adopted new articles of faith and covenant, which included the touchstone of New Divinity polity—the repudiation of halfway practices.[61] At Dartmouth, he instructed in the languages as well as in the way of salvation. Moore's fervent preaching and students' avid reading of Edwards's sermons combined to inspire a revival in spring 1815.[62]

Moore, then, came to Williams imbued with New Divinity theology and evangelistic zeal. In one of his first sermons—probably at his inauguration—he sounded a familiar refrain voiced by nearly every college president of his day:

58. See Durfee, *Williams Biographical Annals*, 139–42.

59. See Sewall, *Life of Prof. Albert Hopkins*, 21, 23–24; Rudolph, *Mark Hopkins and the Log*, 96–97.

60. For a biographical profile of Moore, see Sprague, *Annals of the American Pulpit*, 2:392–97.

61. See Moore, *Articles of faith*, 6–7.

62. See Humphrey, *Memoir of Rev. Nathan W. Fiske*, 16–17.

> An object of equal importance with that of the improvement of intellectual powers, and in many respects of infinitely greater importance in the course of education, is religion and the morality of the Gospel. . . . We are never to forget that an essential and primary object of this Institution is the promotion of piety and Christian knowledge.

At the same time, he spoke in the New Divinity vernacular by appealing to "the affections" as "the grand spring, by which we are animated."[63] In other sermons preached during his presidency, Moore laid bare his New Divinity convictions. He urged upon his listeners "the absolute necessity of regeneration or a change of heart"; he distinguished between "speculative" knowledge (reason) and heart knowledge (the affections); and he affirmed that "those who die in the Lord have that universal, impartial, and disinterested love which is the immediate fruit of a new heart."[64]

Try as Moore might by preaching the grand themes of New Divinity Calvinism, no student revivals ensued during his tenure at Williams. However, his instruction and sermons lent continued theological support to the missionary endeavor. With the creation of the Society of Inquiry in 1818 (renamed the Mills Society of Inquiry in 1837), Williams students formalized their commitment to missionary outreach. Given the society's membership qualification that a candidate pledge "to devote his life, either to a foreign or domestic mission," a more apt title might have been Society for Dedication to Missions. The "inquiry" aspect of the society pertained to its purpose: "to learn the true religious state of the world, the need of labourers in every part of it; and to learn also our own duty and to encourage each other in the performance of it."[65] To assist students in meeting such lofty goals, the society built up an impressive library containing missionary memoirs, missionary magazines, histories of missions, travel guides, and foreign-language grammars and translations of the Bible.

In the annals of Williams College, President Moore is, at best, recognized as an able administrator but thought to lack energy and vision. At worst, he is known as the president who nearly destroyed the college.

63. Zephaniah Swift Moore, mss. sermons, Small Collections, box 4, folder 1, no. 1, Williamsiana Collection.

64. Zephaniah Swift Moore, mss. sermons, Small Collections, box 4, folder 1, nos. 3, 4, 6, Williamsiana Collection. Among Moore's published sermons, New Divinity themes are most explicit in *The ministers of Christ*.

65. See Articles 2 and 3, "Society of Inquiry, Records, 1820–1834," box 1, folder 5, Williamsiana Collection.

Moore left Williams in 1821 to become the first president of Amherst, a college indebted to the New Divinity men at Williams. When Moore accepted the Williams presidency, several trustees had led him to believe that the college would relocate in the more populous Connecticut River valley. Williams's geographical isolation was increasingly viewed as a severe liability, both in halting the Unitarian menace as well as in competing for students with newly founded colleges (Middlebury in 1800, Union in 1805).[66] Anticipating the move, Moore did little to encourage a sense of permanence at Williamstown. Nor did he attract students—during Fitch's presidency, an average of twenty-two students graduated annually; under Moore, the number dropped to fifteen. The exodus of Moore, who was joined by several trustees and fifteen students, cast doubt on the ability of Williams College to survive.

THE NEW DIVINITY EXTENDED: PRESIDENT GRIFFIN (1821–36)

With Moore's departure, the trustees searched for someone to rescue their underendowed, underenrolled, and nearly undone institution. Two candidates declined the presidency before Edward Dorr Griffin accepted. Unlike the college's past presidents—relative unknowns and untested upon their hiring—Williams knew exactly what it was getting in Griffin.[67] By 1821, Griffin had attained prominence among Congregationalists and Presbyterians as a revivalist and New Divinity apologist. Connecticut born and Yale educated (BA, 1790), Griffin imbibed New Divinity theology under the tutelage of Jonathan Edwards Jr. He served pastorates in New Hartford, Connecticut, and Newark, New Jersey, where hundreds professed salvation under his ministrations. By the end of the first decade of the nineteenth century, Griffin's popularity as a pulpit orator and defender of Edwardseanism had reached its height. In 1809, a year after Andover Theological Seminary opened to counter Unitarian influences at Harvard, Griffin assumed the professorship of homiletics. At the same time, beleaguered Calvinists in Boston enlisted his services to lead the newly formed Park Street Church. There, in his *Park Street Lectures* (1813), Griffin delivered the unvarnished tenets of New Divinity theology.

---

66. On the Unitarian threat, see Cooke, *Recollections of Rev. E. D. Griffin*, 34.

67. For a biographical profile of Griffin, see Kling, *Field of Divine Wonders*, 126–30, including n78 for bibliographical references.

In 1815, Griffin returned to Newark as pastor of the Second Presbyterian Church and then, in 1821, accepted the Williams presidency.

The attraction of presiding over Williams was an intensely personal one for Griffin. Moreover, the circumstances that surrounded his joining Williams reveal the web of personal ties that typified the New Divinity movement. At Yale, Ebenezer Fitch had been Griffin's tutor; in New Hartford, Griffin had been the Reverend Samuel Mills's erstwhile colleague, and thus he knew Samuel Jr. from childhood; in Newark, Samuel Jr., knowing of Griffin's keen interest in missions, briefly studied theology with him in order to gain an influential supporter for his missionary vision; at Boston, Griffin was an ordaining minister at the ABCFM's first commissioning service.

The allure of Griffin to Williams was not one-sided. As early as 1807, Williams students hailed Griffin as a prophet of American missions by reprinting and distributing copies of his sermon *The Kingdom of Christ* (1805). Delivered initially before the Presbyterian General Assembly, Griffin's sermon represented one of the earliest calls for American Protestants to take the lead in foreign missionary endeavors. By his own admission, his career had come full circle. "It filled me with gratitude and wonder," Griffin recalled in 1828, "to discover that the religious destinies of the college which are now opening with such unspeakable interest upon my age, received such an impression from the revivals [in Litchfield County] in which I spent the labours of my youth."[68]

While Griffin's renown provided an immediate boost of confidence to students, trustees, and constituents, the new president clearly understood the college's precarious condition. In his inaugural address, Griffin reminded his audience of the college's hallowed history—of Samuel Mills, the Haystack Prayer Meeting, and the college's gift to the foreign missionary movement. "A college which has been honored and sanctified by the scenes of these events," he noted, "wh. has been so pre-eminently the seat of prayer,—wh. has given so many ministers and missionaries to the Ch.h, will not, I trust, be suffered, to fail."[69] But fail it nearly did.

In 1822, Griffin revived New Divinity curricular demands by assigning "Edwards on the Will" (i.e., Edwards's *Freedom of the Will*) to seniors, only to drop it a year later.[70] In 1825, when the Amherst College charter

68. Griffin, *Sermon preached September 2, 1828*, 21.
69. Edward Dorr Griffin, "Inaugural Address," November 4, 1821, misc. mss., vol. 8, p. 35, Williamsiana Collection.
70. See *Catalogue of the Officers and Students of Williams College, March, 1822*. "On

was finally granted, the new college in the Connecticut valley siphoned off one-third of Williams's students. Enrollment plummeted from 120 to 80. Few believed that remote, isolated Williams could compete with the more favorably situated Amherst. Griffin, however, resorted to what he did best: he saved the college by saving souls. He employed the tried and true formula of New Divinity revivals to reinvigorate the college spiritually and, no doubt, psychologically. As a result of team preaching by visiting pastors, "conference meetings" of prayer, Griffin's exhortations, and Professor Albert Hopkins's assistance, twenty-seven students were converted. According to Griffin, this and other revivals during his presidency exhibited the trademarks of New Divinity revivalism—sane, sober, and divinely initiated.

> The means employed in these revivals have been but two,—the clear presentation of Divine truth and prayer. The meetings have been still and orderly, with no other signs of emotion among the hearers than the solemn look and the silent tear. We have been anxiously studious to guard against delusive hopes.... We have not accustomed them [converts] to the bold and unqualified language that such an one *is* converted, but have used a dialect calculated to keep alive a sense of danger of deception.[71]

The 1825 revival emboldened Griffin to solicit funds for the previously proposed building of a chapel with renewed vigor and confidence. This signal of divine blessing—revival—now assured Griffin, his constituents, and potential donors that the college would survive. Griffin raised the needed $25,000, the chapel was built, and the college experienced four more revivals during his presidency.

As in the past, many converts from these revivals dedicated themselves to careers of Christian ministry. To that end, they pursued some form of theological education. Their choice of advanced instruction once again illustrates both the potent presence of the New Divinity at Williams as well as the broader pattern of New Divinity institutional networking. Prior to the opening of Andover Theological Seminary in 1808, 70 percent (thirty-eight of fifty-five) of Williams alumni who entered the

---

the Will" did not appear in subsequent catalogues and was replaced by Leslie's "Letters on Deism." See also Perry, *Williamstown and Williams College*, 426.

71. Edward D. Griffin, quoted in Durfee, *History of Williams College*, 238. On the New Divinity understanding of religious experience, see Rabinowitz, *Spiritual Self in Everyday Life*, chaps. 1–5; Kling, *Field of Divine Wonders*, chap. 7.

ministry apprenticed with a New Divinity pastor-teacher.[72] Beginning with the graduating class of 1807, ministerial and missionary candidates sought opportunities for professional theological education at Andover and then at Princeton following the opening of that seminary in 1812. At the same time, the New Divinity schools of the prophets continued to draw their fair share. Between 1807 and 1822, of the 120 Williams alumni seeking theological education, thirty-five studied with a New Divinity man, forty-two studied at Andover, and eleven at Princeton. Given the Edwardsean character of Andover, well over half (ca. 65 percent) of the Williams alumni pursued theological training under the New Divinity educational canopy.

However, by the early 1820s, the tide was shifting. Few Williams students preferred schools of the prophets to seminaries, although as late as 1835 the Theological Society debated whether students should prepare for the ministry at a theological seminary or under private instruction.[73] Whichever choice was made, President Griffin did all he could to ensure that Williams students pursued theological education within the New Divinity nexus by recommending they study at Auburn Theological Seminary under James Richards, professor of theology from 1823 to 1846. The two men had known each other since the early 1800s when they ministered at Presbyterian churches in New Jersey. Subsequently, they maintained close ties through similar career trajectories (moving from prestigious pastorates to college or seminary positions) but more critically, through their shared Edwardsean convictions.[74] When Richards accepted a professorship at Auburn, Griffin sent Williams graduates to study under his direction. The results, Griffin wrote to Richards, "pleased" him.[75] Forty-five Williams graduates attended Auburn between 1824 and 1837, the second highest number among institutions sending students to the seminary.[76]

---

72. Calculations are based on data gathered from Durfee, *Williams Biographical Annals*.

73. "Theological Society Proceedings, 1829–1842" (July 12, 1835), box 1, folder 3, Williamsiana Collection.

74. On Richards's theological views, see Sprague, *Annals of the American Pulpit*, 4:99–112; Adams, *History of Auburn Theological Seminary*, 73; Gridley, "Biographical Sketch," 86–87; Richards, *Lectures on Mental Philosophy*, 97–153, 476–501; Marsden, *Evangelical Mind*, 44–45.

75. Edward Dorr Griffin to James Richards, December 18, 1828, new misc. mss., box 1.3, folder 51, Williamsiana Collection.

76. *General Bibliographical Catalogue*, 22–77.

In the final years of Griffin's presidency, despite his own concerted efforts, the New Divinity agenda languished. Against the perceived theological defection of Nathaniel W. Taylor at Yale Divinity School, Griffin responded with what became the last comprehensive defense of New Divinity theology, *The Doctrine of Divine Efficiency, defended against certain Modern Speculations* (1833). Against the feared "new measures" of Charles Finney introduced at the Williamstown church, Griffin countered by founding a college church upon New Divinity principles. Neither effort amounted to much. His book was considered recondite, even irrelevant; and under the new president, Mark Hopkins—whom Griffin opposed—the college soon drifted from its New Divinity moorings. Hopkins, along with an increasing number of his generation, viewed Christianity less as a system of doctrine than as a moralistic pattern for living. His theology, remarked Richard Birdsall, was "vague and unobtrusive," far removed from the doctrinalism of President Griffin and his New Divinity predecessors.[77] While evangelical in sympathy and supportive of continued revivals at Williams (led primarily by his brother Albert), the new president shifted the locus of Calvinism from understanding to intuition, thus gutting the vitals of New Divinity theology.[78]

In addition, student demographics conspired to emancipate Williams from its New Divinity grip. Up through Griffin's presidency, students had shared similar backgrounds and religious convictions. During Hopkins's tenure, however, the geographic draw of students shifted from nearby rural villages to the urban business centers of New York, Brooklyn, Albany, and Troy. Once a college for aspiring clergymen and missionaries, by the end of the Hopkins presidency in 1872 Williams had been ineluctably (for it was bereft of an explicit religious mission) transformed by the forces of an increasingly secular society. Those pious, impoverished students, educated through the beneficence of the American Education Society, had vanished. In their place came more sophisticated students from prosperous backgrounds, aspiring to material success of their own.[79]

77. Birdsall, *Berkshire County*, 69.

78. See Rudolph, *Mark Hopkins and the Log*, 118–32. The difference between Griffin and Hopkins is a good example of what Richard Rabinowitz in *The Spiritual Self in Everyday Life* designates as the movement from "a doctrinalist economy of experience" to "moralism" (see introduction, chap. 6).

79. Rudolph, *Mark Hopkins and the Log*, 71–72, 213. Originally organized in 1815 as the American Society for the Education of Pious Youth for the Gospel Ministry and renamed the American Education Society in 1820, the society raised funds for the college expenses of young men intending to enter the ministry.

CONCLUSION

Modern historians of Williams have understated, even denigrated, the influence of the New Divinity upon the college. They have been inclined to view its men and the overall movement as a temporary and even irrelevant aside in the making of a modern, secular liberal arts college. Arthur Latham Perry, Unitarian foe of dogmatism and depravity, likened the New Divinity presence to "mushrooms in a fertile soil," which, thankfully, "decayed into speedy forgetfulness."[80] Frederick Rudolph, in more measured tones, fully recognized the place of evangelical religion in Williams's early history, but he omitted any reference to New Divinity, considered the revivalist ethos a fetter of the mind, and, perhaps most significantly, failed to link the New Divinity men to a discernible *movement*.[81]

This essay has challenged such interpretations. The early history of Williams is largely a religious history, a chapter in the history of an expanding religious movement whose impact transcended the college and its regional identity. The formation of Williams coincided with the maturation of the New Divinity movement to yield an institution with a distinctly Edwardsean cast. While the founding documents of Williams provided no clue as to the religious direction of the college, New Divinity presidents, board members, and students guided the college for well over four decades. From Williams—and the larger New Divinity context—issued the trinity of antebellum evangelicalism: revivalism, millennial fervor, and social reform. From Williams, the Edwardsean axiom of disinterested benevolence extended throughout the world in missionary outreach. The New Divinity, of course, did not have an exclusive hold on the American evangelical identity, but at places such as Williams its reach was manifest.

The career of Nathan Brown provides a fitting coda to the legacy of the New Divinity.[82] Brown typified the young men for whom the college had been established, those "rough hewn ... great unpolished bumpkins who had grown up farm boys," as Nathaniel Hawthorne described them

---

80. Perry, *Williamstown and Williams College*, 419.

81. Rudolph, *Mark Hopkins and the Log*. Rudolph employed such terms as "conservative," "orthodox," and "evangelical." In an earlier piece, written during his student days at Williams, Rudolph credited Griffin with saving the college from extinction but then concluded that, because Griffin's contributions were primarily religious, they "have not been lasting" in their impact. See Rudolph, "Edward Dorr Griffin," 44.

82. On Brown, see Durfee, *Williams Biographical Annals*, 434–35; and [Brown], *Whole World Kin*.

on a visit to Williamstown.[83] Brown entered Williams in 1824 during the early years of Griffin's presidency. His academic interests gravitated toward mathematics taught by Chester Dewey, Williams's most popular and influential teacher. But it was under the spell of Griffin's eloquent sermons that Brown dedicated his life to missionary service. In his baccalaureate address to the members of Brown's 1827 graduating class, Griffin harked back to the original missionary impetus of the college and appealed to the New Divinity principle of self-sacrifice.

> I long to see every class go forth in the spirit of a Mills and a Hall, a Richards and a Robbins determined to make their influence felt on the other side of the globe. Will you not, my dear pupils, carry this spirit with you? Will not every one of you say, with an eye lifted to your dying Lord, "Here am I soul and body, here am I, send me, if it be to the ends of the earth."[84]

Brown carried that spirit with him to the ends of the earth, serving first in Burma for two years with Adoniram Judson, then in Assam from 1834 to 1855. There, he translated the New Testament and parts of the Old into Assamese and used his philological skills to produce Assamese religious literature, including catechisms and hymns. Brown's efforts bore the fruit of Christian witness. In 1985, members of the Assam Association of North America gathered at Williams College to commemorate the one hundredth anniversary of Brown's death.[85] The spiritual ancestors of New Divinity–inspired missionary outreach, in their recent pilgrimage to Williams, recall those first decades in the college's history of New Divinity ascendancy.

---

83. Hawthorne, *American Notebooks*, 50.

84. Griffin, *Sermon, preached September 2, 1827*, 21–22.

85. I am indebted to John M. Hyde, professor of history at Williams, for sharing his unpublished paper, "The Education of Nathan Brown."

Bibliography

Adams, John Quincy. *A History of Auburn Theological Seminary, 1818-1918*. Auburn, NY: Auburn Seminary Press, 1918.

Allmendinger, David F., Jr. *Paupers and Scholars: The Transformation of Student Life in Nineteenth-Century New England*. New York: St. Martin's, 1975.

American Board of Commissioners for Foreign Missions. *First Ten Annual Reports of the American Board of Commissioners for Foreign Missions, with Other Documents of the Board*. Boston: Crocker and Brewster, 1834.

"Analysis of the Book of Daniel." *Connecticut Evangelical Magazine* 4 (1803) 46–53.

[Anderson, Rufus]. *Memorial Volume of the First Fifty Years of the American Board of Commissioners for Foreign Missions*. Boston: American Board of Commissioners, 1861.

Andrew, John A., III. *Rebuilding the Christian Commonwealth: New England Congregationalists and Foreign Missions, 1800-1830*. Lexington, KY: University Press of Kentucky, 1976.

Backus, Charles. *The Faithful Ministers of Jesus Christ Rewarded: A sermon, delivered at the ordination of the Rev. Azel Backus [. . .] April 6, 1791*. Litchfield, CT: [1791].

———. *The High Importance of Love to Jesus Christ in the Minister of the Gospel: A sermon, delivered at the ordination of the Reverend John Hubbard Church [. . .] October 31, 1799*. Amherst, NH: N.p., 1799.

———. *Ministers Serving God in the Gospel of His Son: A sermon delivered at the ordination of the Rev. Timothy Mather Cooley [. . .] February 3, 1796*. West Springfield, MA: N.p., 1796.

———. *Qualifications and Duties of the Christian Pastor: A Sermon, delivered [. . .] October 29, 1795, at the ordination of the Reverend Freegrace Reynolds [. . .]*. Boston, 1795.

———. *The Scripture Doctrine of Regeneration Considered, in Six Discourses*. Hartford, CT: Hudson and Goodwin, 1800.

Bainton, Roland. *Yale and the Ministry: A History of Education for the Christian Ministry at Yale from the Founding in 1701*. New York, 1957.

Barrett, Justin L. *Born Believers: The Science of Children's Religious Belief*. New York: Free, 2012.

———. *Cognitive Science, Religion, and Theology: From Human Minds to Divine Minds*. Templeton Science and Religious Series. West Conshohocken, PA: Templeton Press, 2011.

———. "Dumb Gods, Petitionary Prayer and the Cognitive Science of Religion." In *Current Approaches in the Cognitive Science of Religion*, edited by Ilkka Pyysiäinen and Veikko Anttonen, 93–109. London: Continuum, 2002.

———. "Exploring the Natural Foundations of Religion." *Trends in Cognitive Sciences* 4 (2000) 29–34.

———. "Theological Correctness: Cognitive Constraint and the Study of Religion." *Method and Theory in the Study of Religion* 11 (1999) 325–39.

———. *Why Would Anyone Believe in God?* Lanham, MD: Alta Mira, 2004.

Barrett, Justin L., and Frank C. Keil. "Conceptualizing a Nonnatural Entity: Anthropomorphism in God Concepts." *Cognitive Psychology* 31 (1996) 219–47.

Barshinger, David P. *Jonathan Edwards and the Psalms: A Redemptive-Historical Vision of Scripture.* New York: Oxford University Press, 2014.

Barshinger, David P., and Douglas A. Sweeney, eds. *Jonathan Edwards and Scripture: Biblical Exegesis in British North America.* New York: Oxford University Press, 2018.

Beardslee, John. "John Henry Livingston and the Rise of the American Mission Movement." *Historical Highlights* 8 (1989) 1–21.

Beaver, R. Pierce. "Missionary Motivation through Three Centuries." In *Reinterpretation in American Church History*, edited by Jerald Brauer, 113–51. Chicago: University of Chicago Press, 1968.

Bebbington, David W. *Evangelicalism in Modern Britain: A History from the 1730s to the 1980s.* Grand Rapids: Baker, 1992.

———. "Introduction." In *Evangelicalism: Comparative Studies of Popular Protestantism in North America, the British Isles, and Beyond, 1700–1990*, edited by Mark A. Noll et al., 3–15. New York: Oxford University Press, 1994.

———. "Remembered around the World: The International Scope of Edwards's Legacy." In *Edwards at Home and Abroad: Historical Memories, Cultural Movements, Global Horizons*, edited by David W. Kling and Douglas A. Sweeney, 177–200. Columbia, SC: University of South Carolina Press, 2003.

Beck, Peter. *The Voice of Faith: Jonathan Edwards's Theology of Prayer.* Guelph, ON: Joshua Press, 2010.

Beecher, Lyman. *The Autobiography of Lyman Beecher.* Edited by Barbara C. Cross. 2 vols. Cambridge: Belknap, 1961.

Beeke, Joel R., and Brian G. Najapfour, eds. *Taking Hold of God: Reformed and Puritan Perspectives on Prayer.* Grand Rapids: Reformation Heritage, 2011.

Bellamy, Joseph. *The Works of Joseph Bellamy, D.D. [. . .] With a Memoir of His Life and Character.* 2 vols. Boston: Doctrinal Tract and Book Society, 1850–53.

Bentley, William. *The Diary of William Bentley, D.D., Pastor of the East Church, Salem, Massachusetts.* 4 vols. 1905–15. Reprint, Gloucester, MA: Smith, 1963.

Bering, Jesse. *The Belief Instinct: The Psychology of Souls, Destiny, and the Meaning of Life.* New York: Norton, 2011.

Berk, Stephen E. *Calvinism versus Democracy: Timothy Dwight and the Origins of American Evangelical Orthodoxy.* Hamden, CT: Archon, 1974.

Birdsall, Richard D. *Berkshire County: A Cultural History.* New Haven: Yale University Press, 1959.

———. "Ezra Stiles versus the New Divinity Men." *American Quarterly* 17 (1965) 248–58.

———. "The Second Great Awakening and the New England Social Order." *Church History* 39 (1970) 345-64.

Birney, Hugh, Jr. "The Life and Letters of Asahel Nettleton, 1783-1844." PhD diss., Hartford Theological Seminary, 1943.

Bloch, Ruth H. *Visionary Republic: Millennial Themes in American Thought, 1756-1800.* New York: Cambridge University Press, 1985.

Boudry, Maarten, and Johan De Smedt. "In Mysterious Ways: On Petitionary Prayer and Subtle Forms of Supernatural Causation." *Religion* 41 (2011) 449-69.

Brauer, Jerald C. "Conversion: From Puritanism to Revivalism." *Journal of Religion* 58 (1978) 227-43.

Breitenbach, William. "The Consistent Calvinism of the New Divinity Movement." *William and Mary Quarterly* 41 (1984) 241-64.

———. "New Divinity Theology and the Ideal of Moral Accountability." PhD diss., Yale University, 1978.

———. "Piety and Moralism: Edwards and the New Divinity." In *Jonathan Edwards and the American Experience*, edited by Nathan O. Hatch and Harry S. Stout, 177-204. New York: Oxford University Press, 1989.

———. "Unregenerate Doings: Selflessness and Selfishness in New Divinity Theology." *American Quarterly* 34 (1982) 479-502.

[Brown, Elizabeth W.]. *The Whole World Kin: A Pioneer Experience among remote tribes, and other Labors of Nathan Brown.* Philadelphia: Hubbard Bros., 1890.

Brown, Richard D. *Knowledge Is Power: The Diffusion of Information in Early America, 1700-1865.* New York: Oxford University Press, 1989.

Brown, Robert E. "The Bible." In *The Princeton Companion to Jonathan Edwards*, edited by Sang Hyun Lee, 87-102. Princeton: Princeton University Press, 2005.

———. "Edwards, Locke, and the Bible." *Journal of Religion* 79 (1999) 361-84.

———. *Jonathan Edwards and the Bible.* Bloomington, IN: Indiana University Press, 2002.

Burton, Asa. *The Life of Asa Burton Written by Himself.* Edited by Charles Latham Jr. Thetford, VT: First Congregational Church, 1973.

———. *A Sermon, preached at the Ordination of the Rev. Timothy Clark [. . .] January 1, 1800.* Windsor, VT: N.p., 1800.

Bushman, Richard L. "Jonathan Edwards as Great Man: Identity, Conversion, and Leadership in the Great Awakening." *Soundings: An Interdisciplinary Journal* 52 (1969) 15-46.

Butler, Jon. "Enthusiasm Described and Decried: The Great Awakening as Interpretative Fiction." *Journal of American History* 69 (1982) 305-25.

Byrd, James P. "Jonathan Edwards, War, and the Bible." In *Jonathan Edwards and Scripture: Biblical Exegesis in British North America*, edited by David P. Barshinger and Douglas A. Sweeney, 192-211. New York: Oxford University Press, 2018.

Caldwell, Patricia. *The Puritan Conversion Narrative: The Beginnings of American Expression.* New York: Cambridge University Press, 1983.

Calvin, John. *Institutes of the Christian Religion.* Edited by John T. McNeill. 2 vols. Library of Christian Classics. Philadelphia: Westminster, 1960.

Catalogue of Books, in the Library of Williams College. Bennington, VT: Haswell, 1794.

Catalogue of Books, in the Library of Williams College. Stockbridge, MA: Willard, 1802.

Catalogue of Books, in the Library of Williams College. Stockbridge, MA: Willard, 1812.

Catalogue of Books, in the Library of Williams College. Albany, NY: Websters and Skinners, 1821.

Catalogue of Books, in the Library of Williams College. Williamstown, MA: Bannister, 1828.

Catalogue of the Officers and Students of Williams College, March, 1822. [Williamstown, MA], 1822.

Chai, Leon. *Jonathan Edwards and the Limits of Enlightenment Philosophy.* New York: Oxford University Press, 1998.

Chamberlain, Ava. "Self-Deception as a Theological Problem in Jonathan Edwards's 'Treatise Concerning Religious Affections.'" *Church History* 63 (1994) 541–56.

Chaney, Charles L. *The Birth of Missions in America.* South Pasadena, CA: William Carey Library, 1976.

———. "God's Glorious Work: The Theological Foundations of the Early Missionary Societies in America, 1787–1817." PhD diss., University of Chicago, 1973.

Chauncy, Charles. "Enthusiasm Described and Caution'd Against." In *The Great Awakening: Documents Illustrating the Crisis and Its Consequences,* edited by Alan Heimert and Perry Miller, 228–56. Indianapolis: Bobbs-Merrill, 1967.

———. "Seasonable Thoughts on the State of Religion." In *The Great Awakening: Documents Illustrating the Crisis and Its Consequences,* edited by Alan Heimert and Perry Miller, 291–304. Indianapolis: Bobbs-Merrill, 1967.

Chun, Chris. *The Legacy of Jonathan Edwards in the Theology of Andrew Fuller.* Leiden: Brill, 2012.

Claghorn, George S. "Introduction." In *WJE,* 16:3–27. New Haven: Yale University Press, 1998.

———. "Transcribing a Difficult Hand: Collecting and Editing Edwards's Letters over Thirty-Five Years." In *The Legacy of Jonathan Edwards: American Religion and the Evangelical Tradition,* edited by D. G. Hart et al., 217–27. Grand Rapids: Baker, 2003.

Clark, Kelly James, and Justin L. Barrett. "Reformed Epistemology and the Cognitive Science of Religion." *Faith and Philosophy* 27 (2010) 174–89.

Clark, Sereno D. *The New England Ministry Sixty Years Ago: The Memoir of John Woodbridge, D.D.* Boston: Lee and Shepard, 1877.

Cohen, Charles Lloyd. *God's Caress: The Psychology of Puritan Religious Experience.* New York: Oxford University Press, 1986.

Conforti, Joseph A. "David Brainerd and the Nineteenth-Century Missionary Movement." *Journal of the Early Republic* 5 (1985) 309–29.

———. "The Invention of the Great Awakening, 1795–1842." *Early American Literature* 26 (1991) 99–118.

———. *Jonathan Edwards, Religious Tradition, and American Culture.* Chapel Hill, NC: University of North Carolina Press, 1995.

———. "Mary Lyon, the Founding of Mount Holyoke College, and the Cultural Revival of Jonathan Edwards." *Religion and American Culture* 3 (1993) 69–89.

———. "The Rise of the New Divinity in Western New England, 1740–1800." *Historical Journal of Western Massachusetts* 8 (1980) 37–47.

———. *Samuel Hopkins and the New Divinity Movement: Calvinism, the Congregational Ministry, and Reform between the Great Awakenings.* Grand Rapids: Eerdmans, 1981.

Cooke, Parsons. *Recollections of Rev. E. D. Griffin, or, Incidents Illustrating his Character*. Boston: Sabbath School Society, 1855.

Corr, Donald Philip. "'The Field Is the World': Proclaiming, Translating, and Serving by the American Board of Commissioners for Foreign Missions, 1810–1840." PhD diss., Fuller Theological Seminary, 1993.

Cragg, Gerald R. "Training in the Ministry—The Older Tradition." *Andover Newton Quarterly* 8 (1968) 223–34.

Crawford, Michael J. "New England and the Scottish Revivals of 1742." *American Presbyterians* 69 (1991) 23–32.

———. *Seasons of Grace: Colonial New England's Revival Tradition in Its British Context*. New York: Oxford University Press, 1991.

Crisp, Oliver D., and Douglas A. Sweeney, eds. *After Jonathan Edwards: The Courses of the New England Theology*. New York: Oxford University Press, 2012.

Crump, David. "Are Practical Prayers Pagan Prayers?" *Expository Times* 120 (2009) 231–35.

———. *Knocking on Heaven's Door: A New Testament Theology of Petitionary Prayer*. Grand Rapids: Baker Academic, 2006.

Dahlquist, John T. "Nathanael Emmons: His Life and Work." PhD diss., Boston University, 1963.

Davidson, James West. *The Logic of Millennial Thought: Eighteenth-Century New England*. New Haven: Yale University Press, 1977.

Davies, Ronald E. "The Great Commission from Calvin to Carey." *Evangel* 14 (1996) 44–49.

———. "Jonathan Edwards: Missionary Biographer, Theologian, Strategist, Administrator, Advocate—and Missionary." *International Bulletin of Missionary Research* 21 (1997) 60–67.

Davis, Henry. *A Sermon, delivered before the American Board of Commissioners for Foreign Missions*. Boston: Armstrong, 1816.

De Jong, James A. *As the Waters Cover the Sea: Millennial Expectations in the Rise of Anglo-American Missions, 1640–1810*. Kampen: Kok, 1970.

Delattre, Roland A. "Recent Scholarship on Jonathan Edwards." *Religious Studies Review* 24 (1998) 369–75.

Dexter, Franklin B. *Biographical Sketches of the Graduates of Yale College: With Annals of the College History*. 6 vols. New York, 1885–1912.

Duffy, John. *Epidemics in Colonial America*. Baton Rouge: Louisiana State University Press, 1953.

Durfee, Calvin. *A History of Williams College*. Boston: Williams, 1860.

———. *Sketch of the Late Rev. Ebenezer Fitch, D.D., First President of Williams College*. Boston: Massachusetts Sabbath School Society, 1865.

———. *Williams Biographical Annals*. Boston: Lee and Shepard, 1871.

Edman, Laird R. O. "Applying the Science of Faith: The Cognitive Science of Religion and Christian Practice." *Journal of Psychology and Christianity* 34 (2015) 240–51.

Edwards, Jonathan. *Apocalyptic Writings*. Edited by Stephen J. Stein. WJE 5. New Haven: Yale University Press, 1977.

———. *The "Blank Bible."* Edited by Stephen J. Stein. WJE 24. New Haven: Yale University Press, 2006.

———. "A Divine and Supernatural Light." In *The Sermons of Jonathan Edwards: A Reader*, edited by Wilson H. Kimnach et al., 121–40. New Haven: Yale University Press, 1999.

———. *Ecclesiastical Writings*. Edited by David D. Hall. *WJE* 12. New Haven: Yale University Press, 1994.

———. *Ethical Writings*. Edited by Paul Ramsey. *WJE* 8. New Haven: Yale University Press, 1989.

———. *A Faithful Narrative of the Surprising Work of God*. Boston, 1737.

———. *Freedom of the Will*. Edited by Paul Ramsey. *WJE* 1. New Haven: Yale University Press, 1957.

———. *The Glory and Honor of God*. Edited by Michael D. McMullen. The Previously Unpublished Sermons of Jonathan Edwards 2. Nashville: Broadman & Holman, 2004.

———. *The Great Awakening*. Edited by C. C. Goen. *WJE* 4. New Haven: Yale University Press, 1972.

———. *A History of the Work of Redemption*. Edited by John F. Wilson. *WJE* 9. New Haven: Yale University Press, 1989.

———. *Jonathan Edwards: Containing 16 Sermons Unpublished in Edwards' Lifetime*, Edited by Don Kister. Morgan, PA: Soli Deo Gloria, 2004.

———. *Letters and Personal Writings*. Edited by George S. Claghorn. *WJE* 16. New Haven: Yale University Press, 1998.

———. *The Life of David Brainerd*. Edited by Norman Pettit. *WJE* 7. New Haven: Yale University Press, 1984.

———. "The Mind." In *A Jonathan Edwards Reader*, edited by John E. Smith et al., 22–34. New Haven: Yale University Press, 1995.

———. *The "Miscellanies": Nos. a–z, aa–zz, 1–500*. Edited by Thomas A. Schafer. *WJE* 13. New Haven: Yale University Press, 1994.

———. *The "Miscellanies": Nos. 501–832*. Edited by Ava Chamberlain. *WJE* 18. New Haven: Yale University Press, 2000.

———. *The "Miscellanies": Nos. 833–1132*. Edited by Amy Plantinga Pauw. *WJE* 20. New Haven: Yale University Press, 2002.

———. *The "Miscellanies": Nos. 1153–1360*. Edited by Douglas A. Sweeney. *WJE* 23. New Haven: Yale University Press, 2004.

———. "Much in Deeds of Charity." In *The Sermons of Jonathan Edwards: A Reader*, edited by Wilson H. Kimnach et al., 197–211. New Haven: Yale University Press, 1999.

———. *The Nature of True Virtue*. In *A Jonathan Edwards Reader*, edited by John E. Smith et al., 244–65. New Haven: Yale University Press, 1995.

———. *Notes on Scripture*. Edited by Stephen J. Stein. *WJE* 15. New Haven: Yale University Press, 1998.

———. *Original Sin*. Edited by Clyde A. Holbrook. *WJE* 3. New Haven: Yale University Press, 1970.

———. "Personal Narrative." In *A Jonathan Edwards Reader*, edited by John E. Smith et al., 281–96. New Haven: Yale University Press, 1995.

———. "The Reality of Conversion." In *The Sermons of Jonathan Edwards: A Reader*, edited by Wilson H. Kimnach et al., 83–104. New Haven: Yale University Press, 1999.

———. "Resolutions." In *A Jonathan Edwards Reader*, edited by John E. Smith et al., 274–81. New Haven: Yale University Press, 1995.
———. *Scientific and Philosophical Writings*. Edited by Wallace E. Anderson. *WJE* 6. New Haven: Yale University Press, 1980.
———. *Sermons and Discourses, 1720–1723*. Edited by Wilson H. Kimnach. *WJE* 10. New Haven: Yale University Press, 1992.
———. *Sermons and Discourses, 1723–1729*. Edited by Kenneth P. Minkema. *WJE* 14. New Haven: Yale University Press, 1997.
———. *Sermons and Discourses, 1730–1733*. Edited by Mark Valeri. *WJE* 17. New Haven: Yale University Press, 1999.
———. *Sermons and Discourses, 1734–1738*. Edited by M. X. Lesser. *WJE* 19. New Haven: Yale University Press, 2001.
———. *Sermons and Discourses, 1739–1742*. Edited by Harry S. Stout and Nathan O. Hatch. *WJE* 22. New Haven: Yale University Press, 2003.
———. *Sermons and Discourses, 1743–1758*. Edited by Wilson H. Kimnach. *WJE* 25. New Haven: Yale University Press, 2006.
———. *The Sermons of Jonathan Edwards: A Reader*. Edited by Wilson H. Kimnach et al. New Haven: Yale University Press, 1999.
———. *Sinners in the Hands of an Angry God*. In *The Sermons of Jonathan Edwards: A Reader*, edited by Wilson H. Kimnach et al., 49–65. New Haven: Yale University Press, 1999.
———. *A Treatise Concerning Religious Affections*. Edited by John E. Smith. *WJE* 2. New Haven: Yale University Press, 1959.
———. *Typological Writings*. Edited by Wallace E. Anderson and David Watters. *WJE* 11. New Haven: Yale University Press, 1993.
———. "Untitled Volume, Notes on Conversion from Various Authorities." Jonathan Edwards Collection, Series I. Writings of Jonathan Edwards. Notebooks and Memoranda, Box 21, Folder 1262, Beinecke Rare Book and Manuscript Library, Yale University, New Haven, Connecticut. https://archives.yale.edu/repositories/11/archival_objects/205574.
———. *The Works of Jonathan Edwards Online*. Jonathan Edwards Center at Yale University. http://edwards.yale.edu/archive.
———. *The Works of President Edwards*. 10 vols. New York: Franklin, 1968.
———. *Writings on the Trinity, Grace, and Faith*. Edited by Sang Hyun Lee. *WJE* 21. New Haven: Yale University Press, 2002.
Edwards, Jonathan, Jr. *All Divine Truth Profitable: Illustrated in a Sermon preached [...] January 11th, 1792, at the Ordination of the Rev. Dan Bradley*. New Haven, 1792.
———. *The Duty of Ministers of the Gospel to Preach the Truth; illustrated in a sermon: delivered at the ordination of the Rev. Edward Dorr Griffin [...] June 4th, A.D. 1795*. Hartford, CT: N.p., 1795.
Ehrat, Christoph. "Jonathan Edwards' *Treatise Concerning Religions Affections* and Its Application to Prayer." *Crux* 24 (1988) 11–16.
Ehrhard, James. "Asahel Nettleton: The Forgotten Evangelist." *Reformation and Revival* 6 (1997) 67–93.
Elsbree, Oliver S. *The Rise of the Missionary Spirit in America, 1790–1815*. Williamsport, PA: Williamsport, 1928.
Emmons, Nathanael. *A Discourse, delivered [...] November 4, 1795, at the Ordination of the Reverend James Tufts*. Brattleborough, VT: N.p., 1797.

———. *A Discourse, preached at the Ordination of the Rev. Eli Smith* [. . .] *November 27th, 1793*. Worcester, MA: N.p., 1794.

———. "Memoir of Nathanael Emmons, D.D. written by himself." In *The Works of Nathanael Emmons, D.D.: With a Memoir of His Life*, edited by Jacob Ide, 1:ix–xxxvii. Boston: Crocker & Brewster, 1842.

———. *A Sermon, Delivered* [. . .] *January 4, 1797, at the Ordination of the Rev. John Smith*. Concord, NH: N.p., 1797.

———. "Two Sermons." In *The Atonement: Discourses and Treatises*, edited by Edwards A. Park, 111–36. Boston: Congregational Board of Publications, 1859.

———. *The Works of Nathanael Emmons, D.D.: With a Memoir of His Life*. Edited by Jacob Ide. Vol. 1. Boston: Crocker & Brewster, 1842.

Eversley, Walter L. "The Pastor as Revivalist." In *Edwards in Our Time: Jonathan Edwards and the Shaping of American Religion*, edited by Sang Hyun Lee and Allen C. Guelzo, 113–30. Grand Rapids: Eerdmans, 1999.

Fawcett, Arthur. *The Cambuslang Revival: The Scottish Evangelical Revival of the Eighteenth Century*. London: Banner of Truth Trust, 1971.

Ferm, Robert L. *Jonathan Edwards the Younger, 1745–1801: A Colonial Pastor*. Grand Rapids: Eerdmans, 1976.

Field, Peter S. *The Crisis of the Standing Order: Clerical Intellectuals and Cultural Authority in Massachusetts, 1780–1833*. Amherst: University of Massachusetts Press, 1998.

Fiering, Norman. *Jonathan Edwards's Moral Thought and Its British Context*. Chapel Hill, NC: University of North Carolina Press, 1981.

Finke, Roger, and Laurence R. Iannaccone. "Supply-Side Explanations for Religious Change." *Annals of the American Academy of Political and Social Science* 527 (1993) 27–39.

Finke, Roger, and Rodney Stark. *The Churching of America, 1776–1990: Winners and Losers in Our Religious Economy*. New Brunswick, NJ: Rutgers University Press, 1992.

Fischer, Austin. *Young, Restless, No Longer Reformed*. Eugene, OR: Cascade, 2014.

Fitch, Ebenezer. "Historical Sketch of the Life and Character of Colonel Ephraim Williams, and of Williams College, Founded in 1793 [. . .]." *Collections of the Massachusetts Historical Society* 9 (1802) 47–53.

———. *Useful knowledge and religion, recommended to the pursuit and improvement of the young; in a discourse addressed to the candidates for the baccalaureate in Williams College. September 1, 1799* [. . .]. Pittsfield, MA: Smith, 1799.

Foster, Charles I. *An Errand of Mercy: The Evangelical United Front, 1790–1837*. Chapel Hill, NC: University of North Carolina Press, 1960.

Foster, Frank Hugh. *A Genetic History of the New England Theology*. Chicago: University of Chicago Press, 1907.

Fuess, Claude M. *Amherst: The Story of a New England College*. Boston: Little, Brown, 1935.

Fuller, Andrew. *The Gospel Worthy of All Acceptation*. Northampton, MA: Dicey, 1787.

Gambrell, Mary Latimer. *Ministerial Training in Eighteenth-Century New England*. New York: Columbia University Press, 1937.

General Bibliographical Catalogue of Auburn Theological Seminary, 1818–1918. Auburn, NY: Auburn Seminary Press, 1918.

Godell, C. L. "John Smalley." *Congregational Quarterly* 15 (1873) 351–64.

Goen, Clarence C. "Changing Conceptions of Protestant Theological Education in America." *Foundations* 6 (1963) 293–310.

———. "Editor's Introduction." In *The Great Awakening*, by Jonathan Edwards, 1–95. WJE 4. New Haven: Yale University Press, 1972.

Goodsell, Fred Field. *You Shall Be My Witnesses: An Interpretation of the History of the American Board, 1810–1960*. Boston: American Board of Commissioners for Foreign Missions, 1959.

Grasso, Christopher. *A Speaking Aristocracy: Transforming Public Discourse in Eighteenth-Century Connecticut*. Chapel Hill, NC: University of North Carolina Press, 1999.

Gribbin, William. *The Churches Militant: The War of 1812 and American Religion*. New Haven: Yale University Press, 1973.

Gridley, Samuel. "Biographical Sketch." In *Lectures on Mental Philosophy and Theology*, by James Richards, 9–96. New York: Dodd, 1846.

Griffin, Edward D. *The Causal Power in Regeneration Proper upon the mind*. North Adams, MA: N.p., 1834.

———. *The Doctrine of Divine Efficiency, defended against certain Modern Speculations*. New York: Leavitt, 1833.

———. *Foreign Missions: A Sermon, preached May 9, 1819 [. . .] in the Garden-Street Church, New York*. New York: Seymour, 1819.

———. *The Kingdom of Christ: A Missionary Sermon preached before the General Assembly of the Presbyterian Church in Philadelphia, May 23, 1805*. Andover, MA: Andover Society of Inquiry Respecting Missions, 1821.

———. *A Letter to a Friend on the Connexion between the New Doctrines and the New Measures*. Albany, NY: N.p., 1833.

———. *A Letter to the Rev. Ansel D. Eddy [. . .] on the Narrative of the Late Revivals of Religion*. Williamstown, MA: N.p., 1832.

———. "Letter to the Rev. Dr. William Sprague." In *Lectures on Revivals of Religion*, by William Buell Sprague, 359–60. 2nd ed. New York, 1833.

———. *A Series of Lectures, delivered in Park Street Church, Boston, on Sabbath Evening*. Boston: Willis, 1813.

———. *A Sermon, preached October 20, 1813, at Sandwich, Massachusetts, at the Dedication of the Meeting House*. Boston, 1813.

———. *Sermon, preached September 2, 1827, before the Candidates for the Bachelor's Degree in Williams College*. Williamstown, MA: Bannister, 1827.

———. *A Sermon preached September 14, 1826, before the American Board of Missions at Middletown, Connecticut*. Middletown, CT: E. & H. Clark, 1826.

———. *A Sermon preached September 2, 1828, at the Dedication of the New Chapel connected with Williams College, Massachusetts*. Williamstown, MA: Bannister, 1828.

———. *Sermons of the late Rev. Edward D. Griffin, D.D., to which is prefixed a memoir of his life*, by William B. Sprague, D. D. 2 vols. Albany, NY: N.p., 1838.

Grigg, John A. *The Lives of David Brainerd: The Making of an American Evangelical Icon*. New York: Oxford University Press, 2009.

Grob, Gerald N. *The Deadly Truth: A History of Disease in America*. Cambridge: Harvard University Press, 2002.

Guelzo, Allen C. *Edwards on the Will: A Century of American Theological Debate*. Middletown, CT: Wesleyan University Press, 1989.

———. "Oberlin Perfectionism and Its Edwardsean Origins, 1835–1870." In *Jonathan Edwards' Writings: Text, Context, Interpretation*, edited by Stephen J. Stein, 159–74. Bloomington, IN: Indiana University Press, 1996.

Haber, Samuel. *The Quest for Authority and Honor in the American Professions, 1750–1900*. Chicago: University of Chicago Press, 1991.

Haidt, Jonathan. *The Righteous Mind: Why Good People Are Divided by Politics and Religion*. New York: Vintage, 2013.

Hall, David D. "Editor's Introduction." In *Ecclesiastical Writings*, by Jonathan Edwards, 68–77. WJE 12. New Haven: Yale University Press, 1994.

———. *The Faithful Shepherd: A History of the New England Ministry in the Seventeenth Century*. New York: Norton, 1974.

Hall, Peter Dobkin. *The Organization of American Culture, 1700–1900: Private Institutions, Elites, and the Origins of American Nationality*. New York: New York University Press, 1982.

Hall, Timothy D. *Contested Boundaries: Itinerancy and the Reshaping of the Colonial American Religious World*. Durham, NC: Duke University Press, 1994.

Hallock, William A. *"Light and Love." A Sketch of the Life and Labors of the Rev. Justin Edwards, D.D.* [. . .]. New York: American Tract Society, 1855.

Hambrick-Stowe, Charles E. *The Practice of Piety: Puritan Devotional Disciplines in Seventeenth-Century New England*. Chapel Hill, NC: University of North Carolina Press, 1982.

Hammond, Geordan, and David Ceri Jones, eds. *George Whitefield: Life, Context, and Legacy*. Oxford: Oxford University Press, 2016.

Haroutunian, Joseph. *Piety versus Moralism: The Passing of the New England Theology*. New York: Holt, 1932.

Hart, Levi. *The Christian Minister, or Faithful Preacher of the Gospel described, a Sermon delivered at the Ordination of the Reverend Mr. Joel Benedict* [. . .] *21st of February, 1771*. New London, CT: N.p., 1771.

Hawthorne, Nathaniel. *The American Notebooks*. Edited by Randall Stewart. New Haven: Yale University Press, 1932.

Helm, Paul. "Jonathan Edwards, John Locke, and *The Religious Affections*." *Jonathan Edwards Studies* 6 (2016) 3–15.

Hewitt, John H. *Williams College and Foreign Missions*. Boston: Pilgrim, 1914.

Hofstadter, Richard, and Walter P. Metzger. *The Development of Academic Freedom in the United States*. New York: Columbia University Press, 1955.

Holifield, E. Brooks. *The Covenant Sealed: The Development of Puritan Sacramental Theology in Old and New England, 1570–1720*. New Haven: Yale University Press, 1974.

Hooker, Asahel. *The Immoral and Pernicious Tendency of Error. Illustrated in a Sermon, delivered at the Ordination of the Rev. James Beach* [. . .] *Jan. 1st. 1806*. Hartford, CT: N.p., 1806.

Hoopes, James. "Jonathan Edwards's Religious Psychology." *Journal of American History* 69 (1983) 849–65.

Hopkins, Albert. "Revivals of Religion at Williams College." *American Quarterly Register* 13 (1841) 344–51.

Hopkins, Samuel. *The Life and Character of the late Reverend Mr. Jonathan Edwards, President of the College of New-Jersey*. Boston: Kneeland, 1765.

———. "Serious Address." In *Sketches of the Life of the Late Rev. Samuel Hopkins, D.D.*, edited by Stephen West, 168–216. Hartford, CT: Hudson and Goodwin, 1805.

———. *Sketches of the Life of the Late Rev. Samuel Hopkins, D.D.* Edited by Stephen West. Hartford, CT: Hudson and Goodwin, 1805.

———. *The Works of Samuel Hopkins, D.D.* 3 vols. Boston: Doctrinal Tract and Book Society, 1852.

Humphrey, Heman. *Memoir of Rev. Nathan W. Fiske, professor of intellectual and moral philosophy in Amherst College [. . .]* Amherst, MA: J. S. & C. Adams, 1850.

[Humphrey, Zephaniah Moore]. *Memorial Sketches: Heman Humphrey, Sophia Porter Humphrey.* Philadelphia: Lippincott, 1869.

Hutchison, William R. *Errand to the World: American Protestant Thought and Foreign Missions.* Chicago: University of Chicago Press, 1987.

Hwang, Sung Chul. "The Bible and Christian Experience in the Revival Movements of Charles G. Finney and Asahel Nettleton." PhD diss., Southwestern Baptist Seminary, 2006.

Hyde, John M. "The Education of Nathan Brown." Paper presented at a meeting of the Assam Association of North America in Williamstown, MA, on September 28, 1985, to commemorate the 100th anniversary of the death of Nathan Brown.

Jedrey, Christopher M. *The World of John Cleaveland: Family and Community in Eighteenth-Century New England.* New York: Norton, 1979.

Johnson, Dominic. *God Is Watching You: How the Fear of God Makes Us Human.* New York: Oxford University Press, 2016.

Jones, David Ceri. *"A Glorious Work in the World": Welsh Methodism and the International Evangelical Revival, 1735–1750.* Cardiff: University of Wales Press, 2004.

———. "'Sure the Time Here Now Is Like New England': What Happened when Welsh Calvinistic Methodists Read Jonathan Edwards?" In *Jonathan Edwards and Scotland*, edited by Kelly Van Andel et al., 49–62. Edinburgh: Dunedin Academic Press, 2011.

Jones, James W. *Can Science Explain Religion? The Cognitive Science Debate.* New York: Oxford University Press, 2016.

Judson, Ephraim. *On Preaching the Word. A sermon delivered in Williamstown, June 17, 1795, at the ordination of the Reverend Ebenezer Fitch, president of Williams College [. . .].* Stockbridge, MA: Andrews, 1796.

Kang, Sung Ho. "The Evangelistic Preaching of Asahel Nettleton and Charles G. Finney in the Second Great Awakening and Applications for Contemporary Evangelism." PhD diss., Southwestern Baptist Seminary, 2004.

Kelemen, Deborah. "Are Children 'Intuitive Theists'"? *Psychological Science* 15 (2004) 295–301.

Keller, Charles Roy. *The Second Great Awakening in Connecticut.* New Haven: Yale University Press, 1942.

Kelley, Brooks Mather. *Yale: A History.* New Haven: Yale University Press, 1974.

Kennedy, Earl William. "From Providence to Civil Religion: Some 'Dutch' Reformed Interpretations of America in the Revolutionary Era." *Reformed Review* 29 (1976) 111–23.

Kidd, Thomas S. *The Great Awakening: The Roots of Evangelical Christianity in Colonial America.* New Haven: Yale University Press, 2007.

———. "'The Very Vital Breath of Christianity': Prayer and Revival in Provincial New England." *Fides et Historia* 36 (2004) 19–33.

Kimnach, Wilson H. "General Introduction to the Sermons." In *Sermons and Discourses, 1720–1723*, by Jonathan Edwards, 1–258. WJE 10. New Haven: Yale University Press, 1992.

Kimnach, Wilson H., et al. *Jonathan Edwards's "Sinners in the Hands of an Angry God."* New Haven: Yale University Press, 2010.

Kirkpatrick, Lee A. *Attachment, Evolution, and the Psychology of Religion.* New York: Guilford, 2005.

Kling, David W. *A Field of Divine Wonders: The New Divinity and Village Revivals in Northwestern Connecticut, 1791–1822.* University Park, PA: Pennsylvania State University Press, 1993.

Kling, David W., and Douglas A. Sweeney, eds. *Jonathan Edwards at Home and Abroad: Historical Memories, Cultural Movements, Global Horizons.* Columbia, SC: University of South Carolina Press, 2003.

Kreider, Glenn. "Jonathan Edwards's Theology of Prayer." *Bibliotheca Sacra* 160 (2003) 434–56.

Kuklick, Bruce. *Churchmen and Philosophers: From Jonathan Edwards to John Dewey.* New Haven: Yale University Press, 1985.

———. "Jonathan Edwards and American Philosophy." In *Jonathan Edwards and the American Experience*, edited by Nathan O. Hatch and Harry S. Stout, 246–59. New York: Oxford University Press, 1989.

Lambert, Frank. "The First Great Awakening: Whose Interpretive Fiction?" *New England Quarterly* 68 (1995) 650–59.

———. *Inventing the "Great Awakening."* Princeton: Princeton University Press, 1999.

———. *"Pedlar in Divinity": George Whitefield and the Transatlantic Revivals, 1737–1770.* Princeton: Princeton University Press, 1994.

Land, Steven J. *Pentecostal Spirituality: A Passion for the Kingdom.* Sheffield: Sheffield Academic Press, 1993.

Laurence, David. "Jonathan Edwards, John Locke, and the Canon of Experience." *Early American Literature* 15 (1980) 107–23.

———. "Jonathan Edwards, Solomon Stoddard, and the Preparationist Model of Conversion." *Harvard Theological Review* 72 (1979) 267–83.

Lee, Eliza Buckminster. *Memoirs of Rev. Joseph Buckminster, D.D., and his son, Rev. Joseph Stevens Buckminster.* Boston: Crosby and Nichols, 1849.

Lesser, M. X. "An Honor Too Great: Jonathan Edwards in Print Abroad." In *Edwards at Home and Abroad: Historical Memories, Cultural Movements, Global Horizons*, edited by David W. Kling and Douglas A. Sweeney, 297–319. Columbia, SC: University of South Carolina Press, 2003.

———. *Reading Jonathan Edwards: An Annotated Bibliography in Three Parts, 1729–2005.* Grand Rapids: Eerdmans, 2008.

Lewis, C. S. *Letters to Malcolm: Chiefly on Prayer.* New York: Harcourt, Brace, & World, 1964.

"List of Books Recommended by Dr. Tappan to Theological Students." *The Panoplist, or, The Christian's Armory* 2 (1807) 325–26.

Livingston, John Henry. *The Everlasting Gospel.* New York: T. and J. Swords, 1804.

Lowe, Wolfgang Eberhard. "The First American Foreign Missionaries: 'The Students,' 1810–1820." PhD diss., Brown University, 1962.

Lucas, Sean Michael. *God's Grand Design: The Theological Vision of Jonathan Edwards*. Wheaton, IL: Crossway, 2011.

Luhrmann, T. M., et al. "The Absorption Hypothesis: Learning to Hear God in Evangelical Christianity." *American Anthropologist* 112 (2010) 66–78.

———. *When God Talks Back: Understanding the American Evangelical Relationship with God*. New York: Knopf, 2012.

Luther, Martin. *A Commentary on St. Paul's Epistle to the Galatians*. In *Martin Luther: Selections from His Writings*, edited by John Dillenberger, 99–165. Garden City, NY: Anchor, 1961.

Lyttle, David. "The Sixth Sense of Jonathan Edwards." *Church Quarterly Review* 167 (1966) 50–59.

Marsden, George M. *The Evangelical Mind and the New School Presbyterian Experience: A Case Study of Thought and Theology in Nineteenth-Century America*. New Haven: Yale University Press, 1970.

———. *Jonathan Edwards: A Life*. New Haven: Yale University Press, 2003.

———. "Old, Rested, and Reformed: Reflections on the Recovery of Edwards." *Jonathan Edwards Studies* 10 (2020) 120–28.

———. *A Short Life of Jonathan Edwards*. Grand Rapids: Eerdmans, 2008.

Marshall, Ian. "Taking Louisbourg by Prayer: Responses of Jonathan Edwards and Benjamin Franklin to a Military Episode in Colonial American History." *University of Dayton Review* 20 (1989) 3–19.

Mathews, Donald G. "The Second Great Awakening as an Organizing Process, 1780–1830: An Hypothesis." *American Quarterly* 21 (1969) 23–43.

May, Henry F. *The Enlightenment in America*. New York: Oxford University Press, 1976.

May, Sherry Pierpont. "Asahel Nettleton: Nineteenth-Century American Revivalist." PhD diss., Drew University, 1969.

McCloy, Frank Dixon. "The History of Theological Education in America." *Church History* 31 (1962) 449–53.

McClymond, Michael J. *Encounters with God: An Approach to the Theology of Jonathan Edwards*. New York: Oxford University Press, 1998.

———. "Spiritual Perception in Jonathan Edwards." *Journal of Religion* 77 (1997) 195–216.

McClymond, Michael J., and Gerald R. McDermott. *The Theology of Jonathan Edwards*. New York: Oxford University Press, 2012.

McCoy, Genevieve. "Edwardsean Spirituality and the Nez Perce." Paper presented at the Spring Meeting of the American Society of Church History, Nashville, TN, April 26, 1997.

———. "'Reason for a Hope': Evangelical Women Making Sense of Late Edwardsian Calvinism." In *Jonathan Edwards's Writings: Text, Context, Interpretation*, edited by Stephen J. Stein, 175–92. Bloomington, IN: Indiana University Press, 1996.

———. "The Women of the ABCFM Oregon Mission and the Conflicted Language of Calvinism." *Church History* 64 (1995) 62–82.

McCullough, Donald. *If Grace Is So Amazing, Why Don't We Like It?* San Francisco: Josey-Bass, 2005.

McDermott, Gerald R. *One Holy and Happy Society: The Public Theology of Jonathan Edwards*. University Park, PA: Pennsylvania State University Press, 1992.

———. "A Possibility of Reconciliation: Jonathan Edwards and the Salvation of Non-Christians." In *Edwards in Our Time: Jonathan Edwards and the Shaping of*

American Religion, edited by Sang Hyun Lee and Allen C. Guelzo, 173–202. Grand Rapids: Eerdmans, 1999.

———. *Seeing God: Twelve Reliable Signs of True Spirituality*. Downers Grove, IL: InterVarsity, 1995.

McGiffert, Michael, ed. *God's Plot: Puritan Spirituality in Thomas Shepard's Cambridge*. Rev. and expanded ed. Amherst: University of Massachusetts Press, 1994.

Mead, Sidney E. "The Rise of the Evangelical Conception of the Ministry." In *The Ministry in Historical Perspectives*, edited by H. Richard Niebuhr and Daniel D. Williams, 207–49. New York: Harper & Brothers, 1956.

Millar, Robert. *A History of the Propagation of Christianity and the Overthrow of Paganism*. 2 vols. 3rd ed. London, 1731.

Miller, Glenn T. *Piety and Intellect: The Aims and Purposes of Ante-Bellum Theological Education*. Atlanta, GA: Scholars, 1990.

Miller, Perry. *Jonathan Edwards*. 1949. Reprint, Westport, CT: Greenwood Press, 1973.

Mills, Samuel J. "The Religious Sentiments of Christ." In *Sermons on Important Subjects, Collected from a number of ministers, in some of the Northern States of America*, 1–36. Hartford, CT: Hudson and Goodwin, 1797.

Minkema, Kenneth P. "Jonathan Edwards in the Twentieth Century." *Journal of the Evangelical Theological Society* 47 (2004) 659–87.

———. "Preface to the Period." In *The Great Awakening*, by Jonathan Edwards, 3–47. WJE 14. New Haven: Yale University Press, 1997.

———. "Whitefield, Jonathan Edwards, and Revival." In *George Whitefield: Life, Context, and Legacy*, edited by Geordan Hammond and David Ceri Jones, 115–31. Oxford: Oxford University Press, 2016.

Moody, Josh. *Jonathan Edwards and the Enlightenment: Knowing the Presence of God*. Lanham, MD: University Press of America, 2005.

Moore, Zephaniah Swift. *Articles of faith, and form of covenant, adopted by the Congregational Church in Leicester, Mass., October 3, 1805, while under the pastoral care of Rev. Zephaniah Swift Moore [. . .]*. Concord, NH: Moore, 1823.

———. *The ministers of Christ dependent on divine influences for success in preaching the gospel. A sermon preached at the ordination of the Rev. Simeon Colton, to the pastoral care of the church in Palmer, Mass., June 19, 1811 [. . .]*. Brookfield, MA: Merriam, 1811.

Morgan, Edmund S. "The American Revolution as an Intellectual Movement." In *Paths of American Thought*, edited by Arthur M. Schlesinger Jr. and Morton White, 11–33. Boston: Houghton Mifflin, 1963.

———. *Visible Saints: The History of a Puritan Idea*. Ithaca, NY: Cornell University Press, 1965.

Morimoto, Anri. *Jonathan Edwards and the Catholic Vision of Salvation*. University Park, PA: Pennsylvania State University Press, 1995.

Morris, James. *Memoirs of James Morris of South Farms in Litchfield*. New York: Aline Brothier Morris Fund, 1933.

Mullen, Robert Bruce. "Science, Miracles and the Prayer-Gauge Debate." In *When Science and Christianity Meet*, edited by David C. Lindberg and Ronald L. Numbers, 203–24. Chicago: University of Chicago Press, 2003.

Murray, Iain H. *Jonathan Edwards: A New Biography*. Edinburgh: Banner of Truth, 1987.

Najapfour, Brian G. *Jonathan Edwards: His Doctrine of and Devotion to Prayer.* Caledonia, MI: Biblical Spirituality, 2013.

Naylor, Natalie A. "The Theological Seminary in the Configuration of American Higher Education: The Ante-Bellum Years." *History of Education Quarterly* 17 (1977) 17–30.

Neele, Adriaan C. "The Reception of Edwards's *A History of the Work of Redemption* in Nineteenth-Century Basutoland." *Journal of Religion in Africa* 45 (2015) 68–93.

Nelson, Ricky Charles. "The Relationship between Soteriology and Evangelistic Methodologies in the Ministries of Asahel Nettleton and Charles G. Finney." PhD diss., Southwestern Baptist Seminary, 1997.

Nettleton, Asahel. *Remains of the Late Rev. Asahel Nettleton, D.D.* [. . .]. Compiled by Bennet Tyler. Hartford, CT: N.p., 1865.

———. *Temperance and Revivals.* New York, 1829.

Newton, [Roger]. "A View of God, as Creator and Governor of the World." In *Sermons, on Various Important Doctrines and Duties of the Christian Religion*, 73–86. Northampton, MA: Butler, 1799.

Noll, Mark A. *America's God: From Jonathan Edwards to Abraham Lincoln.* New York: Oxford University Press, 2002.

———. "The Contested Legacy of Jonathan Edwards in Antebellum Calvinism: Theological Conflict and the Evolution of Thought in America." *Canadian Review of American Studies* 19 (1988) 149–64.

———. "Jonathan Edwards and Nineteenth-Century Theology." In *Jonathan Edwards and the American Experience*, edited by Nathan O. Hatch and Harry S. Stout, 115–37. New York: Oxford University Press, 1989.

———. "Moses Mather (Old Calvinist) and the Evolution of Edwardseanism." *Church History* 49 (1980) 273–85.

———. *The New Shape of World Christianity: How American Experience Reflects Global Faith.* Downers Grove, IL: IVP Academic, 2009.

———. *One Nation under God? Christian Faith and Political Action in America.* New York: Harper and Row, 1989.

Noll, Mark A., et al., eds. *Evangelicalism: Comparative Studies of Popular Protestantism in North America, the British Isles, and Beyond, 1700–1990.* New York: Oxford University Press, 1994.

Novak, Steven J. *The Rights of Youth: American Colleges and Student Revolt, 1798–1815.* Cambridge: Harvard University Press, 1977.

O'Brien, Susan. "Eighteenth-Century Publishing Networks in the First Years of Transatlantic Evangelicalism." In *Evangelicalism: Comparative Studies of Popular Protestantism in North America, the British Isles, and Beyond, 1700–1990*, edited by Mark A. Noll et al., 38–57. New York: Oxford University Press, 1994.

———. "A Transatlantic Community of Saints: The Great Awakening and the First Evangelical Network, 1735–1755." *American Historical Review* 91 (1986) 811–32.

Olmsted, Denison. *Memoir of John Treadwell, LL.D., Late Governor of Connecticut.* Boston: Marvin, 1843.

Orr, J. Edwin. *The Eager Feet: Evangelical Awakenings, 1790–1830.* Chicago: Moody, 1975.

Ostrander, Rick. *The Life of Prayer in a World of Science: Protestants, Prayer, and American Culture, 1870–1930.* New York: Oxford University Press, 2000.

Park, Edwards A. *A Memoir of Nathanael Emmons; with sketches of his friends and pupils.* Boston: Congregational Board of Publications, 1861.
Pauw, Amy Plantinga. "Editor's Introduction." In *The "Miscellanies": Nos. 833–1132*, by Jonathan Edwards, 1–39. WJE 20. New Haven: Yale University Press, 2002.
———. "Edwards as American Theologian: Grand Narratives and Pastoral Narratives." In *Jonathan Edwards at 300: Essays on the Tercentenary of His Birth*, edited by Harry S. Stout et al., 14–24. Lanham, MD: University Press of America, 2005.
Perkins, Nathan. *A Discourse delivered at the Ordination of the Rev. William F. Miller [...], Nov. 30, 1791.* Hartford, CT: Babcock, 1792.
———. *A Sermon, preached at the installation of the Rev. Mr. Solomon Wolcott [...] May 24th, 1786.* Hartford, CT: N.p., [1786].
Perry, Alan Frederick. "The American Board of Commissioners for Foreign Missions and the London Missionary Society in the Nineteenth Century: A Study of Ideas." PhD diss., Washington University, 1974.
Perry, Arthur Latham. *Williamstown and Williams College.* New York: Scribner's Sons, 1899.
Peterson, Owen. *A Divine Discontent: The Life of Nathan S. S. Beman.* Macon, GA: Mercer University Press, 1986.
Pettit, Norman. "Editor's Introduction." In *The Life of David Brainerd*, by Jonathan Edwards, 1–85. WJE 7. New Haven: Yale University Press, 1985.
———. *The Heart Prepared: Grace and Conversion in Puritan Spiritual Life.* New Haven: Yale University Press, 1966.
Phillips, Clifton J. *Protestant America and the Pagan World: The First Half Century of the American Board of Commissioners for Foreign Missions, 1810–1860.* Cambridge: East Asia Research Center, Harvard University, 1969.
Piggin, Stuart. "The Expanding Knowledge of God: Jonathan Edwards's Influence on Missionary Thinking and Promotion." In *Jonathan Edwards at Home and Abroad: Historical Memories, Cultural Movements, Global Horizons*, edited by David W. Kling and Douglas A. Sweeney, 266–96. Columbia, SC: University of South Carolina Press, 2003.
———. *Making Evangelical Missionaries, 1789–1858.* Abingdon: Courtenay, 1984.
Porter, Noah. *A Sermon, delivered at the funeral of the Hon. John Treadwell, Esq.* Hartford, CT: Goodwin, 1823.
Rabinowitz, Richard. *The Spiritual Self in Everyday Life: The Transformation of Personal Religious Experience in Nineteenth-Century New England.* Boston: Northeastern University Press, 1989.
Ramsey, Paul. "Editor's Introduction." In *Freedom of the Will*, by Jonathan Edwards, 1–128. WJE 1. New Haven: Yale University Press, 1957.
Rankin, Jeremiah Eames. "Tell It to Jesus." https://hymnary.org/text/are_you_weary_are_you_heavyhearted.
Rice, Howard L., and Lamar Williamson Jr., eds. *A Book of Reformed Prayers.* Louisville, KY: Westminster John Knox Press, 1998.
Richards, James. *Lectures on Mental Philosophy and Theology.* New York: Dodd, 1846.
———. *The Spirit of Paul the Spirit of Missions. A Sermon, preached at New Haven, (CT) before the American Board of Commissioners for Foreign Missions.* Boston: Armstrong, 1814.
Richards, Thomas C. *Samuel J. Mills: Missionary Pathfinder, Pioneer, and Promoter.* Boston: Pilgrim, 1906.

Richardson, Leon Burr. *History of Dartmouth College*. 2 vols. Hanover, NH: Dartmouth College, 1932.
Robbins, Thomas. *The Diary of Thomas Robbins, D.D., 1796-1854*. Edited by Increase Tarbox. 2 vols. Boston, 1886-87.
Robert, Dana L. *American Women in Mission: A Social History of Their Thought and Practice*. Macon, GA: Mercer University Press, 1996.
———. "'The Crisis of Missions': Premillennial Mission Theory and the Origins of Independent Evangelical Missions." In *Earthen Vessels: American Evangelicals and Foreign Missions, 1880-1980*, edited by Joel A. Carpenter and Wilbert R. Shenk, 29-46. Grand Rapids: Eerdmans, 1990.
Robson, David W. *Educating Republicans: The College in the Era of the American Revolution, 1750-1800*. Westport, CT: Greenwood, 1985.
Rogers, Mark. "Edward Dorr Griffin and the Edwardsian Second Great Awakening." PhD diss., Trinity Evangelical Divinity School, 2012.
Rohrer, James R. *Keepers of the Covenant: Frontier Missions and the Decline of Congregationalism, 1774-1818*. New York: Oxford University Press, 1995.
Rooy, Sidney H. *The Theology of Missions in the Puritan Tradition*. Grand Rapids: Eerdmans, 1965.
Rudolph, Frederick. "Edward Dorr Griffin: An Historical Sketch." *Sketch* (1940) 20-21, 39-44.
———. *Mark Hopkins and the Log: Williams College, 1836-1872*. New Haven: Yale University Press, 1956.
Sandeen, Ernest R. *The Roots of Fundamentalism: British and American Millenarianism, 1800-1930*. Grand Rapids: Baker, 1978.
Sassi, Jonathan D. *A Republic of Righteousness: The Public Christianity of the Post-Revolutionary New England Clergy*. New York: Oxford University Press, 2001.
Scott, Donald M. *From Office to Profession: The New England Ministry, 1750-1850*. Philadelphia: University of Pennsylvania Press, 1978.
Schmidt, Leigh Eric. *Holy Fairs: Scottish Communions and American Revivals in the Early Modern Period*. Princeton: Princeton University Press, 1989.
Sewall, Albert C. *Life of Prof. Albert Hopkins*. New York: Randolph, 1879.
Shea, Daniel B. *Spiritual Autobiography in Early America*. Madison, WI: University of Wisconsin Press, 1988.
Shepard, Thomas. *The Parable of the Ten Virgins*. Edited by John Adams Albro. The Works of Thomas Shepard 2. 1853. Reprint, Hildesheim: Olms, 1971.
———. *The Sincere Convert*. Edited by John Adams Albro. The Works of Thomas Shepard 1. 1853. Reprint, Hildesheim: Olms, 1971.
Shewmaker, William O. "The Training of the Protestant Ministry in the United States of America, before the Establishment of Theological Seminaries." *Papers of the American Society of Church History* 6 (1921) 71-202.
Shiels, Richard D. "The Connecticut Clergy in the Second Great Awakening." PhD diss., Boston University, 1976.
Simonson, Harold P. "Jonathan Edwards and His Scottish Connections." *Journal of American Studies* 21 (1987) 353-76.
Simpson, Samuel. "Early Ministerial Training in America." *Papers of the American Society of Church History* 2 (1910) 117-29.
Sloan, Douglas, ed. *The Great Awakening and American Education: A Documentary History*. New York: Teachers College Press, Columbia University, 1973.

———. *The Scottish Enlightenment and the American College Ideal.* New York: Teachers College Press, Columbia University, 1971.
Slone, D. Jason. *Theological Incorrectness: Why Religious People Believe What They Shouldn't.* New York: Oxford University Press, 2004.
Smith, John E. "Editor's Introduction." In *A Treatise Concerning Religious Affections*, by Jonathan Edwards, 1–83. WJE 2. New Haven: Yale University Press, 1959.
———. *Jonathan Edwards: Puritan, Preacher, Philosopher.* Notre Dame: University of Notre Dame Press, 1993.
———. "Testing the Spirits: Jonathan Edwards and the Religious Affections." *Union Seminary Quarterly Review* 37 (1981–82) 27–37.
Smith, R. *Recollections of Nettleton, and the Great Revival of 1820.* Albany, NY: N.p., 1848.
Spilka, Bernard, and Kevin L. Ladd. *The Psychology of Prayer: A Scientific Approach.* New York: Guilford, 2013.
Sprague, William B. *Annals of the American Pulpit: Congregationalists.* 9 vols. New York: Carter & Bros., 1857–69.
Spring, Gardiner. *Death and Heaven: A Sermon preached in Newark at the interment of the Rev. Edward D. Griffin, D.D.* New York: Taylor, 1838.
———. *Memoir of Samuel John Mills.* 2nd ed. New York: Saxton and Miles, 1842.
Spring, Samuel. *A Sermon, preached at New Haven, CT before the American Board of Commissioners for Foreign Missions.* Boston: Armstrong, 1818.
Stanley, Brian. *The Global Diffusion of Evangelicalism: The Age of Billy Graham and John Stott.* Downers Grove, IL: IVP Academic, 2013.
Steele, Richard B. *"Gracious Affection" and "True Virtue" according to Jonathan Edwards and John Wesley.* Metuchen, NJ: Scarecrow, 1994.
Stein, Stephen J. "Editor's Introduction." In *Apocalyptic Writings*, by Jonathan Edwards, 1–93. WJE 5. New Haven: Yale University Press, 1977.
———. "Editor's Introduction." In *The "Blank Bible,"* by Jonathan Edwards, 1–117. WJE 24. New Haven: Yale University Press, 2006.
———. "Editor's Introduction." In *Notes on Scripture*, by Jonathan Edwards, 1–46. WJE 15. New Haven: Yale University Press, 1998.
———. "Edwards as Biblical Exegete." In *The Cambridge Companion to Jonathan Edwards*, edited by Stephen J. Stein, 181–95. Cambridge: Cambridge University Press, 2007.
———. "'For Their Spiritual Good': The Northampton, Massachusetts, Prayer Bids of the 1730s and 1740s." *William and Mary Quarterly* 37 (1980) 261–85.
———. "Introduction." In *Jonathan Edwards's Writings: Text Context, Interpretation*, edited by Stephen J. Stein, ix–xix. Bloomington, IN: Indiana University Press, 1996.
———. "Jonathan Edwards and the Rainbow: Biblical Exegesis and Poetic Imagination." *New England Quarterly* 47 (1974) 440–56.
———. "The Quest for the Spiritual Sense: The Biblical Hermeneutics of Jonathan Edwards." *Harvard Theological Review* 70 (1997) 99–113.
———. "The Spirit and the Word: Jonathan Edwards and Scriptural Exegesis." In *Jonathan Edwards and the American Experience*, edited by Nathan O. Hatch and Harry S. Stout, 118–30. New York: Oxford University Press, 1988,
Stievermann, Jan. "Faithful Translations: New Discoveries on the German Pietist Reception of Jonathan Edwards." *Church History* 83 (2014) 324–66.

Stiles, Ezra. *The Literary Diary of Ezra Stiles*. Edited by Franklin B. Dexter. 3 vols. New York: Scribner's Sons, 1901.
Stoddard, Solomon. *Question: Whether God is not angry with the Country for doing so little towards the Conversion of the Indians?* Boston: Green, 1723.
Stoever, William K. B. "Godly Mind: Puritan Reformed Orthodoxy and John Locke in Jonathan Edwards's Conception of Gracious Cognition and Conviction." *Jonathan Edwards Studies* 4 (2014) 327–52.
Story, Ronald. *The Forging of an Aristocracy: Harvard and the Boston Upper Class, 1800–1870*. Middletown, CT: Wesleyan University Press, 1980.
Stout, Harry S. *The Divine Dramatist: George Whitefield and the Rise of Modern Evangelicalism*. Grand Rapids: Eerdmans, 1991.
———. "Edwards and Revival." In *Understanding Jonathan Edwards: An Introduction to America's Theologian*, edited by Gerald R. McDermott, 37–52. New York: Oxford University Press, 2009.
———. "Edwards as Revivalist." In *Cambridge Companion to Jonathan Edwards*, edited by Stephen J. Stein, 125–43. Cambridge: Cambridge University Press, 2007.
———. "The Puritans and Edwards." In *Jonathan Edwards and the American Experience*, edited by Nathan O. Hatch and Harry S. Stout, 142–59. New York: Oxford University Press, 1989.
———. "Religion, Communications, and the Ideological Origins of the American Revolution." In *Religion in American History: A Reader*, edited by Jon Butler and Harry S. Stout, 89–108. New York: Oxford University Press, 1998.
Stout, Harry S., et al., eds. *The Jonathan Edwards Encyclopedia*. Grand Rapids: Eerdmans, 2017.
Strong, Nathan. *A Sermon, delivered at the Consecration of the New Brick Church in Hartford, December 3, 1807*. Hartford, CT: Hudson and Goodwin, 1808.
Strong, William E. *The Story of the American Board: An Account of the First Hundred Years of the American Board of Commissioners for Foreign Missions*. Boston: Pilgrim, 1910.
Sweeney, Douglas A. "Edwards and His Mantle: The Historiography of the New England Theology." *New England Quarterly* 71 (1998) 97–119.
———. "Edwards and the Bible." In *Understanding Jonathan Edwards: An Introduction to America's Theologian*, edited by Gerald R. McDermott, 63–82. Oxford: Oxford University Press, 2009.
———. "Edwards Studies Today." In *The Oxford Handbook of Jonathan Edwards*, edited by Douglas A. Sweeney and Jan Stievermann, 568–81. Oxford: Oxford University Press, 2021.
———. *Edwards the Exegete: Biblical Interpretation and Anglo-Protestant Culture on the Edge of the Enlightenment*. New York: Oxford University Press, 2016.
———. "The Evangelical Supernatural in Early Modern Europe: Cotton Mather and Jonathan Edwards on the Miracles of Jesus." In *The Bible in Early Transatlantic Pietism and Evangelicalism*, edited by Ryan P. Holeston et al., 131–47. University Park, PA: Pennsylvania State University Press, 2022.
———. "Evangelical Tradition in America." In *Cambridge Companion to Jonathan Edwards*, edited by Stephen J. Stein, 217–38. New York: Cambridge University Press, 2007.
———. *Jonathan Edwards and the Ministry of the Word*. Downers Grove, IL: IVP Academic, 2009.

———. "'Longing for More and More of It'? The Strange Career of Jonathan Edwards's Exegetical Exertions." In *Jonathan Edwards at 300: Essays on the Tercentenary of His Birth*, edited by Harry S. Stout et al., 25–37. Lanham, MD: University Press of America, 2005.

———. *Nathaniel Taylor, New Haven Theology, and the Legacy of Jonathan Edwards*. New York: Oxford University Press, 2003.

———. "Nathaniel William Taylor and the Edwardsian Tradition: A Reassessment." In *Jonathan Edwards's Writings: Text Context, Interpretation*, edited by Stephen J. Stein, 139–58. Bloomington, IN: Indiana University Press, 1996.

———. "New Divinity." In *The Jonathan Edwards Encyclopedia*, edited by Harry S. Stout et al., 400–404. Grand Rapids: Eerdmans, 2017.

Sweeney, Douglas A., and Allen C. Guelzo, eds. *The New England Theology: From Jonathan Edwards to Edwards Amasa Park*. Grand Rapids: Baker, 2006.

Sweeney, Douglas A., and Jan Stievermann, eds. *The Oxford Handbook of Jonathan Edwards*. Oxford: Oxford University Press, 2021.

Sweeney, Kevin M. "River Gods and Related Minor Deities: The Williams Family and the Connecticut River Valley, 1637–1790." 2 vols. PhD diss., Yale University, 1986.

Sweet, William Warren. *Religion in the Development of American Culture, 1765–1840*. New York: Scribner, 1952.

Tannenbaum, Rebecca J. *Health and Wellness in Colonial America*. Santa Barbara, CA: Greenwood, 2012.

Tennent, Gilbert. *The Danger of an Unconverted Ministry*. In *The Great Awakening: Documents Illustrating the Crisis and Its Consequences*, edited by Alan Heimert and Perry Miller, 71–99. Indianapolis: Bobbs-Merrill, 1967.

The Theological Questions of President Edwards, Senior, and Dr. Edwards, His Son. Providence, RI: N.p., 1822.

Thornbury, John F. "Asahel Nettleton's Conflict with Finneyism." *Reformation and Revival* 8 (1999) 103–19.

———. *God Sent Revival: The Story of Asahel Nettleton and the Second Great Awakening*. Grand Rapids: Evangelical, 1977.

Tracy, Joseph. *History of the American Board of Commissioners for Foreign Missions*. 2nd ed. Boston: Dodd, 1842.

Tracy, Patricia. *Jonathan Edwards, Pastor: Religion and Society in Eighteenth-Century Northampton*. New York: Hill and Wang, 1979.

Trumbull, Benjamin. *A Sermon, delivered at the Ordination of the Rev. Lemuel Taylor [. . .] May 7th, 1789*. New Haven, CT: N.p., 1793.

Tyler, Bennet. *Nettleton and His Labours: The Memoirs of Dr. Asahel Nettleton*. 1854. Reprint, Carlisle, PA: Banner of Truth Trust, 1975.

Vaill, Joseph. "Theological Education in Connecticut, Seventy Years Ago." *Congregational Quarterly* 6 (1864) 137–42.

Valeri, Mark. *Law and Providence in Joseph Bellamy's New: England: The Origins of the New Divinity in Revolutionary America*. New York: Oxford University Press, 1994.

———. "The New Divinity and the American Revolution." *William and Mary Quarterly* 46 (1989) 741–69.

Van Andel, Kelly. "The Geography of Sinfulness: Mapping Subjectivity on the Mission Frontier." In *Jonathan Edwards and Scotland*, edited by Kelly Van Andel et al., 89–99. Edinburgh: Dunedin Academic Press, 2011.

van den Berg, Johannes. *Constrained by Jesus' Love: An Inquiry into the Motives of the Missionary Awakening in Great Britain in the Period between 1698 and 1815.* Kampen: Kok, 1956.
van Vlastuin, Willem. "Alternative Viewpoint: Edwards and Revival." In *Understanding Jonathan Edwards: An Introduction to America's Theologian,* edited by Gerald R. McDermott, 53–61. New York: Oxford University Press, 2009.
———. "Prayer." In *The Jonathan Edwards Encyclopedia,* edited by Harry S. Stout et al., 455–57. Grand Rapids: Eerdmans, 2017.
Visala, Aku. *Naturalism, Theism, and the Cognitive Study of Religion: Religion Explained?* Ashgate Science and Religion Series. Farnum: Ashgate, 2011.
Wainwright, William J. *Reason and the Heart: A Prolegomenon to a Critique of Passional Reason.* Ithaca, NY: Cornell University Press, 1995.
Walls, Andrew F. "The Evangelical Revival, the Missionary Movement, and Africa." In *Evangelicalism: Comparative Studies of Popular Protestantism in North America, the British Isles, and Beyond, 1700–1990,* edited by Mark A. Noll et al., 310–30. New York: Oxford University Press, 1994.
———. "Missions and Historical Memory: Jonathan Edwards and David Brainerd." In *Edwards at Home and Abroad: Historical Memories, Cultural Movements, Global Horizons,* edited by David W. Kling and Douglas A. Sweeney, 248–65. Columbia, SC: University of South Carolina Press, 2003.
Warch, Richard. "The Shepherd's Tent: Education and Enthusiasm in the Great Awakening." *American Quarterly* 30 (1978) 177–98.
Ward, W. R. *Early Evangelicalism: A Global Intellectual History.* Cambridge: Cambridge University Press, 2006.
———. *The Protestant Evangelical Awakening.* Cambridge: Cambridge University Press, 1992.
Ward, W. Reginald, and Richard P. Heizenrater, eds. *The Works of John Wesley.* Vol. 19, *Journal and Diaries II (1738–1743).* Nashville: Abingdon, 1990.
Washburn, Joseph. *Sermons on Practical Subjects* [. . .]. Hartford, CT: Lincoln & Gleason, 1807.
Watts, Isaac, and John Guyse. "Preface." In *The Great Awakening,* by Jonathan Edwards, 130–42. WJE 4. New Haven: Yale University Press, 1972.
Weber, Donald. *Rhetoric and History in Revolutionary New England.* New York: Oxford University Press, 1988.
Westerkamp, Marilyn J. *Triumph of the Laity: Scots-Irish Piety and the Great Awakening, 1625–1760.* New York: Oxford University Press, 1988.
Westra, Helen Petter. "'Above All Others': Jonathan Edwards and the Gospel Ministry." *American Presbyterians* 67 (1989) 209–19.
———. "Divinity's Design: Edwards and the Work of Revival." In *Edwards in Our Time: Jonathan Edwards and the Shaping of American Religion,* edited by Sang Hyun Lee and Allen C. Guelzo, 131–57. Grand Rapids: Eerdmans, 1999.
Wheeler, Rachel M. "Edwards as Missionary." In *The Cambridge Companion to Jonathan Edwards,* edited by Stephen J. Stein, 196–214. New York: Cambridge University Press, 2007.
Wilson, John F. "Editor's Introduction." In *A History of the Work of Redemption,* by Jonathan Edwards, 1–109. WJE 9. New Haven: Yale University Press, 1989.

———. "History, Redemption, and the Millennium." In *Jonathan Edwards and the American Experience*, edited by Nathan O. Hatch and Harry S. Stout, 131–41. New York: Oxford University Press, 1988.

Winiarski, Douglas L. *Darkness Falls on the Land of Light: Experiencing Religious Awakenings in Eighteenth-Century New England*. Chapel Hill, NC: University of North Carolina Press, 2017.

———. "Jonathan Edwards, Enthusiast? Radical Revivalism and the Great Awakening in the Connecticut Valley." *Church History* 74 (2005) 683–739.

———. "Religious Experiences in New England." In *Modern Christianity to 1900*, edited by Amanda Porterfield, 209–32. A People's History of Christianity 6. Minneapolis: Fortress, 2007.

Winship, Michael P. *Making Heretics: Militant Protestantism and Free Grace in Massachusetts, 1636–1641*. Princeton: Princeton University Press, 2002.

———. *The Times and Trials of Anne Hutchinson: Puritans Divided*. Lawrence, KS: University Press of Kansas, 2005.

Winter, R. Milton. "Presbyterians and Prayers for the Sick: Changing Patterns of Pastoral Ministry." *American Presbyterians* 64 (1986) 141–55.

Winslow, Ola E. *Jonathan Edwards, 1703–1758*. New York: Macmillan, 1941.

Woods, Leonard. *History of the Andover Theological Seminary*. Boston: Osgood, 1885.

———. *Memoirs of American Missionaries, formerly connected with the Society of Inquiry Respecting Missions, in the Andover Theological Seminary*. Boston: Pierce and Parker, 1833.

———. "A Sermon, delivered at the Tabernacle in Salem, Feb. 6, 1812, on Occasion of the Ordination of the Rev. Messrs. Samuel Newell, A.M.; Adoniram Judson, A.M.; Samuel Nott, A.M.; Gordon Hall, A.M.; and Luther Rice, A.B.; Missionaries to the Heathen in Asia." In *Pioneers in Mission: The Early Missionary Ordination Sermons, Charges, and Instructions*, edited by R. Pierce Beaver, 257–68. Grand Rapids: Eerdmans, 1966.

Worcester, Samuel M. *The Life and Labors of Rev. Samuel Worcester, D.D.* 2 vols. Boston: Crocker and Brewster, 1852.

Wright, Conrad. *The Beginnings of Unitarianism in America*. Boston: King, 1955.

Wuthnow, Robert. *Boundless Faith: The Global Outreach of American Churches*. Berkeley: University of California Press, 2009.

Yale, Cyrus. *The Godly Pastor. Life of the Rev. Jeremiah Hallock, of Canton, CT to which is added a sketch of the Life of Moses Hallock, of Plainfield, Mass*. New York: American Tract Society, [1854].

Yancey, Philip. *What's So Amazing about Grace?* Grand Rapids: Zondervan, 2002.

Yeager, Jonathan M. *Jonathan Edwards and Transatlantic Print Culture*. New York: Oxford University Press, 2016.

Zakai, Avihu. *Jonathan Edwards's Philosophy of History: The Reenchantment of the World in the Age of Enlightenment*. Princeton: Princeton University Press, 2003.

Index

JE = Jonathan Edwards

ABCFM. *See* American Board of Commissioners for Foreign Missions
affections, religious. *See under* Edwards, Jonathan
Allen, Timothy, 164
Alline, Henry, 46
American Board of Commissioners for Foreign Missions
   education of missionaries for, 148, 152–53, 159
   expansion of, 145–51
   influence of the New Divinity on, 128–31, 138–39
   origins of, xxvi, 106–7, 116n19, 117, 150–51, 154–56, 181
   religious context of, 131–35, 143–44
   See also missions, international; New Divinity movement
American Education Society, 204
American Home Missionary Society, 114n11
American Tract Society, 36, 102
Ames, William, 46
Amherst College, 148, 151, 183, 190, 200, 201–2
Anderson, Rufus, 129
Andover Theological Seminary
   center of ministerial training, 107, 148, 160, 177–79, 202–3
   missions and, 129, 147, 154
   New Divinity influence on, 148, 152, 187, 196
   origins of, xxvi, 148, 155, 200
   Society of Inquiry on the Subject of Missions, 118, 143, 153
Andrews, Josiah, 122
anti-intellectualism, 31
Appleton, Nathaniel, 160
Arminianism, 21, 55, 79, 136
atheism, 60, 61–62
atonement (limited vs. unlimited), 125, 141, 153
Auburn Theological Seminary, 179, 203
Augustine, Saint, 21, 69

Backus, Azel, 159n4, 168, 170, 175
Backus, Charles
   education of, 168
   pastor-teacher, role as, 147, 166, 167 fig. 2, 168, 170, 172, 178, 198
   qualifications for the ministry, views on, 175
   the will, views on, 136
   writings of, 192, 196
baptism, 7, 8, 138
Baptist Missionary Society, 104, 145–46n63
Barrett, Justin
   children, views on, 65n26
   cognitive science, views on, 58
   conceptual control, views on, 85

Barrett, Justin (*continued*)
   failed petitionary prayer, views on, 68
   God's sovereignty, views on, 80
   religion, 60–61, 63
Barshinger, David, 44n35
Bartlett, Phebe, 196
Baxter, Richard, 5, 46, 96, 174
Bayley, Kiah, 133–34
Beaver, R. Pierce, 144
Bebbington, David, 95–96, 135
Beck, Peter, 76
Becker, Carl, 132
Beecher, Lyman, 115, 126
Bellamy, Joseph
   education of, 168
   influence on New Divinity by, 173
   pastor-teacher, role as, 147, 151, 160, 166, 167 fig. 2, 168, 170n20, 171–72
   prayers for JE by, 73–74
   pure church principles of, 147, 188
   revivals and, 112
   writings of, 192
Bentley, William, 130, 148, 149n73, 166
Bering, Jesse, 59, 61–62
Bible, the
   influence on JE, 38–40, 45
   JE's interpretation of, xxiv, 43
   JE's use of, 16–17, 28–29, 51–57
   missionaries' use of, 141
   New Divinity and, 171, 175, 176
   prayers in, 74, 79n92, 82–83
   scholars on JE's use of, 38–39
   source of religious authority, 94, 135
   See also under Edwards, Jonathan
Billings, Edward, 186
Birdsall, Richard, xiv, xv, 204
Blank Bible, The (Edwards), 97
Bloch, Ruth, 143
Bloom, Paul, 59
Boudry, Maarten, 84–85
Boyer, Pascal, 59

Brainerd, David
   expulsion of from Yale, 163
   influence of, 36, 106, 133, 149, 153, 155
   missionary, life as, 95, 103–4, 107
   prayer life of, 72
   See also Life of David Brainerd, The
Brauer, Jerald, xviii
Breitenbach, William, xv
Brethren, the. *See under* Williams College
Brown, Nathan, 205–6
Brown University (Rhode Island College), 157
Burr, Aaron, Sr., 21
Burton, Asa, 147, 166, 167 fig. 2, 168, 173, 178
Bushman, Richard, 58n1
Byrd, James, 82

Caldwell, Patricia, 5
Calvin, John, 60, 69, 70, 75, 96, 97
Calvin College, 80
Calvinism
   God's sovereignty, views on, 80–81, 86
   "hard doctrines" of, 18, 45, 118, 125
   limited atonement, views on, 141
   New Divinity and, 183
   Old, 148, 165, 185, 187
   Williams College and, 189, 204
Cape Breton (Nova Scotia). *See* King George's War
Carey, William
   evangelization, views on, 104, 139–40, 145–46n63
   JE's influence on, 100–101, 105, 106, 140
   modern Protestant missions and, 90, 118
Catlin, Jacob, 168, 178n36, 190, 192
Chauncy, Charles, 12–13, 86
children (theology of), 60–61, 65
Chun, Chris, 104

INDEX 231

Claghorn, George, 40
Clap, Thomas, 163, 165
Cleaveland, Ebenezer, 163
Cleaveland, John, 163, 165
cognitive science
 confirmation bias, 69
 field of, 58–59
 God-awareness, 59
 human proclivity to theological incorrectness, 63, 79–80, 87
 two-system model of religious reasoning, xxv, 62–70, 80–81, 86–87
 See also prayer, petitionary; religion (as a natural phenomenon)
Cohen, Charles, 12
Collins, Daniel, 178n36, 189–90
Communion. *See* Edwards, Jonathan: Communion; Half-Way Covenant; Puritans, New England; Stoddard, Solomon: Communion
Concerning the End for Which God Created the World (Edwards), 119
confirmation bias, 69
Conforti, Joseph, xiv–xv, 187
Congregationalism
 decline of, 145, 183
 education of ministers in, 161–62, 163, 165, 168, 174
 New Divinity movement and, 135, 157, 166, 183, 188
 Old Lights vs. New Lights in, 10–11, 163, 164–65
 revivals among, 9
 See also missions, international; schools of the prophets
Connecticut Missionary Society, 114n11, 150, 154, 159
conversion, religious
 American evangelical culture and, 10, 12
 defined by JE, 41
 first conversion, 55–56

 JE's usage of "conversion," 40, 48–49, 49 fig. 1, 51
 New Divinity ministers and, 175, 176–77, 196
 ongoing process of, 55–57
 role of the Bible in conversion, xxiv, 38–48
 scholarship on, 22–23
 See also Bible, the; conversion narratives; Edwards, Jonathan: conversion experience of; Edwards, Jonathan: conversion, views on; Great Awakening, the; new birth, the; Puritanism, English; Puritanism, New England; revivals, American
conversion narratives, 3–4, 5–6, 8. *See also* conversion, religious; Edwards, Jonathan, conversion experience of; Nettleton, Asahel; Half-Way Covenant; Puritans, New England
Cooley, Timothy Mather, 178n36
covenant. *See* Edwards, Jonathan: national covenant; Half-Way Covenant; Puritanism, New England: covenant theology of
Crawford, Michael, 93–94
Crump, David, 79n92
cultural scaffolding, 68–70, 86, 87

Daggett, Naphtali, 165
Dartmouth College, 157, 178, 183, 198
Davenport, James, 11, 124, 164
Davidson, James, 144
Davis, Emerson, 178n36
Davis, Henry, 139, 159n4, 168
Dawkins, Richard, 59
De Jong, James, 155
De Smedt, Johan, 84–85
Dellatre, Roland, 17
Dennett, Daniel, 59
Dewey, Chester, 197–98, 206

disinterested benevolence. *See under* Edwards, Jonathan; Hopkins, Samuel
Distinguishing Marks of a Work of the Spirit of God (Edwards), 23, 50, 94–95
Doddridge, Philip, 192
Dwight, Timothy (JE's grandson), 112

education of ministers. *See* Andover Theological Seminary; Congregationalism; Edwards, Jonathan: education of ministers; England: education of ministers in; Presbyterianism: education of ministers in; schools of the prophets; Whitefield, George: education of ministers; Williams College; Yale College
Edwards, Elizabeth (daughter of JE), 75
Edwards, Esther (mother of JE), 15
Edwards, Jonathan
American revivals, views on, 23–25, 28, 73, 89, 111–12
Apostle Paul, views on, 48, 51, 56, 158
Communion, views on, 20, 28
conversion, views on, xxiv, 13–15, 16, 21–22, 23–37, 38–57, 95, 112, 122
conversion experience of, 14–19, 44–46, 71
death of, 21
conversion in Scripture, views on, 41–44
cosmic redemption, views on, 44n35, 86, 88–89, 95, 111–12, 117, 127, 128
David Brainerd, views on, 72, 99, 163
disinterested benevolence, views on, 107–8, 117, 141–42
early life of, 15, 17–18, 71

education of ministers, views on, 163, 164
exegesis by, 43–44
the Fall, views on, 53, 104
glory of God, views on, 25–26, 30, 35, 57
God's sovereignty, views on, 17, 18, 20, 23, 45, 78–79
grace, views on, 21–22, 31, 47–48, 52, 56, 77, 104–5
Great Awakening and, 21–24
holiness, views on, 19
human agency, views on, 81–86
humiliation, views on, 20, 29, 32–33, 45, 48
hypocrisy, views on, 34, 54, 79
immediate repentance, views on, 137
intellectual influences on, 38, 133
international revivals, views on, 89–90, 98–103
knowledge found in Scripture, views on, 26, 31–32, 35, 47–48
legacy of, xiii–xvi, 4, 111–14, 126–27
the life of prayer, views on, 70–75
love, views on, 28, 31, 33, 34, 35, 107
mercy and justice, views on, 34–35
the millennium, views on, 57, 97, 98, 102, 113–14, 137
mission work of, 20
the national covenant, views on, 81–86
nature, views on, 18–19
the new birth, views on, 28, 33n81, 40, 47
petitionary prayer, views on, 67, 70, 72–73, 74–86, 89, 98–101
piety, views on, 24, 25, 35, 36
pastor of Stockbridge church, 20–21

INDEX 233

pastor-teacher, role as, 166, 167 fig. 2, 168, 172
president of College of New Jersey (Princeton), 21
the Psalms, views on, 44
pure church ecclesiology, views on, 29, 113, 147, 185, 186
religion as a natural phenomenon, views on, 60n7
religious affections, views on, 17, 24–28, 29–37, 50, 76
religious experience, views on, 24–37, 46–48, 50, 95
republished works of, 148–49
scholarship on, xiii–xvi, xvii, xix, xxiii–xxiv
the Song of Songs, views on, 43–44
spirituality of, 18–19, 46
theology of (general), 20, 30, 195
the will, views on, 26–28, 35, 52–53, 103, 136, 158
See also Bible; Carey, William; conversion; Great Awakening; Griffin, Edward Dorr; missionary movement, international; New Divinity movement; Northampton; revivals, American; revivals, international; schools of the prophets; Second Great Awakening; Stoddard, Solomon; Whitefield, George
Edwards, Jonathan, Jr. (son of JE)
education of, 159n4, 168
John Ryland Jr. on, 119, 133
pastor-teacher, role as, 167 fig. 2, 168, 172, 200
Edwards, Jonathan, works of. See specific titles
Edwards, Justin, 196
Edwards, Mary (daughter of JE), 74
Edwards, Sarah Pierpont (wife of JE), 16, 36n91, 71
Edwards, Timothy (father of JE), 15, 46, 48, 89, 112
Edwards, Timothy (son of JE), 74
Edwardseans. See New Divinity movement
election, doctrine of, 6, 64, 103, 125, 138, 141
Eliot, John, 103–4, 151
Emmons, Nathanael
education of, 168
library of, 173
ministerial associations and, 147
pastor-teacher, role as, 147, 166, 167 fig. 2, 169, 170, 172, 178
theology of, 135, 141, 177, 195
writings of, 192
England, 3, 89
education of ministers in, 161
Methodist movement in, 22
revivals in, 90, 92, 98, 113
See also King George's War; missionary movement, international
Enlightenment, the, 24, 40, 95, 135–36, 139
Erasmus, 96
Erskine, Ebenezer, 89
Erskine, John, 100
evangelical movement, American
emergence of, 4
New Divinity theology and, 37, 115, 138, 139, 143, 205
transatlantic aspects of, 10, 89–91, 102, 106, 132–35
See also conversion, religious; missions, American; missions, international; missions in America; New Divinity movement
experimental religion, 29, 35, 94, 113

Faithful Narrative of the Surprising Work of God, A (Edwards)
conversion, views on, 23, 29, 50
influence on Asahel Nettleton, 121, 122
influence on international revivals, xxv, 89, 91–94

Fall, the. *See under* Edwards, Jonathan
Fermin, Giles, 46
Fiering, Norman, 78
Finke, Roger, 145, 145n62
Finney, Charles, 116, 126–27, 204
Fischer, Austin, 80–81n98
Fisk, Ezra, 190
Fitch, Ebenezer, 178n36, 183, 189, 190–98, 200, 201
folk beliefs. *See* cognitive science: two-system model of religious reasoning
Fowler, Abraham, 169
Franklin, Benjamin, 83, 86, 173
Freedom of the Will (Edwards)
  Allen Guelzo on, xvi
  human will, views on, 113, 136, 158
  influence on Justin Edwards, 196
  influence on international missions, 95, 103–4
  Williams College curriculum and, 201
Frelinghuysen, Theodore, 89
Fuller, Andrew, 100, 103–4, 106, 118, 133

Gambrell, Mary, 161
Garrick, David, 12
Gelston, Maltby, 172
Germany
  publications in, 91, 93, 101, 105
  revivals in, xxv, 22, 89, 93
glory of God, 119–20, 142, 149. *See also* Edwards, Jonathan: disinterested benevolence; Edwards, Jonathan: glory of God
God, 63, 77–79, 81–86. *See also* cognitive science; Edwards, Jonathan, love; glory of God; God's sovereignty; grace; redemption; salvation
God's sovereignty
  difficulty believing in, 80–81
  human agency and, 81–86
  New Divinity on, 135–36, 158

petitionary prayer and, 68–70
William Carey on, 104, 140
See also under Edwards, Jonathan
Goen, Clarence C., 38, 159
grace (of God)
  common, 30
  counterintuitive nature of, 64–65
  means of, 21, 52, 121, 122, 139–41, 152
  New Divinity on, 113, 176
  Solomon Stoddard on, 8
  See also Edwards, Jonathan: grace; Puritanism, New England: conversion narratives
Great Awakening (New England)
  aftermath of, 99, 135
  American higher education, role in, 157–60
  defined, 9–10
  division within, 10–13, 28
  human agency, role of, 80–81
  JE and, 21–24, 28, 35
  legacy of, 157, 159, 175
  scholarship on, xiii–xvi, 9
  See also Edwards, Jonathan: Great Awakening and; George Whitehead; Second Great Awakening
Great Commission, the, 96, 101, 103, 140, 152. *See also* missionary movement, international; missions in America
Griffin, Edward Dorr, xxv
  Andover faculty, role as, 148
  education of, 159n4, 168
  JE's influence on, 116–21, 126–27, 195n47
  pastor-teacher, role as, 167 fig. 2, 201
  preaching of, xxv, 115–16, 176
  revivalist, role as, 114–21, 122
  revivals, views on, 124
  scholarship on, 117
  theology of, 126–27

transatlantic connections of, 133
writings of, 118–21, 126–27,
  133, 152–53, 192, 201
  See also Williams College:
  President Edward Dorr
  Griffin and
Guelzo, Allen, xvi
Guyse, John, 92

Half-Way Covenant, 7, 8, 20, 113,
  147, 185
Hall, David D., 168n17
Hall, Edward, 5
Hall, Gordon, 129, 147–48, 149, 168
Hallock, Homan, 152
Hallock, Jeremiah, 169
Hallock, Moses, 152, 194n43
Hamilton College, 148, 178
Hansen, Collin, 80
Haroutunian, Joseph, xiii–xiv
Harris, Howell, 89, 90, 92
Hart, Levi, 167 fig. 2, 168, 169, 176
Hart, William, 12
Harvard College, 146, 161, 162, 173,
  189, 200
Hatheway, Deborah, 73
Hawthorne, Nathaniel, 205–6
Haystack Prayer Meeting. *See under*
  Williams College
*History of the Work of Redemption,
  A* (Edwards)
  divine intervention, views on,
    85–86
  influence on international
    missions, 97, 101–3, 106,
    108
  influence on Protestant culture,
    119
  the millennium, views on, 98,
    102, 113–14, 137
  redemption, views on, 120n38
Holifield, Brooks, 8
holiness. *See under* Edwards,
  Jonathan
Hooker, Asahel, 166–67, 167 fig. 2,
  169, 170, 172
Hooker, Thomas, 48
Hopkins, Albert, 197, 198, 202, 204

Hopkins, Mark, 204
Hopkins, Samuel
  disinterested benevolence, views
    on, 107–8, 117, 128, 141–43,
    182
  education of, 147, 166, 189
  JE's prayer life, views on, 70–71,
    72
  letter to Andrew Fuller, 106, 133
  missionary movement and, 117,
    129–30, 151, 155, 182
  New Divinity and, 147, 165, 188
  number of New Divinity clergy,
    views on, 165–66
  pastor-teacher, role as, 166, 168,
    172
  preaching of, 176
  scholarship on, xiv
  theology of, xv, 135, 144, 151,
    195
  writings of, 173, 191–92
Horne, Melville, 106
human agency. *See under* Edwards,
  Jonathan
*Humble Attempt to Promote Explicit
  Agreement, An* (Edwards)
  human role, views on, 102
  influence on Edward Dorr
    Griffin, 120–21
  influence on international
    missions, 95, 106, 133
  the millennium, views on, 113,
    137
  prayer, views on, 72, 75, 89,
    99–101
Humble Inquiry, An (Edwards), 185
Hume, David, 173
humiliation. *See under* Edwards,
  Jonathan
Humphrey, Heman, 169, 190
Hutchinson, Anne, 6
Hyde, Alvan
  New Divinity debates and,
    195n47
  pastor-teacher, role as, 167 fig. 2,
    168, 178, 190
  vice president of Williams
    College, role as, 178n36, 189

hypocrisy. *See under* Edwards, Jonathan

itinerancy. *See under* revivals, American

James, William, 13
Jonathan Edwards Center. *See under* Yale College
Jonathan Edwards Encyclopedia (Stout et al.), xxiii
Jones, Griffith, 89
Judson, Adoniram, Jr., 106, 129, 134, 206
Judson, Adoniram, Sr., 151
Judson, Ann "Nancy," 106, 129
Judson, Ephraim, 160, 167 fig. 2, 178, 191

Kelemen, Deborah, 60
Kidd, Thomas, 10
King, Jonas, 152
King George's War, 82–86
kingdom of Christ. *See* Great Commission; millennialism
Kling, David, xiv, xv, xvi
Knapp, Isaac, 190
Kreider, Glenn, 78
Kuklick, Bruce, xv
Kuypers, Gerardus, 93

Lesser, M. X., xxiii
Lewis, C. S., 68
Life of David Brainerd, The (Edwards)
    Andover Theological Seminary curriculum and, 148
    influence on Asahel Nettleton, 122
    influence on Justin Edwards, 196
    influence on missionaries, 105–6, 108, 128, 133, 149
    piety, views on, 36, 72
    See also Edwards, Jonathan: David Brainerd
"Little Awakening" (Connecticut River Valley, 1734–35), 49, 73, 88–89

Livingston, John H., 118, 152n87
Locke, John, 26, 38
Loomis, Harvey, 147–48, 168
Lord Herbert of Cherbury, 173
love of God. *See* Edwards, Jonathan: love
Luhrmann, T. M., 62–63
Luther, Martin, 32, 64
Lutherans, 9, 90, 93
Lyon, Mary, 107, 187

Mabille, Adolph, 102
Marsden, George, xxiii, 84
Marsden, Samuel, 106
Marshman, Joshua, 145–46n63
Marty, Martin, xviii
Martyn, Henry, 105–6
Massachusetts Missionary Society, 114n11, 159
Mastricht, Peter van, 33n81, 46
Mather, Cotton, 67, 72
Mathews, Donald, 132
May, Henry, 182
McClymond, Michael, xxiii, 17, 33n81, 46
McCulloch, William, 89, 91, 94
McDermott, Gerald, xxiii, 33n81, 39n3
McGiffert, Michael, 6
McWhorter, Andrew, 118
mercy and justice. *See under* Edwards, Jonathan
Methodism, 145, 146, 183
Middlebury College, 139, 148, 151
Millar, Robert, 97
millennium, the
    Edward Dorr Griffin on, 117–18, 120–21
    optimism and, 132, 143–44, 150
    See also under Edwards, Jonathan
Miller, Glenn, 159
Miller, Samuel, 133
Mills, Samuel J., Jr.
    Andover Theological Seminary, student at, 153
    Edward Dorr Griffin and, 118, 201

missionary movement and, 129, 151–54, 155, 181, 194
theology of, 184
Williams College, choice of, 151–52, 184, 193–94
See also Williams College: Haystack Prayer Meeting
Mills, Samuel J., Sr., 118, 141, 152, 161, 201
"Mind, The" (Edwards), 33n82
Minkema, Kenneth, xxiii, 46, 49n50, 84n110
miracles, 22, 53, 56, 83n107, 85, 140
missionary movement, international
  Catholics and the, 96
  education of missionaries, 145–46, 159–60
  Edward Dorr Griffin and, 117–21
  England and the, 100–101, 105–6, 118, 132–33, 134–35
  JE as transitional figure in the, 90, 129–30
  JE's influence on the, xxv, 89–108, 117, 121, 155, 181–84
  missionary societies and the, 101, 106, 150, 159
  origins of the, 90, 96, 150
  Protestant denominations and the, 103–4, 129, 145–46
  Samuel Hopkins as transitional figure in the, 129–30
  scholarship on the, 119, 128, 155–56
  Scotland and the, 100
  transatlantic network of the, 90–92, 106–7, 155
  See also American Board of Commissioners of Foreign missions; Andover Theological Seminary; Great Commission, the; Mills, Samuel J., Jr.; redemption; schools of the prophets; Williams College
missionary movement in America, xxvi, 96, 107, 114, 145, 150. *See also* Brainerd, David;

Life of David Brainerd; New Divinity movement; salvation
Moody, Josh, 78n87
Moore, Zephaniah Swift, 159n4, 168, 183, 191, 198–200
Moravian missionaries, 20, 89, 90, 96
Morgan, Edmund, 7, 8
Morimoto, Anri, 30–31
Morris, James, 151, 193
Morrison, Robert, 106
Morse, Jedidiah, 155
Mount Holyoke Female Seminary, 107, 183, 187
Mullen, Robert Bruce, 83n107
Murray, Iain, 72

Narrative of Surprising Conversions, A (Edwards), 196
nature. *See under* Edwards, Jonathan
Nature of True Virtue, The (Edwards), 30
Netherlands, 89, 90, 93
Nettleton, Asahel, xxv–xxvi, 114–16, 121–27
new birth, the, 11–12, 94, 95, 135, 138–39. *See also under* Edwards, Jonathan
New Divinity movement
  culture of the, xviii, 130, 146–51, 165–69, 182–84, 188
  decline of the, 180
  defined, xiiin1, 135, 157–58
  ideal pastor in the, 173–77
  JE's influence on the, 113–14, 126–27, 148–49, 173
  scholarship on the, xiii–xvi, xvii, 182–83
  theology of the, 112–13, 125, 135–44, 158, 171, 194–95
  third-generation disciples of JE and the, xv, xxv–xxvi, 14, 112
  See also under American Board of Commissioners for Foreign Missions; Andover Theological Seminary;

New Divinity movement (*continued*)
  Bible; Congregationalism; conversion narratives; evangelical movement; God's sovereignty; grace; missionary movement, international; revivals, American; schools of the prophets; Second Great Awakening; Williams College; Yale College
New England Theology. *See* New Divinity movement
Newell, Harriet Atwood, 129
Newell, Samuel, 129
Niebuhr, Reinhold, 70
Noll, Mark, xv, 142
Northampton (Massachusetts)
  JE and his congregation in, 54, 74, 101–2, 147, 174
  JE's ouster from Northampton church in, 19–20, 29, 185–86
  pastor-teachers in, 167 fig. 2
  prayer requests of JE's congregation in, xxv, 66–69
  revivals in, 21, 23, 88–89, 91–93
  Solomon Stoddard's congregation in, 8
  See also *Faithful Narrative*
Nott, Rosanne Peck, 129
Nott, Samuel, 129

Original Sin (Edwards), 103, 104–5
Ostrander, Rick, 70
Oxford Handbook of Jonathan Edwards (Sweeney and Stievermann), xxiii

Packard, Theophilus, 167 fig. 2, 190
Parish, Elijah, 134
Park, Edwards A., 148, 182
Parsons, Levi, 108, 143, 152
pastor-teachers. *See under* Backus, Charles; Bellamy, Joseph; Edwards, Jonathan; Edwards, Jonathan, Jr.; Emmons, Nathanael; Griffin, Edward Dorr; Hopkins, Samuel; Hyde, Alvan; Northampton; schools of the prophets; West, Stephen
Perkins, Nathan, 175, 167 fig. 2
Perkins, William, 5
Perry, Arthur Latham, 182n4, 205
"Personal Narrative" (Edwards), 15–20, 29, 30, 71, 121–22
Pettit, Norman, 36n91
Pietism, xxv, 22, 89, 91, 93, 96, 97
piety, Protestant, xiv–xv, 36, 153, 163–65, 175–76, 197. *See also* Edwards, Jonathan: piety
Piggin, Stuart, 98, 141n43
Porter, Ebenezer, 148, 167 fig. 2, 168
prayer, life of. *See under* Edwards, Jonathan
prayer, petitionary
  against enemies in war, 81–86
  cognitive science and, 65–70
  failed, 68–70
  God's response to, 77–78
  health-related, 65–67
  revivals and, 98–101
  theologically correct, 75–81
  See also Bible, the; cognitive science; Edwards, Jonathan: petitionary prayer; Edwards, Jonathan: religious affections
praying societies. *See* revivals, international: concerts of prayer and
predestination. *See* election (limited vs. unconditional)
Presbyterianism
  education of ministers in, 162, 163, 179
  missions and, 118, 146
  Old Sides vs. New Sides in, 10, 163
  prayer requests in, 65–67
  revivals among, 9, 115
  See also Davenport, James; Erskine, John; Tennent, George
Prince, Thomas, 46–47, 91
Princeton College, 21, 157, 203

Princeton Theological Seminary, 178, 179, 194n44, 203
providential history, 83–84, 112, 113–14, 137
Psalms, the. *See under* Edwards, Jonathan
pure church ecclesiology. *See under* Edwards, Jonathan
Puritanism, English, 3–4, 9, 168n17
Puritanism, New England
   Communion, views on, 8
   conversion narratives in, 3–7
   conversion morphology of, 5, 17, 29, 44, 45–46, 55, 122
   covenant theology of, 81–86, 138, 185
   devotional practices of, 71–72, 95
   fracturing of, 163–65
   higher education of preachers, views on, 161–63
   missions and, 96, 139
   prayer, views on, 68, 70
   See also Half-Way Covenant; piety; prayer, petitionary

Rabinowitz, Richard, 204n78
"Reality of Conversion, The" (Edwards), 51–52
redemption, cosmic
   Edward Dorr Griffin on, 119–21, 152
   New Divinity and, 196
   God's plan for, 39–40, 97–98, 101–2
   See also Edwards, Jonathan: cosmic redemption; grace; salvation
religion (as a natural phenomenon), 59–62. *See also* atheism; cognitive science; Edwards, Jonathan: religion as a natural phenomenon; theology (intuitive vs. doctrinal)
religious affections. *See under* Edwards, Jonathan

Religious Affections, The (Edwards). *See Treatise Concerning Religious Affections*
religious authority, 24, 131–32, 135
religious experience. *See under* Edwards, Jonathan
repentance, immediate. *See under* Edwards, Jonathan
revivals, American
   divisions within, 163
   emphasis on moment of conversion, 33
   New England and, 9, 89, 137, 183
   Middle Colonies and, 9, 89
   itinerancy and, 10–12, 23, 28, 124, 150
   JE's influence on, xxv, 112–14, 127, 168, 196
   legacy of, 10
   New Divinity approach to, xxv–xxvi, 124, 127, 132, 137, 149–50
   origins of, 22–23
   religious enthusiasm in, 10, 12–13, 25
   work of God, viewed as, 50, 73
   See also Edwards, Jonathan: religious affections; Edwards, Jonathan: American revivals; Great Awakening; "Little Awakening"; Nettleton, Asahel; Second Great Awakening; Whitehead, George; Williams College
revivals, international
   concerts of prayer and, 98–101, 113, 124
   evangelical view of conversion and, 37
   England and, 91, 92
   Germany and, 91, 93
   JE's influence on, 90–92, 95–98, 101–3, 108m 132–33
   Netherlands and, 93
   network of reading communities, 91

revivals, international (*continued*)
  new genre of revival literature, 91–92, 94
  Scotland and, 91, 93–94, 95
  Wales and, 92–93, 94–95
  See also under Edwards, Jonathan; *Faithful Narrative of the Surprising Work of God, A* (Edwards); Griffin, Edward Dorr; prayer, petitionary
Rice, Luther, 129
Richards, James, 142–43, 152, 179, 203
Richards, William, 152
Robbins, Ammi Ruhamah, 151–52, 160, 178n36, 190, 194
Robbins, Philemon, 160, 165
Robbins, Thomas, 160–61
Robe, James, 94
Rowland, Daniel, 89, 92
Rudolph, Frederick, 205
Rutger's University (Queen's College), 157
Ryland, John, Jr., 100, 105, 118, 119, 133

salvation, 64, 81, 103. *See also* Edwards, Jonathan: grace; grace: means of; redemption, cosmic
Sandeen, Ernest, 118, 143
Schaefer, Thomas, xix
schools of the prophets
  curricula of, 169–74
  defined, 147–48, 158
  influence of, 158–60, 165–69
  JE's influence on, 168
  libraries of, 172–73
  origins of, 160–65
  pastor-teachers, role of New Divinity, 166–67, 167 fig. 2, 168
  professionalization of education of ministers and, 177–80
  scholarship on, xxvi, 159, 177
  transitional phase of, 178–80, 203

  See also Andover Theological Seminary; *names of individual pastor-teachers*; New Divinity movement
Schwartz, Christian Frederick, 106
Scotland, 72, 89, 90, 93–95, 100, 106
Second Great Awakening (ca. 1790–1835)
  influence of, xiv, 107
  JE's influence on, 111–27
  origins of, 149–50
  New Divinity and, 159, 177
  revivalists of, xxv–xxvi, 182
  scholarship on, 112, 114
seminaries, establishment of modern, 158–59, 178–79
sense of the heart. *See* Edwards, Jonathan: will, the
"Serenity Prayer," 70
Shea, Daniel, 15–16
Shepard, Samuel, 178n36
Shepard, Thomas, 4–7, 17, 32, 46, 55
Shepherd's Tent, 164
sin, original, 104–5, 113, 125, 136–37, 158
Sinners in the Hands of an Angry God (Edwards), 14, 94
Sloan, Douglas, 159
Slone, Jason, 80–81
Smalley, John, 147, 167 fig. 2, 168, 172, 173, 192
Smith, John E., 29, 39
Snell, Thomas, 190
Society of Inquiry on the Subject of Missions. *See under* Andover Theological Seminary
Some Thoughts Concerning the Present Revival (Edwards), 23–24, 50, 73, 99, 164
Song of Songs. *See under* Edwards, Jonathan
sovereignty of God. *See* God's sovereignty
Spring, Samuel, 134, 140, 155
Springer, Gardiner, 115
Stark, Rodney, 145, 145n62
Stein, Stephen, 13, 66, 67–68, 69
Steinmetz, Johann Adam, 91, 93

INDEX 241

Stiles, Ezra, 147, 165, 166, 188, 190
Stoddard, Solomon (grandfather of JE)
   Communion, views on, 8
   conversion, views on, 46
   death of, 19
   evangelization, views on, 96–97
   influence on JE, 15, 20, 28, 46, 48, 112
   revivals led by, 89
Stout, Harry, 89, 112
Strong, Nathan, 192
Stuart, Moses, 148
supernatural, the, 61–62, 63–64, 85
Sutcliff, John, 100, 145n63
Sweeney, Douglas, xiii–xvi, xix, 130
Sweeney, Kevin, 186
Swift, Job, 178n36, 190, 192
Swift, Seth, 178n36, 190, 193

Tappan, David, 173
Taylor, Nathaniel William, 116, 126–27, 195n47, 204
teachers. *See* pastor-teachers
"Tell It to Jesus," 77
Tennent, Gilbert, 11, 89, 163
Tennent, William, 89, 163
theism, 60
Theological Institute of Connecticut, 116nn19–20
Theological Society. *See under* Williams College
theology (intuitive vs. doctrinal), 62–65, 68–70, 79–81
Treadwell, John, 154–55
Treatise Concerning Religious Affections, A (Edwards)
   conversion, views on, 57
   influence on Justin Edwards, 196
   influence on the New Divinity, 123, 124, 148
   prayer, views on, 78
   religious experience, views on, 13, 24–37, 47–48
   revivals, views on, 50, 123, 124
   scholarship on, 38–39
   use of the Bible in, 38–39

Trumbull, Benjamin, 167 fig. 2, 170, 192
Tyler, Bennet, 121, 123

Union College, 148, 151, 178, 200
Unitarianism, 146, 154, 183, 189, 200

Wales, 90, 92–93, 98, 113
Walls, Andrew, 90, 101, 129–30
War of 1812, 134–35
Ward, W. R., 92
Ward, William, 145–46n63
Watts, Isaac, 92
Wayland, Francis, xxvi, 115n16
Weil, Simone, 64n24
Wesley, Charles, 89
Wesley, John, 36, 89, 90, 92
West, Stephen
   pastor-teacher, role as, 161, 167 fig. 2, 172, 173
   influence on the New Divinity, 147, 173, 188
   Williams College and, 178n36, 189, 190n32, 192, 198
   writings of, 173, 192
Westminster Confession, 67
Westminster Shorter Catechism, 30
Wheeler, Rachel, 104–5
Wheelock, Eleazar, 51, 157
Whitby, Daniel, 173
Whitefield, George
   education of ministers, views on, 163
   JE and, 73, 90
   marketing tactics of, 11, 22–23
   prayer, views on, 72
   preaching tours of, 11–12, 51, 57, 89, 124
will, human, 103, 149n73. *See also* Edwards, Jonathan: will, the
Willard, Josiah, 97
Williams, Edward, 141n43
Williams, Ephraim, Jr., xxvi, 184–86
Williams, Ephraim, Sr., 185
Williams, Israel, 186
Williams, Solomon, 185

Williams, William (American), 186–87, 191
Williams, William (Welsh), 94
Williams College
    Brethren, the, at, 118, 152–53, 194
    curriculum of, 191–93, 201
    disciplining students at, 196–97
    founding of, xxvi, 184–90
    Haystack Prayer Meeting at, 129, 152, 168, 181, 183, 201
    missionary spirit of, 181–82, 205–6
    New Divinity influence on, xxvi, 151–53, 178–79, 182–84, 187, 202–6
    New Light vs. Old Light Calvinists at, 185–86, 191–92
    origins of, 184–87
    President Ebenezer Fitch and, 190–98
    President Edward Dorr Griffin and, 115–16, 179, 198, 200–204, 205n81, 206
    President Zephaniah Swift Moore and, 198–200
    presidents and board members of, 189–90
    revivals at, 193, 197–99, 202
    scholarship on, 205
    Society of Inquiry at, 199
    Theological Society at, 153, 194–96, 203
    See also American Board of Commissioners for Foreign Missions; Calvinism: Old; Griffin, Edward Dorr; Mills, Samuel J., Jr.
Williston, Payson, 170
Woods, Leonard, 135, 139, 141, 198
Worcester, Samuel, 155

Yale College
    cost of, 193–94
    curriculum of, 161
    education of future college presidents by, 148, 159
    education of ministers by, 158, 162, 164–65, 178
    JE as student, tutor, rector at, 18, 19
    Jonathan Edwards Center at, xvii, 14
    New Divinity and, 123, 146, 148, 158, 164–65, 188
    New Haven Theology, 116n20
    Old Lights and, 163–64
    Williams College board and, 190
Yale Divinity School, 178
Yancey, Philip, 64n24

Zakai, Avihu, 14, 44–45, 112

www.ingramcontent.com/pod-product-compliance
Lightning Source LLC
Chambersburg PA
CBHW071248230426
43668CB00011B/1640